Overseas

Average rates of exchange

Average for year ending	31.12.96	31.3.97	31.12.97	31.3.98	31.12.98	31.3.99
Algeria (Dinar)	85·7181	88·6549	95·3397	96·3977	97·8645	99·2018
Argentina (Peso)	1·5609	1·5855	1·6385	1·6432	1·658	1·6539
Australia ($A)	1·9952	2·0129	2·2087	2·3021	2·638	2·6643
Austria (Schilling)	16·5372	17·3392	19·9796	20·4914	20·5069	20·2487
Bahrain (Dinar)	0·589	0·5983	0·618	0·6198	0·6254	0·6239
Bangladesh (Taka)	64·3978	66·3433	71·8156	73·2702	77·9876	78·6191
Barbados (BD$)	3·1399	3·1913	3·2969	3·3067	3·3458	3·334
Belgium (Franc)	48·3809	50·7632	58·5873	60·0947	60·1307	59·3682
Bolivia (Boliviano)	7·9464	8·1664	8·6305	8·736	9·1699	9·2559
Botswana (Pula)	5·1291	5·4936	5·9396	6·0386	7·0147	7·2987
Brazil (Real)	1·5705	1·6232	1·7525	1·7894	1·9252	2·1975
Brunei ($)	2·1949	2·2324	2·4208	2·5236	2·7657	2·7821
Burma (Kyat)	9·178	9·4811	10·2315	10·2881	10·3702	10·3445
Burundi (Franc)	405·1671	403·9885	520·8658	589·9479	733·8387	775·3835
Canada (Can$)	2·1643	2·1936	2·2669	2·3028	2·4588	2·4873
Cayman Islands (CI$)	1·3065	1·3286	1·3583	1·3589	1·3762	1·3714
Chile (Peso)	644·0859	657·2934	687·7897	703·7922	764·0855	777·2736
China (Renminbi Yuan)	12·9393	13·1517	13·5969	13·596	13·7424	13·6737
Colombia (Peso)	1,616·58	1,651·973	1,872·778	1,997·295	2,367·175	2,451·284
Congo Dem Rep (Zaire)						
(Congolese Franc)	73,656·37	127,788·8	225,418·1	221,423·4658	224,147·7	223,581·9
Costa Rica (Colon)	321·0629	337·0134	379·4464	389·5695	427·8467	436·6955
Cuba (Peso)			34·1751	35·8312	38·1782	37·9873
1.1.96–30.11.96	1·5484					
1.12.96–31.12.96	31·1923					
1.4.96–30.11.96		1·5541				
1.12.96–31.3.97		31·1678				
Cyprus (£)	0·7253	0·7499	0·8404	0·8559	0·8596	0·8521
Czechoslovakia (Koruna)	42·245	43·4344	51·8142	54·4364	53·3515	53·0363
Denmark (Krone)	9·0577	9·4616	10·8156	11·0912	11·1015	10·9556
Ecuador (Sucre)	4,946·143	5,312·16	6,490·7567	6,850·581	9,258·9275	11,008·15
Egypt (£)	5·3159	5·3971	5·5689	5·591	5·6636	5·6512
El Salvador (Colon)	13·6261	13·8569	14·358	14·3648	14·5292	14·4518
EMS (ECU)	1·2478	1·2911	1·4492	1·4797	1·4783	
Ethiopia (Birr)	9·1336	9·4883	10·668	10·8539	11·472	11·5096
European Union (Euro)						1·4647
Fiji Islands (F$)	2·1868	2·2158	2·3537	2·5122	3·3017	3·3113
Finland (Markka)	7·1751	7·4542	8·5027	8·7589	8·8624	8·7562
France (Franc)	7·9905	8·3433	9·5568	9·7851	9·7681	9·6473
French Cty/Africa						
(CFA franc)	794·5833	829·7642	952·8192	973·84	979·1458	967·5958
French Pacific Is						
(CFP franc)	144·5258	150·4152	173·0895	177·1803	177·7411	175·5382
Gambia (Dalasi)	15·3013	15·585	16·3181	16·4068	17·0422	17·3619
Germany						
(Deutsche mark)	2·3506	2·4642	2·8391	2·912	2·9147	2·878
Ghana (Cedi)	2,542·721	2,694·739	3,362·86	3,578·286	3,846·755	3,869·185
Greece (Drachma)	376·2084	389·8525	447·1124	461·9111	489·8869	486·6462
Grenada/Wind. Isles						
(EC$)	4·2176	4·284	4·4259	4·4389	4·4788	4·4677
Guyana (G$)	217·3761	221·3241	232·4098	234·4382	244·0337	249·2911
Honduras (Lempira)	17·7612	19·0761	21·3249	21·5222	22·3154	22·518
Hong Kong (HK$)	12·0795	12·2759	12·6824	12·7128	12·8378	12·8158
Hungary (Forint)	231·6071	247·7858	304·2664	319·3189	357·4845	363·4616
Iceland (Krona)	104·1897	107·3178	116·2706	117·6784	117·9762	117·0532
India (Rupee)	55·2826	56·2891	59·5592	61·1163	68·432	69·5958
Indonesia (Rupiah)	3,634·018	3,723·169	4,731·619	7,726·729	16,894	16,511·01
Iran (Rial)	4,686·156	4,760·009	4,917·584	4,932·109	4,976·34	4,964
Iraq (Dinar)	0·4857	0·4933	0·5097	0·5112	0·5157	0·5144
Irish Republic (Punt)	0·9755	0·9888	1·0814	1·1239	1·1635	1·1529
Israel (Shekel)	4·9887	5·1515	5·6472	5·7802	6·3147	6·4948
Italy (Lira)	2,408·06	2,473·67	2,788·26	2,858·55	2,876·52	2,843·76

Average rates of exchange — continued

Average for year ending	31.12.96	31.3.97	31.12.97	31.3.98	31.12.98	31.3.99
Jamaica (J$)	55·6957	55·2863	56·2463	57·0217	59·378	60·0323
Japan (Yen)	169·593	178·8762	198·189	201·5651	216·6834	211·499
Jordan (Dinar)	1·1062	1·1258	1·163	1·167	1·1796	1·1771
Kenya (Shilling)	89·1287	89·3362	96·0346	98·695	100·1734	100·8518
Korea South (Won)	1,248·863	1,300·689	1,512·7625	1,829·133	2,269·7583	2,133·946
Kuwait (Dinar)	0·468	0·4768	0·4974	0·5	0·5057	0·5036
Laos (New Kip)	1,431·731	1,456·261	1,616·78	1,849·443	4,477·095	5,453·88
Lebanon (£)	2,454·038	2,476·73	2,524·757	2,523·745	2,515·233	2,501·539
Libya (Dinar)	0·5553	0·5641	0·644	0·6572	0·6447	0·6703
Luxembourg (Franc)	48·3809	50·7632	58·5873	60·0948	60·1307	59·3713
Malawi (Kwacha)	23·9018	24·2698	26·2217	30·098	52·1602	60·5949
Malaysia (Ringgit)	3·9289	3·9661	4·6203	5·2295	6·477	6·4056
Malta (Pound)	0·5638	0·5813	0·6341	0·6432	0·6449	0·64
Mauritius (Rupee)	30·7386	31·7472	34·4037	35·6534	39·7329	40·4902
Mexico (Peso)	11·8748	12·2089	13·0057	13·2708	15·2139	15·8026
Morocco (Dirham)	13·038	13·9962	15·5795	15·827	15·9401	15·7773
Nepal (Rupee)	87·7806	89·7057	93·24	94·678	99·6421	101·4974
Netherlands (Guilder)	2·6339	2·7639	3·1952	3·2795	3·2854	3·2438
N'nd Antilles (Guilder)	2·7857	2·8334	2·9303	2·9315	2·9713	2·9546
New Zealand (NZ$)	2·2698	2·2861	2·4827	2·6109	3·0946	3·1402
Nicaragua (Gold Cordoba)	13·0508	13·6574	15·3967	15·8654	17·05	17·4486
Nigeria (Naira)	34·3652	34·8876	35·9028	35·9815	36·3062	40·8369
Norway (Krone)	10·0835	10·3301	11·594	11·9974	12·5117	12·5348
Oman (Rial Omani)	0·6015	0·611	0·6311	0·633	0·6387	0·6371
Pakistan (Rupee)	56·3789	59·5736	67·3595	69·1708	77·9532	80·1179
Papua New Guinea (Kina)	2·0476	2·0934	2·3387	2·5122	3·4923	3·6339
Paraguay (Guarani)	3,197·293	3,294·955	3,549·4278	3,700·0241	4,488·0871	4,650·0563
Peru (New Sol)	3·8302	4·0024	4·3604	4·4355	4·8575	5·0689
Philippines (Peso)	40·9431	41·6537	48·6631	54·6569	67·8068	65·6731
Poland (Zloty)	4·1814	4·437	5·3532	5·5712	5·8184	5·9455
Portugal (Escudo)	240·8921	250·3734	287·0583	295·8785	298·5344	294·9011
Qatar (Riyal)	5·6853	5·7748	5·9676	5·9875	6·0411	6·0242
Romania (Leu)	4,811·369	6,204·511	11,532·98	12,433·58	14,935·4667	16,801·7
Russia (Rouble) (Market)	7,958·611	8,451·753	9,475·4158		17·6101	24·9644
1.4.97–31.12.97				9,548·9477		
1.1.98–31.3.98				9·9369		
Rwanda (R Franc)	399·0622	443·2439	505·5068	520·114	538·8919	525·5502
Saudi Arabia (Riyal)	5·8584	5·9511	6·1483	6·1663	6·2222	6·2069
Seychelles (Rupee)	7·7512	7·914	8·2395	8·2923	8·7357	8·7682
Sierra Leone (Leone)	1,358·974	1,337·208	1,298·899	1,345·217	2,083·987	2,358·464
Singapore (S$)	2·2125	2·2508	2·4363	2·5424	2·7692	2·7791
Solomon Islands (SI$)	5·4868	5·6318	6·0008	6·4455	7·9247	7·9434
Somali Republic (Shilling)	4,077·322	4,147·178	4,296·9542	4,298·787	4,348·9917	4,327·245
South Africa (Rand)	6·725	7·1191	7·547	7·7471	9·1681	9·6233
Spain/Balic. Isles (Peseta)	197·843	207·5908	239·785	246·1423	247·4537	244·5556
Sri Lanka (Rupee)	86·3735	89·2778	96·6421	98·7092	107·5062	110·1795
Sudan (Dinar)	186·6184	214·1687	244·0676	250·2443	289·0171	301·7498
Surinam (Guilder)	639·3482	648·9861	661·3535	657·9441	665·6281	662·2998
Swaziland (Lilangeni)	5·7303	7·0875	7·5447	7·7058	9·2103	9·6606
Sweden (Krona)	10·4755	10·8837	12·5085	12·8045	13·1769	13·1419
Switzerland (Franc)	1·932	2·0616	2·3751	2·3972	2·4011	2·376
Syria (Pound)	65·2647	66·4698	66·9719	66·3858	68·6522	70·0802

Average rates of exchange — continued

Average for year ending	31.12.96	31.3.97	31.12.97	31.3.98	31.12.98	31.3.99
Taiwan (New T$)	42·887	43·5986	47·0966	49·4721	55·4635	55·1962
Tanzania (Shilling)	884·3338	922·4204	1,000·059	1,017·706	1,081·67	1,099·416
Thailand (Baht)	39·6131	40·4954	51·4646	60·0541	68·2186	64·3246
Tonga Islands (Pa Anga)	1·9941	2·0103	2·2	2·2942	2·6455	2·6829
Trinidad and Tobago (TT$)	9·1599	9·482	10·1211	10·1684	10·3313	10·322
Tunisia (Dinar)	1·5202	1·582	1·8042	1·854	1·8879	1·8719
Turkey (Lira)	128,783·2	152,836·6	251,532·048	295,626·61	436,113·253	483,958·502
Uganda (New Shilling)	1,622·468	1,651·004	1,760·402	1,814·281	2,041·597	2,131
United Arab Emirates (Dirham)	5·7369	5·8274	6·0205	6·0378	6·0927	6·0776
Uruguay (Peso Uruguayo)	12·4152	13·256	15·4775	16·0205	17·3546	17·6704
USA (US$)	1·5619	1·5866	1·638	1·642	1·6573	1·6542
Venezuela (Bolivar)			800·7369	818·8615	908·8414	931·5492
1.1.96–21.4.96	441·5667					
22.4.96–31.12.96	741·0028					
1.4.96–21.4.96		439·8923				
22.4.96–31.3.97		749·6244				
Vietnam (Dong)	17,165·53	17,556·35	19,135·658	19,665·03	22,094·9167	22,451·46
Yemen North (Rial)	198·2838	209·5619	210·8668	208·4937	218·2828	222·6623
Yemen South (Dinar)						
1.1.96–31.3.96	45·9503					
Zambia (Kwacha)	1,885·7	2,011·703	2,167·322	2,288·8509	3,177·2307	3,508·3228
Zimbabwe (Dollar)	15·6631	16·5514	20·043	22·6336	39·4382	48·2683

Rates of exchange on year-end dates

	31.12.96	31.3.97	31.12.97	31.3.98	31.12.98	31.3.99
Australia ($A)	2·1546	2·0948	2·5253	2·5252	2·7126	2·5563
Austria (Schilling)	18·5497	19·2808	20·8157	21·7878	19·4965	20·5755
Belgium (Franc)	54·3586	56·6252	60·9619	63·8841	57·1561	60·3193
Canada (Can$)	2·3456	2·2683	2·3546	2·3815	2·5555	2·4421
Denmark (Krone)	10·0948	10·4364	11·2664	11·8053	10·589	11·1137
European Union (Euro)						1·4953
France (Franc)	8·8966	9·242	9·8985	10·3753	9·294	9·8084
Germany (Deutsche mark)	2·6373	2·7395	2·9585	3·0969	2·7711	2·9245
Hong Kong (HK$)	13·2369	12·7239	12·749	12·9749	12·8895	12·5101
Irish Republic (Punt)	1·0111	1·0337	1·1544	1·2324	1·1159	1·1776
Italy (Lira)	2,602·03	2,739·27	2,909·06	3,052·58	2,743·43	2,895·26
Japan (Yen)	198·631	203·296	213·937	223·31	187·671	191·182
Luxembourg (Franc)	54·3586	56·6252	60·9619	63·8841	57·1561	60·3193
Netherlands (Guilder)	2·9601	3·08	3·3356	3·491	3·1224	3·2952
Norway (Krone)	10·9273	10·8338	12·1302	12·7672	12·6761	12·4765
Portugal (Escudo)	265·679	275·462	302·498	317·152	284·055	299·776
South Africa (Rand)	8·0046	7·2585	8·0071	8·4381	9·7875	9·9845
Spain/Balic. Isles (Peseta)	222·597	232·786	250·784	262·93	235·746	248·793
Sweden (Krona)	11·6848	12·3703	13·0552	13·3872	13·486	13·2744
Switzerland (Franc)	2·2978	2·3655	2·3999	2·5529	2·2852	2·3894
USA (US$)	1·7113	1·642	1·6454	1·6746	1·6638	1·6143

Note: The material on pages 3 to 5 is Crown Copyright.

D1822906

Double taxation agreements (including protocols and regulations)
Taxes on income and capital gains

Agreements terminated or superseded within the last six years are printed in italic. Amending protocols and exchanges of notes are printed in square brackets. Entry into force after 5.4.70 is indicated in the third column.

Country	SI/SR & O	Entry into force
Antigua & Barbuda	1947/2865	
	[1968/1096]	
Argentina	1997/1777	1.8.97
Armenia†	1986/224	30.1.86
Australia	1968/305	3.10.95
	[1980/707]	21.5.80
	(talks 1997)	
Austria*	1970/1947	17.12.70
	[1979/117]	6.2.79
	[1994/768]	1.12.94
Azerbaijan	*1986/224*	*30.1.86*
	1995/762	3.10.95
Bangladesh	1980/708	8.7.80
Barbados	1970/952	26.6.70
	[1973/2096]	12.12.73
Belarus†	1986/224	30.1.86
	1995/2706	
Belgium*	1987/2053	21.10.89
	(talks 1997)	
Belize	1947/2866	
	[1968/573]	
	[1973/2097]	12.12.73
Bolivia	1995/2707	23.10.95
Bosnia Herzegovina‡	1981/1815	16.9.82
Botswana	1978/183	9.2.78
	(talks 1998)	
Brazil	(talks 1997)	
Brunei	1950/1977	
	[1968/306]	
	[1973/2098]	12.12.73
Bulgaria	1987/2054	28.12.87
Canada§§	1980/709	17.12.80
	[1980/1528]	18.12.80
	[1985/1996]	23.12.85
	1980/780 (dividend)	1.7.80
	[1987/2071]	1.1.88
	1996/1782	30.7.96
Chile	(talks 1998)	
China◇	1984/1826	23.12.84
	[1996/3164]	4.3.97
Colombia	(talks 1994)	
Croatia‡	1981/1815	16.9.82
Cyprus	1975/425	18.3.75
	[1980/1529]	15.12.80
Czech Republic§	1991/2876	20.12.91
Denmark	1980/1960	17.12.80
	[1991/2877]	19.12.91
	[1996/3165]	20.6.97
Ecuador	(text agreed)	
Egypt	1980/1091	23.8.80
Estonia	1994/3207	19.12.94
European Economic Community	(Convention and Directives 90/434/EEC, 90/435/EEC, 90/436/EEC: see TA 1988 s 815B)	23.7.90
Falkland Islands	*1984/363*	*27.6.84*
	[1992/3206]	*30.12.92*
	1997/2985	18.12.97
Faroe Islands**	*1950/1195*	
	[1961/579]	
	1969/1068	*31.5.71*
	[1971/717]	*31.5.71*
	1973/1326	*19.12.75*
	[1975/2190]	*19.12.75*
Fiji*	1976/1342	17.8.76

Country	SI/SR & O	Entry into force
Finland	1970/153	
	[1980/710]	25.4.81
	[1985/1997]	20.2.87
	[1991/2878]	23.12.91
	[1996/3166]	8.8.97
France*§§	1968/1869	
	[1973/1328]	6.8.73
	[1987/466]	7.4.87
	[1987/2055]	23.12.87
	(text agreed)	
Gabon	(talks 1986)	
Gambia	1980/1963	5.7.82
Georgia†	1986/224	30.1.86
German Democratic Republic: now part of German Federal Republic		
German Federal Republic*§§	1967/25	
	[1971/874]	1.6.71
	(talks 1994)	(extended to former GDR from 1.1.91)
Ghana (1978 Convention never entered into force)	*1947/2868*	
	1978/785	
	1993/1800	10.8.94
Greece*	1954/142	
Grenada	1949/361	
	[1968/1867]	
Guernsey	1952/1215	
	[1994/3209]	3.1.95
Guyana	1992/3207	18.12.92
Hungary	1978/1056	27.8.78
Iceland	1991/2879	19.12.91
India	*1981/1120*	*21.10.81*
	1993/1801	25.10.93
Indonesia	*1975/2191*	*3.1.76*
	1994/769	14.4.94
Irish Republic*	1976/2151	23.12.76
	[1976/2152]	23.12.76
	[1995/764]	21.9.95
	[1998/3151]	23.12.98
Isle of Man	1955/1205	
	[1991/2880]	19.12.91
	[1994/3208]	3.1.95
Israel	1963/616	
	[1971/391]	25.3.71
Italy	1990/2590	31.12.90
Ivory Coast	1987/169	10.2.87
Jamaica	1973/1329	31.12.73
Japan	1970/1948	25.12.70
	[1980/1530]	31.10.80
Jersey	1952/1216	
	[1994/3210]	3.1.95
Jordan	(talks 1999)	
Kazakhstan	*1986/224*	*30.1.86*
	1994/3211	15.7.96
	[1998/2567]	2.11.98
Kenya*	1977/1299	18.10.77
Kiribati	1950/750	
	[1968/309]	
	[1974/1271]	25.7.74
Korea	*1978/786*	*31.5.78*
	1996/3168	30.12.96
Kuwait	1999/2036	
Kyrgyzstan†	1986/224	30.1.86
Latvia	1996/3167	30.12.96
Lesotho	*1949/2197*	
	[1968/1868]	
	1997/2986	23.12.97

Double taxation agreements — continued

Country	SI/SR & O	Entry into force
Lithuania§§	(talks 1997)	
Luxembourg*	1968/1100	
	[1980/567]	21.5.80
	[1984/364]	19.3.84
Macedonia‡	1981/1815	16.9.82
Malawi	1956/619	
	[1964/1401]	
	[1968/1101]	
	[1979/302]	14.3.79
Malaysia	1973/1330	13.9.73
	[1987/2056]	26.1.88
	1997/2987	8.7.98
Malta	1962/639	
	[1975/426]	18.3.75
	1995/763	27.3.95
Mauritius*	1981/1121	19.10.81
	[1987/467]	26.10.87
Mexico	1994/3212	15.12.94
Moldova†	1986/224	30.1.86
Mongolia	1996/2598	4.12.96
Montserrat	1947/2869	
	[1968/576]	
Morocco	1991/2881	29.11.90
Myanmar*	1952/751	
Namibia*§§	1962/2352	
	[1962/2788]	
	[1967/1489]	
	[1967/1490]	
	(agreement initialled)	
Netherlands*	1967/1063 (dividend)	
	1980/1961	6.4.81
	[1983/1902]	20.12.90
	[1990/2152]	20.12.90
	(talks 1997)	
New Zealand	1984/365	16.3.84
Nigeria	1987/2057	27.12.87
Norway*§§	1985/1998	20.12.85
	(talks 1997)	
Oman◇◇	1998/2568	9.11.98
Pakistan	1987/2058	8.12.87
Papua New Guinea	1991/2882	20.12.91
Philippines	1978/184	9.2.78
Poland	1978/282	25.2.78
Portugal*	1969/599	
Romania	1977/57	17.1.77
Russian Federation†	1986/224	30.1.86
	1994/3213	18.4.97
St Christopher and Nevis	1947/2872	
Serbia and Montenegro‡	1981/1815	16.9.82

Country	SI/SR & O	Entry into force
Sierra Leone	1947/2873	
	[1968/1104]	
Singapore	1967/483	
	[1978/787]	4.8.78
	1997/2988	19.12.97
Slovakia§	1991/2876	20.12.91
Slovenia‡	1981/1815	16.9.82
Solomon Islands	1950/748	
	[1968/574]	
	[1974/1270]	25.7.74
South Africa*	1969/864	
	(talks 2000)	
Spain	1976/1919	25.11.76
	[1995/765]	26.5.95
Sri Lanka	1980/713	21.5.80
Sudan	1977/1719	25.10.77
Swaziland*	1969/380	
Sweden	1984/366	26.3.84
	(talks 1997)	
Switzerland*	1978/1408	7.10.78
	[1982/714]	18.5.82
	[1994/3215]	19.12.94
Tajikistan†	1986/224	30.1.86
Thailand	1981/1546	20.11.81
Trinidad and Tobago	1983/1903	22.12.83
Tunisia	1984/133	8.2.84
Turkey	1988/932	26.10.88
Turkmenistan†	1986/224	30.1.86
Uganda	1952/1213	
	1993/1802	21.12.93
Ukraine	1986/224	30.1.86
	1993/1803	11.8.93
United Arab Emirates	(text agreed)	
USA	1946/1331 (dividend)	
	[1955/499]	
	[1961/985]	
	[1980/779]	22.5.80
	1980/568	25.4.80
	[1994/1418] (dividend)	16.6.94
	[1996/1781] (dividend)	30.7.96
	(talks 1999)	
Uzbekistan	1986/224	30.1.86
	1994/770	10.6.94
Venezuela	1996/2599	31.12.96
Vietnam	1994/3216	15.12.94
Zambia*	1972/1721	29.3.73
	[1981/1816]	14.1.83
Zimbabwe	1982/1842	11.2.83

* Individuals resident in these countries are entitled to personal reliefs, similar to the relief under TA 1988 s 278, under the provisions of double taxation treaties between these countries and the UK. Non-resident nationals of all EEA countries are entitled to personal allowances as from 6 April 1996: see FA 1996 s 145.

** Following its termination by Denmark, the agreement ceased to have effect in the UK from 1 April 1997 for corporation tax and 6 April 1997 for income tax.

† SP 3/92: as an interim measure the Convention with the former USSR is to be regarded as applicable pending negotiation of new Conventions with the successor states. Such conventions have been concluded and are in force with Azerbaijan, Kazakhstan, Russia, Ukraine and Uzbekistan. A convention has been concluded with Belarus, but this has not yet been ratified.

‡ SP 6/93: the treaty with former Yugoslavia is treated as remaining in force between the UK and, respectively, Croatia and Slovenia, until bilateral agreements are signed. The UK also applies that treaty to Bosnia Herzegovina, Macedonia and 'rump' Yugoslavia (i.e. Serbia and Montenegro). Macedonia applies the treaty vis à vis the UK, but the Inland Revenue is not aware of the position taken by Bosnia Herzegovina or Serbia and Montenegro.

§ SP 5/93: the treaty with the former Czechoslovakia is treated as remaining in force between the UK and, respectively, the Czech Republic and Slovakia.

§§ Negotiations with these countries are seen as a priority (IR Press Release of 28 April 1998).

◇The 1984 Agreement does not apply to the Hong Kong Special Administrative Region.

◇◇Certain provisions relating to profits, income and gains from ships and aircraft operated in international traffic take effect from 1 January 1979 (Article 29(2)).

Double taxation agreements — continued

Shipping and air transport profits

Country	SI or SR & O	Country	SI or SR & O
Algeria (air)	1984/362	Jordan	1979/300
Argentina	*1949/1435*	Kuwait (air)**	1984/1825
Armenia (USSR air)*	1974/1269	Kyrgyzstan (USSR air)*	1974/1269
Bahrain (air)	(text agreed)	Lebanon	1964/278
Belarus (USSR air)*	1974/1269	Moldova (USSR air)*	1974/1269
Brazil	1968/572	Oman (air)***	(text agreed)
Cameroon (air)	1982/1841	Qatar (air)	(text agreed)
China (air)	1981/1119	*Russia (USSR air)**	*1974/1269*
Congo Democratic Republic	1977/1298	Saudi Arabia (air)	1994/767
Ethiopia (air)	1977/1297	Tajikistan (USSR air)*	1974/1269
Georgia (USSR air)*	1974/1269	Turkmenistan (USSR air)*	1974/1269
Hong Kong (air)	1998/2566	United Arab Emirates (air)	(text agreed)
Iran (air)	1960/2419	*USSR (air)**	*1974/1269*

* The Revenue has confirmed that this Arrangement will be treated in the same way as the Convention covering income and capital gains SI 1986/224. See note † on p 7.

** To be superseded by the comprehensive Agreement (SI 1999/2036, Art. 30), p 7 above.

*** This agreement was not brought into force. See now the comprehensive Agreement, p 7 above.

Taxes on capital

Country	SI	Country	SI
France	1963/1319	South Africa	1979/576
India	1956/998	Sweden	1981/840
Ireland	1978/1107		1989/986
Italy	1968/304	Switzerland	*1957/426*
Netherlands	1980/706		1994/3214
	[1996/730]	USA	1979/1454
Pakistan	1957/1522		(talks 2000)

Income arising abroad — Schedule D assessment

	Case IV	Case V		
	Securities	Professions, trades, etc	Pensions	Possessions
NON-RESIDENTS	Exempt	Exempt	Exempt	Exempt
RESIDENTS				
1) **Foreign domicile**	Remittance	Remittance	Remittance	Remittance
2) **UK domicile**				
(a) Non Commonwealth citizen[1]	Arising	Arising	90%[3] arising	Arising
(b) Commonwealth citizen[2]				
(i) ordinarily resident	Arising	Arising	90%[3] arising	Arising
(ii) not ordinarily resident	Remittance	Remittance	Remittance	Remittance

[1] But not citizen of the Republic of Ireland.
[2] Or citizen of the Republic of Ireland.
[3] Pensions paid by the governments of the Federal Republic of Germany or of Austria to victims of Nazi persecution are exempt from 6.4.86. Previously 50% exemption.

Schedule E liability of non-resident employees   see p 71.

Tax-free (FOTRA) securities

Under FA 1996 s 154 interest on certain securities ('FOTRA securities') issued by the Treasury is exempt from tax where the beneficial owner is not ordinarily resident in the UK. Except in the case of 3½% War Loan 1952 or after, the exemption does not apply where the securities are held for the purposes of a trade or business carried on in the UK. From 6 April 1998, FOTRA status has been extended to all government stock on the terms of FA 1996 s 154 ((1998) SWTI 440).

General

Certificates of tax deposit

The Series 7 Prospectus came into operation on 1 October 1993.

From 1 October 1993, certificates are not available for purchase for use against corporation tax liabilities, although certificates purchased before that date can be used before 1 October 1999 and set against all liabilities listed in the schedule to the Series 6 Prospectus.

Certificates are available to individuals, trustees, companies or other persons or bodies for the payment of any taxes or other liabilities listed in the schedule to the Prospectus. Minimum first deposit £2,000; subsequent deposits not less than £500.

Interest is paid without deduction of tax and is assessed under Schedule D Case III. It will only be paid for the first 6 years of a deposit. Under the Series 7 Prospectus a deposit bears interest for the first year at the rate in force at the time of the deposit and for each subsequent year at the rate in force on the anniversary of the deposit. No bonus or interest supplement is payable.

Series 7
Deposits of £100,000 or over: rate varies according to number of months held for in relevant year:

A = under £100,000
B = £100,000 or over

From	Amount	Held for (mths in yr)	Pay't of tax %	Cashed %
Series 7 (1.10.93)				
13. 9.94	A	no limit	2	1
	B	under 1	2	1
		1-under 6	4¾	2½
		6-under 9	5	2½
		9-12	5½	2¾
8.12.94	A	no limit	2½	1¼
	B	under 1	2½	1¼
		1-under 3	5¼	2¾
		3-under 6	5½	2¾
		6-under 9	5¾	3
		9-12	6	3
3. 2.95	A	no limit	3	1½
	B	under 1	3	1½
		1-under 6	5¾	3
		6-under 9	6	3
		9-12	6¼	3¼
14.12.95	A	no limit	2½	1¼
	B	under 1	2½	1¼
		1-under 3	5½	2¾
		3-under 9	5	2½
		9-12	4¾	2½
19. 1.96	A	no limit	2¾	1½
	B	under 1	2¾	1½
		1-under 3	5¼	2¾
		3-under 9	4¾	2½
		9-12	4½	2¼
11. 3.96	A	no limit	2½	1¼
	B	under 1	2½	1¼
		1-under 3	5	2½
		3-under 9	4¾	2½
		9-12	4½	2¼
7. 6.96	A	no limit	2¼	1¼
	B	under 1	2¼	1¼
		1-12	4¾	2½
31.10.96	A	no limit	2½	1¼
	B	under 1	2½	1¼
		1-under 3	5¼	2¾
		3–12	5	2½
7. 5.97	A	no limit	2¾	1½
	B	under 1	2¾	1½
		1-under 3	5½	2¾
		3-under 6	5¼	2¾
		6-under 9	5½	2¾
		9-12	5¼	2¾
9. 6.97	A	no limit	3	1½
	B	under 1	3	1½
		1–12	5½	2¾
11. 7.97	A	no limit	3¼	1¾
	B	under 1	3¼	1¾
		1-under 3	6	3
		3-under 9	5¾	3
		9–12	6	3
8. 8.97	A	no limit	4½	2¼
	B	under 1	4½	2¼
		1-under 9	6	3
		9-12	5¾	3
7.11.97	A	no limit	4	2
	B	under 1	4	2
		1-under 6	6½	3¼
		6–12	6¼	3¼
5. 6.98	A	no limit	4	2
	B	under 1	4	2
		1-under 3	6½	3¼
		3-under 9	6¼	3¼
		9–12	6	3
9.10.98	A	no limit	3¾	2
	B	under 1	3¾	2
		1-under 3	6¼	3¼
		3-under 6	5¾	3
		6-under 9	5½	2¾
		9–12	5¼	2¾
6.11.98	A	no limit	3¼	1¾
	B	under 1	3¼	1¾
		1-under 3	5¾	3
		3-under 6	5¼	2¾
		6-under 9	5	2½
		9–12	4¾	2½
11.12.98	A	no limit	3¼	1¾
	B	under 1	3	1½
		1-under 3	5¼	2¾
		3-under 6	4¾	2½
		6-under 9	4½	2¼
		9–12	4¼	2¼
8.1.99	A	no limit	2½	1¼
	B	under 1	2½	1¼
		1-under 3	5	2½
		3-under 6	4½	2¼
		6-12	4	2
5.2.99	A	no limit	1¾	1
	B	under 1	1¾	1
		1-under 3	4½	2¼
		3-under 6	4	2
		6-12	3¾	2
9.4.99	A	no limit	1¾	1
	B	under 1	1¾	1
		1-under 3	4¼	2¼
		3-under 6	4	2
		6–12	3¾	2
11.6.99	A	no limit	1½	¾
	B	under 1	1½	¾
		1–12	4	2
9.9.99	A	no limit	1¾	1
	B	under 1	1¾	1
		1–12	4½	2¼
4.11.99	A	no limit	2	1
	B	under 1	2	1
		1-under 3	5	2½
		3-under 12	4¾	2½
14.1.00	A	no limit	2¼	1¼
	B	under 1	2¼	1¼
		1-under 9	5	2½
		9–12	5¼	2¾
11.2.00	A	no limit	2½	1¼
	B	under 1	2½	1¼
		1-under 3	5¼	2¾
		3-under 6	5	2½
		6–12	5¼	2¾

Due dates of tax

Capital gains tax

From 1996–97:
(TMA 1970 s 59B. There are no provisions for payment on account for capital gains tax.)
Normally 31 January following end of year of assessment.
(See also *Extended due dates* under **Income tax**, below)
Before 1996–97:
Later of *(a)* 1 December following end of year of assessment, and
          (b) 30 days after issue of notice of assessment.

Corporation tax

Generally (accounting periods ending after 30 September 1993: pay and file and self assessment)
(TMA 1970 s 59D, substituted by FA 1998 Sch 19 para 29 for accounting periods ending after 30 June 1999.)
9 months and 1 day after end of accounting period.
Instalments for larger companies (TMA 1970 s 59E, SI 1998/3175)
(Large: profits exceeding upper relevant maximum amount in force at end of accounting period, subject to certain restrictions: reg 3.)
    1st instalment: 6 months and 13 days from start of accounting period (or date of final instalment if earlier);
    (2nd instalment: 3 months after 1st instalment, if length of accounting period allows);
    (3rd instalment: 3 months after 2nd instalment, if length of accounting period allows);
    Final instalment: 3 months and 14 days from end of accounting period.
Transitional provisions (reg 4) percentage of total liability payable by instalments for accounting periods ending:
    after 30 June 1999 but before 1 July 2000: 60%
    after 30 June 2000 but before 1 July 2001: 72%
    after 30 June 2001 but before 1 July 2002: 88%
(balance due and payable in accordance with *Generally* above).
Advance corporation tax (abolished from 6 April 1999) (FA 1998 ss 31, 32, Sch 3)
Tax in respect of franked payments to be included in a return is due 14 days after a return period ends.
Return periods end on 31 March, 30 June, 30 September, 31 December and at the end of each accounting period, when not one of the above.
Close companies: tax on loans to participators
Loans etc made in accounting periods ending after 30 March 1996: 9 months and 1 day after the end of the accounting period. Previously 14 days after the end of the accounting period in which the loan was made. To be included in instalment payments for large companies in respect of accounting periods ending after 30 June 1999 (TMA 1970 s 59E(11), see above).

Income tax

From 1997–98:
(1)   *Payment on account* (TMA 1970 s 59A)*
A payment on account is required where a taxpayer was assessed to income tax in respect of the immediately preceding year in an amount exceeding the amount of tax deducted at source in respect of that year (subject to a de minimis limit, see below). This excess is known as the "relevant amount".
The payment on account is made in 2 equal instalments due on –
   (a) 31 January during the year of assessment, and
   (b) 31 July in the following year of assessment.
No payments on account are required where–
   (a) the aggregate of the relevant amount (see above) and the Class 4 NIC liability for the preceding year is less than £500; or
   (b) more than 80% of the taxpayer's income tax and Class 4 NIC liability for the immediately preceding year was met by tax deducted at source.
From 1996–97:
(2)   *Payment of income tax* (TMA 1970 s 59B)
Balance of income tax due for a year of assessment (after deducting payments on account, tax deducted at source and credits in respect of dividends, etc) is due on:
31 January following end of year of assessment (i.e. the first such payment was due on 31 January 1998).
   Extended due dates:
   (a) If a taxpayer has given notice of liability within 6 months of the end of the year of assessment (as required by TMA 1970 s 7), but a notice to make a return is not given until after 31 October following the end of the year of assessment, the final payment is not due until 3 months after the notice is given (TMA 1970 s 59B(3)).
   (b) If an amended self-assessment is made less than 30 days before the due date (or the extended due date at (*a*) above) the additional tax is payable on or before the day following the end of a 30-day period beginning on the day on which notice of the amendment is given (TMA 1970 s 59B(5)).
   (c) If an assessment other than a self-assessment under TMA 1970 s 9 is made, tax payable under the assessment is due on the day following the end of a 30-day period beginning on the day on which notice of the assessment is given (TMA 1970 s 59B(6)).
For partnership businesses commenced before 6 April 1994 where there has been no subsequent deemed cessation and recommencement, each partner's share of the income tax paid for 1996–97 by the partnership was treated for these purposes as if it had been tax deducted at source.
*(For 1996–97 only:***
(1)   *Payment on account* (TMA 1970 s 59A as amended by FA 1995 Sch 21 para 2)
A payment on account was required where a taxpayer was assessed to income tax in respect of 1995–96 in an amount exceeding the aggregate of (a) the amount of higher-rate tax charged on any income not subject to PAYE or income from which tax had been deducted or was treated as deducted, and which was attributable to the difference between the higher rate and the basic rate (or lower rate in the case of dividend income); (b) tax deducted at source; and (c) the excess of any Schedule E liability over tax deducted under PAYE etc (subject to a de minimis limit, see below). This excess was known as the "relevant amount".
The payment on account was to be made in 2 instalments as follows–
   (a) due on 31 January 1997:
      (i) 100% of 1995–96 tax charged under Schedule A and Schedule D Cases III to VI and
      (ii) 50% of the remainder (including Class 4 NIC)
   excluding tax deducted at source, and
   (b) due on 31 July 1997: 50% of the remainder (including Class 4 NIC).
No payments on account were required where the aggregate of the relevant income (see above) and the Class 4 NIC liability for 1995–96 was less than £500.)
** These rules do not apply to partnership businesses commenced before 6 April 1994 where there has been no subsequent deemed cessation and recommencement. For 1996–97, such partnerships were required to pay tax in two instalments on 1 January and 1 July 1997, as under the old rules (see p 12).

Interest on overdue tax see p 11.   **Repayment supplement** see p 15.
Remission of tax see p 14.

Before 1996–97 (These rules applied also, in the case of Schedule D Cases I, II and V, for 1996–97 to partnerships commenced before 6 April 1994 and which had not undergone a deemed cessation and recommenced subsequently):

Schedule A   Later of   *(a)*   1 January in year of assessment, and
                           (b)   30 days after issue of notice of assessment.

Schedule C   Tax deducted by paying agent and due within 30 days of issue of notice of assessment.

Schedule D Cases I, II and V (trades, professions, etc): 2 equal payments due –
                           (a)   1 January in year of assessment (or 30 days after issue of notice of assessment, if later) and
                           (b)   1 July following year of assessment (or 30 days after issue of notice of assessment, if later).

Schedule D Cases III, IV, V (other than trades, professions) and VI: Later of –
                           (a)   1 January in year of assessment, and
                           (b)   30 days after issue of notice of assessment.

Schedule E   Deductible from emoluments under PAYE
               Assessments: 14 days after application by collector.

Higher rate on income from which income tax has been deducted (other than under PAYE), or is treated as having been deducted or paid, or income chargeable under Schedule F
               Later of   *(a)*   1 December following end of year of assessment, and
                           (b)   30 days after issue of notice of assessment.

Inheritance tax (capital transfer tax)

Chargeable transfers other than on death, made between:
6 April and 30 September – 30 April in next year.
1 October and 5 April – 6 months after end of month in which chargeable transfer is made.

Chargeable events following conditional exemption for heritage etc. property and charge on disposal of trees or underwood before the second death
                           – 6 months after end of month in which chargeable event occurs.

Transfers on death
Earlier of *(a)* 6 months after end of month in which death occurs, and
            (b) delivery of account by personal representatives.

Tax or extra tax becoming payable on death: (1) chargeable transfers and potentially exempt transfers within 7 years of death, or
                           (2) gifts in excess of £100,000 made to political parties before 15 March 1988 and within 1 year of death: due 6 months after end of month in which death takes place.

Interest on overdue tax

Interest on overdue income tax and capital gains tax

(NB: These rules apply with respect to liabilities for 1996–97 and subsequent years and to liabilities for 1995–96 and earlier years assessed after 5 April 1998. However, for partnerships with trades, etc set up and commenced before 6 April 1994, the previous rules continued to apply for the year 1996–97.)

For payments on account (under TMA 1970 s 59A(2)), tax not postponed pending an appeal (under TMA 1970 s 55) and balancing payments (under TMA 1970 s 59B), interest runs from the due date to the date of payment, on the amount outstanding. For the due date, see pp 10, 11. In respect of payments on account, interest is charged on the difference between the amount that ought to have been paid and the amount actually paid.

For amendments to self-assessments (under TMA 1970 s 9(4)–(6)) and discovery assessments (under TMA 1970 s 29), interest normally runs from the annual filing date for the relevant tax year.

Where a claim made under TMA 1970 s 59A(3) or (4) to reduce payments on account proves to be excessive, an underpayment may arise. In such a case, interest is charged on the difference between the amount actually paid and the amount that ought to have been paid if the claim had been made correctly.

Surcharge on unpaid income tax and capital gains tax (TMA 1970 s 59C, amended by FA 1995 s 109)

Applies from 1996–97, and for assessments for 1995–96 or an earlier year of assessment made after 5 April 1998 (FA 1995 s 109(2)). (Tax taken into account in determining certain other penalties (under TMA 1970 ss 7, 93(5), 95 and 95A) is ignored for the purposes of calculating the surcharge.)

28 days: Where income tax or capital gains tax becomes payable and all or part of it remains unpaid the day following 28 days after the due date, the taxpayer is liable to a surcharge of 5% of the unpaid tax.

6 months: The taxpayer is liable to a further surcharge of 5% on any of the tax remaining unpaid 6 months and 1 day from the due date.

Interest is payable on surcharge from the expiry of 30 days beginning on the day on which the surcharge is imposed until the date of payment. It is charged at the rate applying to overdue income tax and capital gains tax (see p 13).

Interest on overdue corporation tax (accounting periods ending after 30 September 1993)

Interest runs from the due date (see p 10) to the date of payment: TMA 1970 s 87A (wording amended by FA 1994 Sch 19 para 24 and SI 1998/3175 reg 7 for accounting periods ending after 30 June 1999) and ss 59D (substituted from the same date) and 59E (inserted from the same date).

For instalment payments by large companies for accounting periods ending after 30 June 1999, a special rate of interest runs from the due date to the earlier of the date of payment and nine months after the end of the accounting period (after which the normal rate applies). SI 1989/1297 regs 32A and 32B (inserted by SI 1998/3176 reg 6).

Interest on inheritance tax

Interest runs from the due date (see above) to the date of payment.

Interest on overdue tax — continued

Interest on PAYE and national insurance

Employer's tax and Class 1 national insurance payable under PAYE (1992–93 and future years)	19 April following deduction year to date of payment
(Settlement agreement: Income Tax (Employments) Regulations 1993 Part VI Ch V)	19 October following year to which agreement relates to date of payment
Class 1A national insurance	19 April following year in which contributions due to date of payment
Class 4 national insurance	See p 10

'Old' rules:

Period for which interest runs: default interest charged under TMA 1970 s 88 (*repealed* with effect for assessments in respect of 1996–97 and subsequent years (1997–98 and subsequent years if the taxpayer is a partnership whose trade etc commenced before 6 April 1994), and for assessments in respect of 1995–96 and earlier years where such assessments are made after 5 April 1998.)

Advance corporation tax	Not applicable
Capital gains tax	1 December following end of tax year for which charged to date of payment
Income tax	
Schedule A	1 January in tax year for which charged to date of payment
Schedule C	*1 January in tax year for which charged to date of payment*
Schedule D Cases I, II and V (foreign trades and professions)	One-half from 1 January in tax year for which charged; one-half from following 1 July to date of payment
Schedule D Cases III, IV, V (other than trades etc), VI	1 January in tax year for which charged to date of payment
Schedule E	1 January in tax year for which charged to date of payment
Higher rate tax	1 December following end of tax year for which charged to date of payment

Period for which interest runs: non-default interest (for partnerships with trades, etc set up and commenced before 6 April 1994, in respect of years before 1997–98, and generally for liabilities in respect of 1995–96 and earlier years assessed before 6 April 1998, only)
(*For due date see pages 10 and 11, above)

Advance corporation tax	Due date* to date of payment
Capital gains tax	See p 12 (below)
Capital transfer tax	Due date* to date of payment
Corporation tax (accounting periods ending after 30 September 1993)	Due date to date of payment
Development land tax	3 months after event giving rise to liability to date of payment
Employer's tax and Class 1 national insurance payable under PAYE (1992–93 and subsequent years)	19 April following deduction year to date of payment
Class 1A national insurance	19 April following year in which contributions due to date of payment
Class 4 national insurance	See p 12 (below)
Income tax	
Schedule A	See p 12 (below)
Schedule C	See p 12 (below)
Schedule D	See p 12 (below)
Schedule E	Due date to date of payment
Higher rate tax	See p 12 (below)
Inheritance tax	Due date* (see above) to date of payment

Capital gains tax, income tax under Schedules A, C, D (for partnerships with trades, etc set up and commenced before 6 April 1994, or liabilities in respect of 1995–96 and earlier years assessed before 6 April 1998, only)

Interest runs from due date for payment (see pp10, 11) until paid *UNLESS* the assessment is under appeal *and* an application is made to postpone the tax (*or* if additional tax not charged by the assessment is found payable on appeal), when the interest runs from the *later* of—

    (a) the original due date (see column *(a)* below), and
    (b) the *earlier* of—   (i) the date on which the tax actually becomes due (see column *(b)* (i) below), and
                     (ii) the date given in TMA 1970 s 86(4) Table (see column *(b)* (ii) below).

Tax	*(a)*	*(b)*(i)		*(b)*(ii)
		(1)	(2)	
	Original due date	*Tax not postponed*	*Tax postponed but payable or additional tax determined payable*	*Date given in TMA 1970 s 86(4) Table*
Capital gains tax Higher rate tax	1 December following y of a†	Due date *(a)*, or 30 days after the determination of the postponement application, if later	Due date *(a)*, or 30 days after issue of notice of total tax due, if later	1 June after end of *next* y of a
Schedule A Schedule D Cases III (except public/foreign dividends) IV, V (other than trades, professions), VI	1 January in y of a†	As above	As above	1 July following y of a
Schedule C Schedule D Case III (public/foreign dividends etc)	30 days from issue of notice of assessment	30 days after determination of postponement application	30 days after issue of notice of total tax due	6 months after due date *(a)*
Schedule D Cases I,II (including Class 4 national insurance contributions), V (foreign trades, professions)	2 equal instalments: 1 Jan in y of a† and 1 July following y of a†	Each instalment: appropriate due date *(a)*, or 30 days after determination of application, if later	Each instalment: appropriate due date *(a)*, or 30 days after issue of notice of total tax due, if later	1 July following y of a

† Or 30 days after issue of notice of assessment, if later; not applicable for the purposes of column *(b)* (i) or (ii).

Prescribed rate

	Rate	Period
(1) **Generally:** Late payment or (from 1 October 1993) repayment of corporation tax for accounting periods ending before 1 October 1993. Income tax (including PAYE due from employer) (before 31 January 1997); capital gains tax (before 31 January 1997). Before 31 January 1997, the rates shown also applied to advance corporation tax; development land tax; Class 1, 1A and 4 national insurance contributions; income tax on company payments; petroleum revenue tax (including advance petroleum revenue tax); stamp duty reserve tax	6.5% 5.75% 6.5% 7.25% 6.25% 7% 6·25% 5·5% 6·25% 7% 7·75% 9·25% 10% 10·75% 11·5% 12·25% 13% 12·25% 11·5% 10·75% 9·75% 7·75% 8·25% 9% 8·25% 9% 9·5% 8·5% 11% 8% 12% 9% 6% 4% 3%	from 6 February 2000 6 March 1999–5 February 2000 6 January 1999–5 March 1999 6 August 1997–5 January 1999 6 February 1996–5 August 1997 6 March 1995–5 February 1996 6 October 1994–5 March 1995 6 January 1994–5 October 1994 6 March 1993–5 January 1994 6 December 1992–5 March 1993 6 November 1992–5 December 1992 6 October 1991–5 November 1992 6 July 1991–5 October 1991 6 May 1991–5 July 1991 6 March 1991–5 May 1991 6 November 1990–5 March 1991 6 November 1989–5 November 1990 6 July 1989–5 November 1989 6 January 1989–5 July 1989 6 October 1988–5 January 1989 6 August 1988–5 October 1988 6 May 1988–5 August 1988 6 December 1987–5 May 1988 6 September 1987–5 December 1987 6 June 1987–5 September 1987 6 April 1987–5 June 1987 6 November 1986–5 April 1987 6 August 1986–5 November 1986 1 May 1985–5 August 1986 1 December 1982–30 April 1985 1 January 1980–30 November 1982 1 July 1974–31 December 1979 19 April 1969–30 June 1974[1] 19 April 1967–18 April 1969 before 19 April 1967
(2) **Income tax, capital gains tax and Class 1, 1A and 4 national insurance contributions:** from 31 January 1997 (SI 1989/1297; SI 1996/3187) **Stamp duty and stamp duty reserve tax:** from 1 October 1999 (SI 1999/2538; SI 1999/2536)	8.5% 7.5% 8.5% 9.5% 8.5%	from 6 February 2000 6 March 1999–5 February 2000 6 January 1999–5 March 1999 6 August 1997–5 January 1999 31 January 1997–5 August 1997
(3) **Corporation tax self assessment:** (accounting periods ending after 30 June 1999) (a) Instalment payments (except where tax still unpaid nine months after end of accounting period)	8% 7.75% 7.5% 7.25% 7% 7.25% 7.5% 8% 8.25%	from 21 February 2000 24 January 2000–20 February 2000 15 November 1999–23 January 2000 20 September 1999–14 November 1999 21 June 1999–19 September 1999 19 April 1999–20 June 1999 15 February 1999–18 April 1999 18 January 1999–14 February 1999 17 January 1999–17 January 1999
(b) Payments other than instalment payments (or for instalment payments still unpaid nine months after end of accounting period)	8.5% 7.5%	from 6 February 2000 6 March 1999–5 February 2000
(4) **Corporation tax pay and file:** (accounting periods ending after 30 September 1993)	6.75% 5.75% 6.5% 7.5% 6.25% 7% 6·25% 5·5% 6·25%	from 6 February 2000 6 March–5 February 2000 6 January 1999–5 March 1999 6 August 1997–5 January 1999 6 February 1996–5 August 1997 6 March 1995–5 February 1996 6 October 1994–5 March 1995 6 January 1994–5 October 1994 1 October 1993–5 January 1994
(5) **Income tax on company payments** (due on or after 14 October 1999)	8.5% 7.5%	from 6 February 2000 14 October 1999–5 February 2000
(6) **Income tax on company payments** (due before 14 October 1999), **advance corporation tax, development land tax, petroleum revenue tax** (including **advance petroleum revenue tax**) and **stamp duty reserve tax** (before 1 October 1999): from 31 January 1997	6.5% 5.75% 6.5% 7.25% 6.25%	from 6 February 2000 6 March 1999–5 February 2000 6 January 1999–5 March 1999 6 August 1997–5 January 1999 31 January 1997–5 August 1997

	Rate	Period
(7) **Inheritance tax** and **capital transfer tax:**	5%	from 6 February 2000
The rates for periods before 16 December 1986	4%	6 March 1999–5 February 2000
applied *unless* the transfer was one listed at (7)	5%	6 October 1994–5 March 1999
below	4%	6 January 1994–5 October 1994
	5%	6 December 1992–5 January 1994
	6%	6 November 1992–5 December 1992
	8%	6 July 1991–5 November 1992
	9%	6 May 1991–5 July 1991
	10%	6 March 1991–5 May 1991
	11%	6 July 1989–5 March 1991
	9%	6 October 1988–5 July 1989
	8%	6 August 1988–5 October 1988
	6%	6 June 1987–5 August 1988
	8%	16 December 1986–5 June 1987
	11%	1 May 1985–15 December 1986
	8%	1 December 1982–30 April 1985
	12%	1 January 1980–30 November 1982
	9%	before 1 January 1980
(8) **Inheritance tax:** chargeable transfers on death or	9%	1 May 1985–15 December 1986
potentially exempt transfers	6%	1 December 1982–30 April 1985
Capital transfer tax: chargeable transfers on death	9%	1 January 1980–30 November 1982
only	6%	before 1 January 1980

[1] The rate of default interest charged under TMA 1970 s 88 for 19 April 1969–30 June 1974 was 4%.

Remission of tax

By concession, arrears of tax may be waived if they result from the Revenue's failure to make proper and timely use of information supplied by the taxpayer or, where it affects the taxpayer's coding, by his or her employer. From 26 April 1994 the concession also applies to information supplied by the DSS affecting the taxpayer's entitlement to a retirement or widow's pension (see Concession A19). The concession only applies where the taxpayer could reasonably have believed that his or her affairs were in order and (unless the circumstances are exceptional) where the taxpayer is notified of the arrears more than 12 months after the end of the tax year in which the Revenue received the information indicating that more tax was due.

Before 11 March 1996, the proportion of arrears which could be remitted was determined by a scale according to the taxpayer's income.

Date of notification of arrears	Taxpayer's gross income*	Proportion remitted
17 February 1993–10 March 1996	£15,500 or below	Whole
	Above £15,500 but not above £18,000	3/4
	Above £18,000 but not above £22,000	1/2
	Above £22,000 but not above £26,000	1/4
	Above £26,000 but not above £40,000	1/10
	Above £40,000	None

Repayment supplement

Calculated as simple interest on the amount of tax repaid. The supplement is tax free. (From 31 January 1997 the rate is determined under SI 1989/1297 as amended by SI 1996/3187, see below.)

These rates apply also to overpaid Class 1, 1A and 4 national insurance contributions but not to overpaid corporation tax for accounting periods ending after 30 September 1993 (see p 16). The rates also apply to overpaid stamp duty and stamp duty reserve tax from 1 October 1999.

Period to which supplement relates	Rate
from 6 February 2000	4%
6 March 1999–5 February 2000	3%
6 January 1999–5 March 1999	4%
6 August 1997–5 January 1999	4·75%
6 February 1997–5 August 1997	4%
6 February 1996–5 February 1997	6·25%
6 March 1995–5 February 1996	7%
6 October 1994–5 March 1995	6·25%
6 January 1994–5 October 1994	5·5%
6 March 1993–5 January 1994	6·25%
6 December 1992–5 March 1993	7%
6 November 1992–5 December 1992	7·75%
6 October 1991–5 November 1992	9·25%
6 July 1991–5 October 1991	10%
6 May 1991–5 July 1991	10·75%
6 March 1991–5 May 1991	11·5%
6 November 1990–5 March 1991	12·25%
6 November 1989–5 November 1990	13%
6 July 1989–5 November 1989	12·25%
6 January 1989–5 July 1989	11·5%
6 October 1988–5 January 1989	10·75%
6 August 1988–5 October 1988	9·75%
6 May 1988–5 August 1988	7·75%
6 December 1987–5 May 1988	8·25%
6 September 1987–5 December 1987	9%
6 June 1987–5 September 1987	8·25%
6 April 1987–5 June 1987	9%
6 November 1986–5 April 1987	9·5%
6 August 1986–5 November 1986	8·5%
6 May 1985–5 August 1986	11%
6 December 1982–5 May 1985	8%
6 January 1980–5 December 1982	12%
6 April 1974–5 January 1980	9%
Before 6 April 1974	6%

'New' rules:
Income tax (TA 1988 s 824; FA 1997 s 92)

From 1996–97 (1997–98 for partnerships whose trade, profession or business commenced before 6 April 1994) repayment supplement applies to:

(a) amounts paid on account of income tax
(b) income tax paid by or on behalf of an individual
(c) surcharges on late payments of tax
(d) penalties incurred by an individual under any provision of TMA 1970

but excluding amounts paid in excess of the maximum the taxpayer is required to pay.

Except for tax deducted at source, the repayment supplement runs *from* the date on which the tax, penalty or surcharge was paid *to* the date on which the order for repayment is issued. For tax deducted at source, repayment supplement runs from 31 January after the end of the tax year for which the tax was deducted.

Capital gains tax (TCGA 1992 s 283; FA 1997 s 92)

From 1996–97 repayment supplement runs *from* the date on which the tax was paid *to* the date on which the order for repayment is issued.

'Old' rules:
Individuals, personal representatives and trusts. (Before 1996–97, or before 1997–98 for partnerships whose trade, profession or business commenced before 6 April 1994.)

Repayments of IT, surtax or CGT made over 12 months after year of assessment to which repayment relates. Calculated *from* later of

(a) end of year of assessment following that for which repayment is made, and
(b) end of year of assessment in which overpayment of tax was made,

to end of tax month in which repayment order issued (TA 1988 s 824 as originally enacted).

Companies: interest on tax overpaid (accounting periods ending after 30 September 1993 and before 1 July 1999) (TA 1988 s 826)

These provisions are amended for accounting periods ending after 30 June 1999, to which corporation tax self-assessment applies. Advance corporation tax is abolished from 6 April 1999 (FA 1998 ss 31, 32, SI 1999/358).

Repayments of corporation tax, repayments of ACT in respect of foreign income dividends, repayments of income tax in respect of payments received, and payments of tax credits in respect of franked investment income received, made after the material date.

Calculated *from* the material date *to* the date the repayment order is issued.

For corporation tax, the material date is the later of

(a) the date on which the tax was paid and

(b) the date on which the tax became, or would have become, due and payable – generally, nine months and one day after the end of the accounting period.

For ACT, the material date is the date on which corporation tax for the accounting period in which the distribution was made became, or would have become, due and payable – generally, nine months and one day after the end of the accounting period.

For repayments of income tax in respect of payments received and payments of tax credits in respect of franked investment income received, the material date is the date on which corporation tax for the accounting period in which the payments or the franked investment income were received became, or would have become, due and payable. Again, this is generally nine months and one day after the end of the accounting period.

This rule is qualified in instances where there is a carry-back of surplus ACT or a carry-back of trading losses for more than 12 months.

Surplus ACT (s 826(7) repealed for accounting periods beginning on or after 6 April 1999 by FA 1998 Sch 3)

Where there is in any accounting period ('the later period') an amount of surplus ACT and a claim is made under TA 1988 s 239(3) to carry this surplus ACT back to an earlier accounting period ('the earlier period'), then interest on any repayment of corporation tax for the earlier period (or of income tax on a payment received in the earlier period) resulting from the claim under s 239(3) begins to run only after the date on which the corporation tax for the *later* period (the period in which the surplus ACT arose) became due and payable.

This rule is in itself subject to modification where the surplus ACT arises because of a trading loss carried back (see below).

A similar rule (s 826(7C)) applies to the carry-back of a non-trading deficit on a company's loan relationships as applies to the carry-back of surplus ACT.

Trading losses carried back for more than 12 months (s 826(7A, 7B))

Where a claim is made under TA 1988 s 393A(1) to set off a loss incurred in a later period against the profits of an earlier period not falling within the 12 months immediately preceding the later period, and

(a) a repayment of corporation tax in respect of that earlier period or a repayment of income tax in respect of a payment received in the earlier period; or

(b) following a claim under TA 1988 s 242 to include surplus franked investment income in profits available for set-off, a payment of the whole or part of the tax credit comprised in franked investment income of the earlier period,

is made, interest in respect of that part of the repayment due to the claim under TA 1988 s 393A(1) or TA 1988 s 242 (so far as it relates to the claim under s 393A(1)) begins to run only after the date on which the corporation tax in respect of the later period (the lossmaking period) became, or would have become, due and payable.

Carry-back of trading loss giving rise to carry-back of surplus ACT (s 826(7AA) repealed for accounting periods beginning on or after 6 April 1999 by FA 1998 Sch 3)

Where

(a) a trading loss carried back under s 393A(1) from a later period ('the lossmaking period') gives rise to an amount of surplus ACT, and that surplus ACT is then carried back under s 239(3) to a still-earlier period and

(b) as a result a repayment of corporation tax for the still-earlier period (or of income tax on a payment received in the still-earlier period) falls to be made

then interest on those repayments begins to run only after the date on which the corporation tax for the *lossmaking period* became due and payable.

A similar rule (s 826(7CA)) applies to the carry-back of surplus ACT following the carry-back of a non-trading deficit on a company's loan relationships.

Rates	
from 6 February 2000	3.5%
6 March 1999–5 February 2000	2.75%
6 January 1999–5 March 1999	3.25%
6 August 1997–5 January 1999	4%
6 February 1996–5 August 1997	3.25%
6 March 1995–5 February 1996	4%

Corporation tax for accounting periods ending after 30 June 1999

SI 1989/1297 regs 3BA and 3BB (inserted by SI 1998/3176 reg 8)

For instalment payments by large companies and early payments by other companies, a special rate of interest runs from the date the excess arises (but not earlier than the due date of the first instalment) to the earlier of the date the repayment order is issued and nine months after the end of the accounting period after which the normal rate of interest applies.

Rates on overpaid instalment payments and on corporation tax paid early (but not due by instalments):	
from 21 February 2000	5.75%
24 January 2000–20 February 2000	5.5%
15 November 1999–23 January 2000	5.25%
20 September 1999–14 November 1999	5%
21 June 1999–19 September 1999	4.75%
19 April 1999–20 June 1999	5%
15 February 1999–18 April 1999	5.25%
18 January 1999–14 February 1999	5.75%
7 January 1999–17 January 1999	6%

Rates on overpaid corporation tax in respect of periods after normal due date (SI 1989/1297 reg 3BB):

from 6 February 2000	5%
6 March 1999–5 February 2000	4%

Penalties

A) Personal tax returns: offences by taxpayers

Offence	Penalty
Failure to give notice of chargeability to income or capital gains tax within 6 months from end of year of assessment (TMA 1970 s 7).	Amount not exceeding tax assessed (either self-assessed under TMA 1970 s 9 or under a TMA 1970 s 29 'discovery' assessment) for that year and not paid before 1 February following that year.
(From 1996–97) Failure to comply with notice requiring return for income tax or capital gains tax (TMA 1970 s 93).	(a) Initial penalty of £100; and (b) upon direction by Commissioners, further penalty not exceeding £60 for each day on which failure continues after notification of direction; (c) if failure continues after six months following filing date, and no application for a direction under (b) has been made, a further penalty of £100. (d) In addition, if failure continues after first anniversary of filing date, and there would have been a liability to tax shown in the return, a penalty not exceeding the liability that would have been shown in the return. (e) If the taxpayer can prove that the liability to tax shown in the return would not have exceeded a particular amount, the sum of penalties under (a) and (c) above are not to exceed that amount.
(From 1996–97) Failure to comply with notice requiring partnership return (TMA 1970 s 93A).	(a) Initial penalty on each 'relevant partner' of £100; and (b) upon direction by Commissioners, further penalty on each relevant partner not exceeding £60 for each day on which failure continues after notification to representative partner of direction; (c) if failure continues after six months following filing date, and no application for a direction under (b) has been made, a further penalty on each relevant partner of £100. NB: A 'relevant partner' is any person who was a partner at any time during the period for which the return is required.
Fraudulently or negligently delivering incorrect return or accounts or making an incorrect statement in connection with a claim for an allowance, deduction or relief (TMA 1970 s 95).	Penalty not exceeding the difference between the amount payable under the return etc and the amount which would have been payable if the return etc had been correct.
(From 1996–97) Fraudulently or negligently delivering incorrect partnership return or accounts or making an incorrect statement or declaration in connection with such a return (TMA 1970 s 95A).	Penalty on each relevant partner not exceeding the difference between the amount payable by him or her under the return, etc and the amount that would have been payable by him or her if the return, etc had been correct. For the meaning of 'relevant partner', see under TMA 1970 s 93A above.

B) Corporation tax returns under pay and file and corporation tax self assessment

Offence	Penalty
Pay and file (accounting periods ending before 1 July 1999)	
Failure to give notice of chargeability to corporation tax within 12 months after end of accounting period (TMA 1970 s 10).	Penalty not exceeding amount of tax unpaid 12 months after end of accounting period (after set-off of income tax credits).
Failure to comply with notice requiring return for corporation tax (TMA 1970 s 94).	(a) If return is delivered within 3 months of due date – £100 (£500 in respect of default for third consecutive period); (b) if return is delivered more than 3 months after due date – £200 (£1,000 in respect of default for third consecutive period); and (c) if return is delivered between 18 months and 2 years after end of return period – an additional penalty of 10% of tax unpaid at end of 18-month period; (d) if return is delivered more than 2 years after end of return period – an additional penalty of 20% of tax unpaid at end of 18-month period.
Fraudulently or negligently delivering incorrect return or accounts or making an incorrect statement in connection with a claim for an allowance, deduction or relief (TMA 1970 s 96).	Penalty not exceeding the difference between the amount payable under the return etc and the amount which would have been payable if the return etc had been correct.

B) Corporation tax returns under pay and file and corporation tax self assessment — continued

Offence	Penalty
Self assessment (accounting periods ending on or after 1 July 1999)	*(For the restriction of penalties where multiple tax-related penalties are payable in respect of the same accounting period see FA 1998 Sch 18 para 90)*
Failure to give notice of chargeability to corporation tax within 12 months after end of accounting period (FA 1998 Sch 18 para 2).	Penalty not exceeding amount of tax payable for that accounting period remaining unpaid 12 months after end of accounting period (taking no account of relief deferred under TA 1988 s 419(4A)).
Failure to deliver a company tax return by the filing date (FA 1998 Sch 18 paras 17, 18).	*Flat-rate penalties* (Unless FA 1998 Sch 18 para 19 (excuse for late delivery of returns) applies) (a) If return is delivered within 3 months of the filing date: £100 (£500 for third successive failure); (b) in any other case: £200 (1,000 for third successive failure); (the increased penalties under (a) and (b) apply with modifications where the first or second period ends before 1 July 1999 (para 17(4)). *Tax-related penalties* (c) If return is delivered between 18 months (or the filing date, if later) and 2 years after the end of the return period: an additional penalty of 10% of the unpaid tax; (d) If return delivered more than 2 years after the end of the return period: an additional penalty of 20% of the unpaid tax. (In determining the amount of unpaid tax no account is taken of relief deferred under TA 1970 s 419(4A)).
Fraudulently or negligently delivering a company tax return which is incorrect (FA 1998 Sch 18 para 20).	An amount not exceeding the amount of tax understated (taking no account of relief deferred under TA 1988 s 419(4A)).
On discovering that a company tax return delivered by it (neither fraudulently nor negligently) is incorrect, a company does not remedy the error without reasonable delay (FA 1998 Sch 18 para 20).	An amount not exceeding the amount of tax understated (taking no account of relief deferred under TA 1988 s 419(4A)).
Fraudulently or negligently making an incorrect return, statement or declaration in connection with a claim for any tax allowance, deduction or relief, or submitting any incorrect accounts in connection with the ascertainment of the company's tax liability (FA 1998 Sch 18 para 89).	Penalty not exceeding the amount of tax understated (excluding relief deferred under TA 1988 s 419(4A)).

C) PAYE returns

Offence	Penalty
Failure to submit return P9D or P11D (benefits in kind) by due date (6 June following tax year 1995–96; 6 July following subsequent tax years) (TMA 1970 s 98 (1)).	(a) An initial penalty not exceeding £300; and (b) a continuing penalty not exceeding £60 for each day on which the failure continues after imposition of the initial penalty.
Fraudulently or negligently submitting incorrect return P9D or P11D (TMA 1970 s 98(2)).	Penalty not exceeding £3,000.
Failure to submit returns P14 (individual end of year summary), P35 (annual return), P38 or P38A (supplementary returns for employees not on P35) by due date (19 May following tax year) (TMA 1970 s 98A).	(a) First 12 months: penalty of £100 for each 50 employees (or part thereof) for each month the failure continues; (b) failures exceeding 12 months: a penalty not exceeding the amount of PAYE or NIC due and unpaid at 19 April following year of assessment. (For late 1995–96 returns, the Revenue will normally limit the amount of the penalty to the total of the tax and NIC that should be reported on the return or to £100, whichever is greater: Revenue Press Release dated 14 June 1996.)
Fraudulently or negligently submitting incorrect form P14, P35, P38 or P38A (TMA 1970 s 98A).	Penalty not exceeding the difference between the amount payable under the return and the amount which would have been payable if the return had been correct.

D) Inheritance tax returns and information

Offence	Penalty
Failure to deliver an account under IHTA 1984, section 216 or 217. (IHTA 1984 s 245; FA 1999 s 108)	(a) An initial penalty not exceeding £100; (b) further penalty not exceeding £60 (where penalty determined by court or Special Commissioners) for each day on which the failure continues after imposition of initial penalty; and (c) if failure continues after six months following the date on which the account is due, and proceedings have not commenced, a further penalty not exceeding £100.
Failure to make a return under IHTA 1984, section 218 or failure to comply with a notice under section 219.	(a) An initial penalty not exceeding £300; and (b) further, penalty not exceeding £60 (where penalty determined by court or Special Commissioners) for each day on which the failure continues after imposition of initial penalty.
Failure to comply with a notice under IHTA 1984, section 219A (1) or (4) (IHTA 1984 s 245A; FA 1999 s 108)	(a) An initial penalty not exceeding £50; and (b) further, penalty not exceeding £30 (where penalty determined by court or Special Commissioners) for each day on which the failure continues after imposition of initial penalty.
The taxpayer fraudulently or negligently delivering, furnishing or producing incorrect accounts, information or documents. (IHTA 1984 s 247(1); FA 1999 s 108)	(a) In the case of fraud, a penalty not exceeding the aggregate of £3,000 and the difference between the amount payable according to the information furnished and the amount that would have been payable if the accounts etc. had been correct; and (b) in the case of negligence, a penalty not exceeding the aggregate of £1,500 and the difference between the amount payable according to the information furnished and the amount that would have been payable if the accounts etc. had been correct.
A person other than the taxpayer fraudulently or negligently delivering, furnishing or producing incorrect accounts, information or documents (IHTA 1984 s 247(3); FA 1999 s 108).	(a) In the case of fraud, a penalty not exceeding £3,000; and (b) in the case of negligence, a penalty not exceeding £1,500.
Any person assisting in or inducing the delivery, furnishing or production of any account, information or document which he knows to be incorrect. (IHTA 1984 s 247(4); FA 1999 s 108).	A penalty not exceeding £3,000.

E) Special returns of information

Offence	Penalty
Failure to comply with a notice to deliver a return or other document, furnish particulars or make anything available for inspection under any of the provisions listed in column 1 of the table in TMA 1970 s 98. (FA 1999, s 89 extends this to corporation tax payments by instalment.)	(a) An initial penalty not exceeding £300 (£3,000 for failure to comply with TA 1988 s 765A(2)(a) or (b)); and (b) a continuing penalty not exceeding £60 (£600 for failure to comply with TA 1988 s 765A(2)(a) or (b)) for each day on which the failure continues after imposition of the initial penalty.
Failure to comply with requirement to furnish information, give certificates or produce documents or records under any of the provisions listed in column 2 of the table in TMA 1970 s 98. (FA 1999, s 86 extends this to advance pricing agreements.)	(a) An initial penalty not exceeding £300; and (b) a continuing penalty not exceeding £60 for each day on which the failure continues after imposition of the initial penalty.
Fraudulently or negligently delivering any incorrect document, information etc required under any of the provisions listed in column 1 or 2 of the table in TMA 1970 s 98.	Penalty not exceeding £3,000.
(Accounting periods ending after 30 June 1999). Failure of a company to produce documents, etc., for the purposes of an enquiry (FA 1998 Sch 18 para 29).	(a) £50; (b) If failure continues after imposition of penalty under (a), an additional penalty for each day the failure continues, not exceeding: (i) £30 if determined by the Revenue under TMA 1970 s 100; and (ii) £150 if determined by the Commissioners under TMA 1970 s 100C.
Fraudulently or negligently making a false or misleading statement in the preparation of, or application to enter into, any advance pricing agreement (FA 1999, s 86).	Penalty not exceeding £10,000.

F) Other offences by taxpayers, agents etc

Offence	Penalty
Failure to retain records as required by TMA 1970 s 12B(1) (TMA 1970 s 12B(5)).	Penalty not exceeding £3,000.
Falsification of documents (TMA 1970 s 20BB).	On summary conviction, a fine not exceeding the statutory maximum (£5,000); on conviction on indictment, imprisonment for a term not exceeding 2 years or a fine or both.
Failure to produce documents required under TMA 1970 s 19A (power to enquire into self-assessment return, etc) (TMA 1970 s 97AA).	(a) Initial penalty of £50; and (b) further penalty not exceeding £30 (where penalty determined by officer of Board) or £150 (where penalty determined by Commissioners) for each day on which failure continues after imposition of initial penalty.
Offences in connection with the supply of information regarding European Economic Interest Groupings—	
(i) failure to supply information	An initial penalty not exceeding £300 per member of the Grouping at the time of failure and after direction by the Commissioners a continuing penalty not exceeding £60 per member of the Grouping at the end of the day for each day on which the failure continues after notification of the direction.
(ii) fraudulent or negligent delivery of an incorrect return, accounts or statement. (TMA 1970 s 98B).	Not exceeding £3,000 for each member of the Grouping at the time of delivery.
Assisting in the delivery of incorrect returns, accounts or information (TMA 1970 s 99).	Not exceeding £3,000.
Fraudulently or negligently giving a certificate of non-liability to income tax for the purposes of receiving interest gross on a bank or building society account, or failing to comply with an undertaking given in such a certificate (TMA 1970 s 99A).	Not exceeding £3,000.
Refusal to allow a deduction of income tax authorised by the Taxes Acts (TMA 1970 s 106).	£50.
Obstruction of officer of the Board in inspection of property to ascertain its market value (TMA 1970 s 111).	Not exceeding level 1 on the standard scale.
Issue by a company of a certificate of approval for enterprise investment scheme relief fraudulently or negligently or without the authority of the inspector (TA 1988 s 306(6)).	Not exceeding £3,000.
False statement to obtain relief for payments to secure a retirement annuity, a purchased life annuity or under a personal pension scheme (TA 1988 ss 619(7), 653, 658(5)).	Not exceeding £3,000.
Creation or transfer of shares or debentures in a non-resident subsidiary company without the consent of HM Treasury (TA 1988 s 766).	On conviction on indictment— (a) imprisonment for not more than 2 years or a fine, or both; or (b) in the case of a UK company, a fine not exceeding the greater of— (i) £10,000; or (ii) three times the tax payable by the company attributable to income and gains arising in the previous 36 months.
Failure by a Lloyd's syndicate's managing agent to comply with notice requiring return of syndicate's profit or loss (FA 1993 Sch 19 para 2(3), (4)).	£60 for each 50 members of syndicate (or part thereof) for each day the failure continues.
Delivery by a Lloyd's syndicate's managing agent fraudulently or negligently of an incorrect return of syndicate profits (FA 1993 Sch 19 para 2(5)).	Not exceeding £3,000 for each member of the syndicate.

F) Other offences by taxpayers, agents etc — continued

Offence	Penalty
Obstructing, molesting or hindering an officer or other person employed in relation to inland revenue in the execution of his duty (Inland Revenue Regulation Act 1890 s 11).	Level 3 on the standard scale.
(Accounting periods ending after 30 June 1999. Deliberately or recklessly failing to pay corporation tax due in respect of total liability of company for accounting period, or fraudulently or negligently making claim for repayment (TMA 1970 s 59E(4); S1 1998/3175 reg 13).	Penalty not exceeding twice amount of interest charged under S1 1998/3175 reg 7.
(Accounting periods ending after 30 June 1999) Failure of a company to keep and preserve records (other than those only required for claims, etc., or dividend vouchers and certificates of income tax deducted where other evidence is available) (FA 1998 Sch 18 para 23).	Penalty not exceeding £3,000.

G) Standard scale penalties under Criminal Justice Act[1]

Level	Amount	
	1.5.84–30.9.92 £	From 1.10.92 £
1	50	200
2	100	500
3	400	1,000
4	1,000	2,500
5 (statutory maximum)	2,000	5,000

[1] Criminal Justice Act 1982 s 37.

Mitigation of penalties

The Board has discretion to mitigate or entirely remit any penalty or to stay or compound any penalty proceedings (TMA 1970 s 102).

Interest on penalties

From 1996–97 penalties under TMA 1970 Parts II (ss 7–12B), IV (ss 28A–43B), VA (ss 59A–59D) and X (ss 93–107) carry interest at the prescribed rate (see p 13): TMA 1970 s 103A. Surcharges on unpaid income tax and capital gains tax carry interest under TMA 1970 s 59C (with effect from 9 March 1998, by virtue of SI 1998/310). As regards corporation tax, the provisions apply for accounting periods ending on or after 1 July 1999.

Stamp duties see page 89.

VAT see page 92.

Time limits for claims and elections

The information in the tables below was originally derived from Tax Digest No 108 "Time limits for claims and elections" (Spring 1992) published by the Institute of Chartered Accountants in England and Wales.

From 1996–97: Whenever possible, a claim or election must be made on the tax return or by an amendment to the return (TMA 1970 s 42 and FA 1998 Sch 18 paras 9, 10, 67 and 79). Exceptions to this general rule are dealt with in TMA 1970 Sch 1A.

Except where another period is expressly prescribed, a claim for relief in respect of income tax and capital gains tax must be made within five years from the 31 January following the year of assessment to which it relates (TMA 1970 s 43(1) as amended). The time limit for claims by companies remains at six years from the end of the accounting period to which it relates (TMA 1970 s 43(1) (b) and, for accounting periods ending after 1 July 1999, FA 1998 Sch 18 para 55).

The tables below set out exceptions to the general limits.

Unless otherwise specified, for income tax and capital gains tax, two-year time limits run from the 31 January in the year of assessment (see FA 1996 s 128). For companies the time limit runs from the end of the accounting period to which the claim relates (TMA 1970 s 43(1) (b), FA 1998 Sch 18 para 55).

Before 1996–97: Except where a longer or shorter period was expressly prescribed, a claim for relief had to be made within six years of the end of the chargeable period to which it related (TMA 1970 s 43(1) as originally enacted).

Income and corporation tax

Claim	Time limit
Sums received in respect of a furnished letting to be assessed under Schedule A to the extent of the rental element (not generally applicable for income tax from 1995–96) (TA 1988 s 15(2)). (Of no application, generally, after 31 March 1998.)	*2 years from end of chargeable period.*
Land managed as one estate at 5 April 1963 – new owner entitled to include notional rent in respect of parts not let and to claim expenses as if those parts were let at a full rent. Applies throughout that person's ownership (TA 1988 s 26(3)). (Of no application for income tax purposes on or after 6 April 2001 or for corporation tax purposes, for accounting periods beginning on or after 1 April 2001.)	12 months after the end of the first year of assessment or accounting period for which the claimant was entitled to claim or such further time as the Board may allow.
Capital allowances on machinery or plant used for the maintenance, repair or management of let property. Applies to all future periods (not generally applicable for income tax from 1995–96 and repealed altogether for income tax for 1997-98 and subsequent years, and for corporation tax for accounting periods ending after 31 March 1997) (TA 1988 s 32(5), (6)).	*Before the date when the assessment in respect of the net income from the property for the year becomes final and conclusive.*
Relief for gifts of plant and machinery to educational establishments (TA 1988 s 84(3), (3A)).	First anniversary of 31 January next following year of assessment in the basis period of which the gift was made (income tax); 2 years from end of accounting period in which the gift was made (corporation tax).
Averaging relief to be available to a person carrying on a trade of farming or market gardening (TA 1988 s 96(8) as amended).	12 months after 31 January next following end of second year which enters into the averaging calculation.
Herd basis to apply (TA 1988 s 97, Sch 5 para 2 as amended).	12 months from 31 January next following first year of assessment for which profits computed by reference to period in which herd was kept (income tax); 12 months from 31 January next following year of assessment in which fell the end of the first period of account in which herd was kept (partnerships); 2 years from end of first accounting period in which herd was kept (corporation tax).
Work in progress at date of discontinuance of profession or vocation to be valued at actual cost (TA 1988 s 101(2), (2A)).	First anniversary of 31 January next following year of assessment in which discontinuance occurred (income tax); 2 years from end of accounting period in which discontinuance occurred (corporation tax).
Post cessation receipts to be charged as if received on the date of discontinuance or change of basis of computation (TA 1988 s 108 as amended).	One year from 31 January following end of year of assessment in which sum received.
Change in persons carrying on a trade, profession or vocation in partnership not to be treated as a discontinuance (not applicable to partnerships commenced after 5 April 1994 or, from 1997–98, to partnerships commenced on or before that date) (TA 1988 s 113(2)).	*2 years from date of partnership change.*
Tax arising upon the exercise of a share option to be payable by instalments, provided that the option was acquired prior to 6 April 1984 (TA 1988 s 137(1)(d), (3)).	60 days after the end of the year in which the exercise occurs.

Claim	Time limit
Election by employee for alternative method to be applied in calculating the cash equivalent of the benefit obtained from a loan (TA 1988 s 160, Sch 7 para 5 as amended).	12 months from 31 January next following year of assessment.
Relief to be given for expenses incurred wholly, exclusively and necessarily in the performance of the duties of an office or employment (TA 1988 s 198(1)).	The date on which the assessment becomes final and conclusive.
Certain subscriptions etc to be deducted from the emoluments of an office or employment (TA 1988 s 201(1)).	The date on which the assessment becomes final and conclusive.
Inspector to be required to issue a return (before 1996-97 an assessment) under Schedule E (TA 1988 s 205(4)).	5 years after 31 October next following year of assessment.
Surplus ACT paid to be carried back for offset against corporation tax liabilities for accounting periods beginning within six years prior to the period of payment (TA 1988 s 239(3)) (repealed with respect to accounting periods beginning after 5 April 1999).	*2 years.*
Surplus franked investment income to be treated as profits chargeable to corporation tax for offset against trading losses and capital allowances (TA 1988 s 242) (Repealed generally with effect for accounting periods beginning after 1 July 1997.)	*2 years.*
Interest and other payments to be treated as group income. Before 6 April 1999, applies also to dividends. Applies until revoked but the company making the payments may give notice to the collector of taxes that it is not to apply to specific payments (TA 1988 ss 247, 248).	3 months prior to date of payment but if the inspector notifies his or her acceptance of the election within three months the election is effective from the date of notification.
Income from jointly owned property to be assessed on husband and wife in unequal shares (TA 1988 s 282B(2)).	Effective from date of declaration.
Relief to be given for the enterprise investment scheme (TA 1988 s 306(1) as amended).	Not earlier than 4 months after the company commences its qualifying activity and no later than fifth anniversary of 31 January next following year of assessment.
Certain expenses to be deducted from the emoluments of a clergyman (TA 1988 s 332(3)).	The date on which the assessment becomes final and conclusive.
Loss sustained in a trade, profession or vocation to be set against other income of the year or the last preceding year. Extended to certain pre-trading expenditure by TA 1988 s 401 (TA 1988 s 380(1) as substituted).	12 months from 31 January next following year of assessment in which loss arose.
Loss sustained in the first 4 years of a new trade, profession or vocation to be offset against other income arising in the 3 years immediately preceding the year of loss. Extended to certain pre-trading expenditure by TA 1988 s 401 (TA 1988 s 381(1)).	First anniversary of 31 January next following year of assessment in which loss sustained.
Loss sustained by a company in a trade in an accounting period ending after 31 March 1991 to be offset against— (a) profits of that accounting period; (b) profits of the preceding three years for losses arising in accounting periods ending before 2 July 1997 and profits of the preceding one year for losses arising in subsequent accounting periods. Extended to certain pre-trading expenditure by TA 1988 s 401 (TA 1988 s 393A(1) (2A)).	2 years or such further period as Board may allow.
Group relief to be given for accounting periods ending after 30 September 1993 and before 1 July 1999. The surrendering company must consent to the claim (TA 1988 s 412, Sch 17A para 2).	2 years after the end of the surrendering company's accounting period or the date on which the relevant assessment becomes final, whichever is later.
Group relief to be given for accounting periods ending after 30 June 1999. The surrendering company must consent to the claim (FA 1998 Sch 18 paras 66 to 77)	The last of: (a) 1 year from the filing date of the claimant company's return for the accounting period for which the claim is made; (b) 30 days after the end of an enquiry into the return; (c) if the Revenue amend the return after an enquiry, 30 days after issue of notice of amendment; (d) if an appeal is made against the amendment, 30 days after the determination of the appeal; (or such later time as the Revenue may allow).

Claim	Time limit
Relief for non-trading deficits on loan relationships in a company in an accounting period ending after 31 March 1996 to be claimed by: (a) offset against profits of the same period; (b) group relief; (c) offset against post 31 March 1996 profits of earlier accounting periods (as for trading losses above); or (d) offset against non-trading profits for the next accounting period, and so on. (FA 1996, s 83)	2 years or such further period as Board may allow.
Averaging treatment to be applied in determining the number of days on which holiday accommodation is let (TA 1988 s 504(6), (6A)).	First anniversary of 31 January next following year of assessment in which accommodation let (income tax); 2 years from end of accounting period in which accommodation let (corporation tax).
UK resident in receipt of a capital sum from the sale of patent rights to be charged to tax for period of receipt (TA 1988 s 524(2), (2A)).	First anniversary of 31 January next following year of assessment in which sum received (income tax); 2 years from end of accounting period in which sum received (corporation tax).
Non-resident in receipt of a capital sum on the sale of non-UK patent rights to be charged to tax as if the sum was received over a period of 6 years (TA 1988 s 524(4) as amended).	First anniversary of 31 January next following year of assessment in which sum is paid.
Consideration for know-how sold together with a trade or part of a trade not to be treated as a payment for goodwill. Time limit runs from the date of the disposal. Both purchaser and vendor must elect (TA 1988 s 531(3)).	2 years.
Certain sums received by an author in respect of the assignment of a copyright to be assessed as if received over a period of up to 3 years (TA 1988 s 534(1), (5) as amended).	1 year from 31 January next following the latest year of assessment in which payment receivable.
Spreading claim made under TA 1988 s 535(1) in respect of sums received by author more than 10 years after first publication of the work to be recalculated on the death of the author or the discontinuance of his or her profession (TA 1988 s 535(8A)).	1 year from 31 January next following year of assessment in which payment receivable.
Sums received by a designer for the assignment of rights in a design to be assessed as if received over a period of up to 3 years (TA 1988 s 537A(5), (5A) as amended).	1 year from 31 January next following the latest year of assessment in which payment receivable.
Loss on disposal by an investment company of shares in a qualifying trading company to be offset against other income of the period of loss or the preceding accounting period (TA 1988 s 573(2)).	2 years.
Loss on disposal by an individual of shares in a qualifying trading company to be offset against other income of the year of loss or the last preceding year (TA 1988 s 574(1) as substituted).	1 year from 31 January next following year of assessment in which loss incurred.
Unremittable overseas income to be excluded from assessment (TA 1988 s 584(2), (6) (as substituted)).	1 year from 31 January next following year of assessment in which income arises (income tax); 2 years from end of accounting period in which income arises (corporation tax).
Relief to be given in respect of a qualifying premium paid under a retirement annuity contract entered into before 1 July 1988 for the immediately preceding year of assessment (or the year before that if no net relevant earnings in the immediately preceding year) (TA 1988 s 619(4) as amended).	31 January next following year of assessment in which premium paid.
Unused relief to be available against a qualifying premium paid under a retirement annuity contract entered into before 1 July 1988 where an assessment becomes final and conclusive more than 6 years after the year to which it relates (TA 1988 s 625(3)).	6 months from the date when the assessment becomes final.
Relief to be given against relevant earnings from Lloyd's underwriting activities in respect of a qualifying premium paid in the next year but two under an approved contract entered into before 1 July 1988 (repealed from 1997–98) (TA 1988 s 627(1), (3)).	*Before the end of the year of assessment in which the premium is paid.*
Relief to be given against relevant earnings from Lloyd's underwriting activities in respect of a contribution paid under approved personal pension arrangements in the next year of assessment but two (repealed from 1997–98) (TA 1988 s 641(2), (4) as amended).	*31 January next following year of assessment in which contributions paid.*

Claim	Time limit
Relief to be given in respect of a contribution paid under approved personal pension arrangements for the immediately preceding year of assessment (or the year before that if no net relevant earnings in the immediately preceding year) (TA 1988 s 641(1), (4) as amended).	31 January next following year of assessment in which contributions paid.
Unused relief to be available for relief against a contribution paid under approved personal pension arrangements where an assessment to tax for a year of assessment becomes final and conclusive more than 6 years after the end of that year (TA 1988 s 642(4)).	6 months from the date when the assessment for the year in question becomes final and conclusive.
Income arising to trustees of maintenance funds for historic buildings not to be treated as the income of the settlor (TA 1988 s 691(2), (4) as amended).	First anniversary of 31 January next following year of assessment to which it relates.
Income of a beneficiary to be adjusted for past years on completion of the administration of a deceased's estate (TA 1988 s 700(1), (3) as amended).	3 years from 31 January next following year of assessment in which the administration is completed.
Controlled foreign company to be deemed not to have made a specified claim (TA 1988 ss 747, 753(4), Sch 24 para 4). (New provisions apply in respect of self-assessment for accounting periods ending after 30 June 1999. (FA 1998, Sch 17)).	60 days from issue of notice of direction.
Controlled foreign company to be deemed to be subject to a direction for an earlier period in which a loss was incurred (TA 1988 s 747, Sch 24 para 9). (New provisions apply in respect of self-assessment for accounting periods ending after 30 June 1999. (FA 1998, Sch 17)).	60 days from issue of direction.
Relief for maintenance payments made under obligations entered into before 15 March 1988 as if the obligation had been entered into after that date (FA 1988 s 39).	First anniversary of 31 January next following first year of assessment for which it is to have effect.
Emoluments to be taxed only in the year of receipt (FA 1989 s 38(6) and SP1/92).	5 April 1991 or (at Board's discretion) 3 months after the issue of a Schedule E assessment for 1988–89 or 1989–90.
Adjustment of employer's Schedule D calculation for emoluments paid subsequently, but within 9 months of the end of the employer's period of account (FA 1989 s 43(5)).	2 years from end of period of account.
Unrelieved trading losses to be set against capital gains (FA 1991 s 72, TA 1988 s 380(1)).	12 months from 31 January next following year of assessment in which loss sustained.
Claim for relief by a trader etc for gifts in kind to low-income countries under the Millennium Gift Aid scheme (FA 1998 s 47(6)).	First anniversary of 31 January next following year of assessment in the basis period of which the gift is made (income tax); 2 years from end of accounting period in which the gift is made (corporation tax).
Capital allowances	
Grant of a long lease of a building to be treated as a sale of the relevant interest by the lessor. Both lessor and lessee must elect (CAA 1990 s 11(1), (3)).	2 years from the date when the lease takes effect.
Part or all of the total of plant and machinery first-year allowances to be disclaimed (CAA 1990 ss 22(7), 140(3), Sch A1 para 7).	Required allowance claimed in tax return (income tax);[2] Required allowance claimed in return (corporation tax).
Part or all of the total of plant and machinery writing down allowances to be disclaimed (CAA 1990 s 24(3), 140 (3), Sch A1 para (7)).	Required allowance claimed in tax return (income tax);[2] Required allowance claimed in return (corporation tax).
Writing down allowance to be available where first year allowance not claimed (CAA 1990 s 25(3) as amended, (3A)). The requirement for notification of expenditure on which allowances may be claimed (FA 94 s 118) is abolished for periods ending on or after 6 April 1998 (income tax) and 1 April 1998 (corporation tax).	First anniversary of 31 January next following year of assessment in which ends chargeable period related to incurring of expenditure (income tax);[1] 2 years from end of chargeable period related to incurring of expenditure (corporation tax).

Claim	Time limit
Part or all of a first year allowance in respect of expenditure on a ship to be postponed to a later period (CAA 1990 s 30(1) as amended, (1A)).	First anniversary of 31 January next following year of assessment in which period of account ends (income tax);[1] 2 years from end of accounting period for which allowance made (corporation tax).
Part or all of a postponed first year allowance in respect of expenditure on a ship to be given in a later period (CAA 1990 ss 30(2), 140(3), Sch A1 para 7). (Now provisions apply in respect of self-assessment for companies for accounting periods ending after 30 June 1999.)	Claim to be made in return (income tax and corporation tax)[2]
Capital allowances to be given in respect of expenditure on machinery or plant used for the maintenance, repair or management of let property. Applies to all future periods (TA 1988 s 32(5)). (Does not generally apply to income tax from the year 1994–95 and repealed altogether for income tax for 1997-98 and subsequent years, and for corporation tax for accounting periods ending after 31 March 1997.)	*Before the date on which the assessment for the period becomes final and conclusive.*
Part or all of a writing down allowance in respect of expenditure incurred after 13 March 1984 on a ship to be postponed to a later period (CAA 1990 s 31(3) as amended, (3A)).	First anniversary of 31 January next following year of assessment in which chargeable period ends (income tax);[1] 2 years from end of chargeable period (corporation tax).
Allowances postponed under CAA 1990 s 31(3) to be treated as writing-down allowances for a subsequent period (CAA 1990 ss 31(4), 140(3), Sch A1 para 7). (Now provisions apply in respect of self-assessment for companies for accounting periods ending after 30 June 1999).	Claim to be made in return (income tax and corporation tax)[2]
Single ship trade treatment not to apply to the whole or part of the expenditure (CAA 1990 s 33 (1) as amended, (5A)).	First anniversary of 31 January next following year of assessment in which chargeable period ends (income tax);[1] 2 years from end of chargeable period (corporation tax).
Machinery or plant to be treated as a short life asset (CAA 1990 s 37(2) as amended, (2A)).	First anniversary of 31 January next following year of assessment in which chargeable period in which qualifying expenditure occurred ends (income tax);[1] 2 years from end of chargeable period (corporation tax).
Transfer of short life asset to a connected person to be treated as taking place at tax written down value (CAA 1990 s 37(9)).	2 years from end of chargeable period in which disposal occurred.
Machinery or plant which becomes a fixture and is subject to an equipment lease to be treated as belonging to equipment lessor. Election to be made by both lessor and lessee but not permitted if they are connected persons (CAA 1990 s 53 (2) as amended, (2A)).	First anniversary of 31 January next following year of assessment in which chargeable period ends (income tax);[1] 2 years from end of chargeable period (corporation tax).
Machinery or plant which has become a fixture on land which is subsequently let to be treated as belonging to lessee. Election to be made by both lessor and lessee but not permitted if they are connected persons (CAA 1990 s 55).	2 years from date on which lease takes effect.
Oilfield abandonment expenditure to be deductible in relation to a ring fence trade (CAA 1990 s 62A(4), (5)).	2 years from end of chargeable period related to incurring of expenditure.
Expenditure on production or acquisition of films etc to be reallocated (CAA 1990 s 68(5) as amended, (5A)).	First anniversary of 31 January next following year of assessment in which relevant period ends (income tax); 2 years from end of relevant period (corporation tax).[1]
Succession to a trade between connected persons to be ignored in computing capital allowances (CAA 1990 s 77(3)).	2 years from the date of the succession.

Claim	Time limit
Acquisition of relevant interest in capital expenditure on agricultural land and buildings to be treated as a balancing event (CAA 1990 s 129(2) as amended).	First anniversary of 31 January next following year of assessment in which chargeable period ends (income tax);[1] 2 years from end of chargeable period (corporation tax).
Claim for income tax capital allowances made in taxing the trade (CAA 1990 s 140(3)).	Claim to be made in return.
Capital allowances given by way of discharge or repayment of tax and offset against income of the specified class: the excess of such allowances to be set against other income of the year and the immediately succeeding year (CAA 1990 s 141(3) as amended). (Repealed with effect from 1997-98.)	*First anniversary of 31 January next following year of assessment.[1]*
Excess of corporation tax capital allowances given by discharge or repayment of tax over the relevant class of income to be set against the profits of that period and the immediately preceding period (CAA 1990 s 145(3)).	2 years.
Claims, amended claims and withdrawals of claims in respect of corporation tax capital allowances for accounting periods ending after 30 September 1993 and before 1 July 1999 (CAA 1990 s 145A, Sch A1 paras 2, 3). (New provisions apply for self-assessment by companies for accounting periods ending after 30 June 1999, see below.)	The latest of — (a) two years after the end of the accounting period; (b) the date on which the company's corporation tax assessment for the period becomes final; and (c) the date on which the determination of the company's losses or the amount available for group relief for the accounting period becomes final.
(Accounting periods ending after 30 June 1999). A claim for capital allowances (FA 1998 Sch 18 para 82).	The last of: (a) 1 year from the filing date of the claimant company's return for the accounting period for which the claim is made; (b) 30 days after the end of an enquiry into the return; (c) if the Revenue amend the return after an enquiry, 30 days after issue of notice of amendment; (d) if an appeal is made against the amendment, 30 days after the determination of the appeal; (or such later time as the Revenue may allow).
Disposal and acquisition of property between persons one of which controls the other or which are under common control to be treated as made at the lower of open market value and tax written down value (CAA 1990 s 158(1)).	2 years from the date of the disposal.

[1] For the purposes of income tax, applies from 1997–98 in respect of trades etc set up and commenced before 6 April 1994 and from 1996–97 for trades etc commenced after 5 April 1994: see FA 1996 s 135(3), Sch 21.

[2] An amended claim may be made in an amended return, the normal time limit for which is the first anniversary of 31 January next following the year of assessment in which the chargeable period ends.

Capital gains

Claim	Time limit
Loss to be allowed where the value of an asset has become negligible (TCGA 1992 s 24(2)).	Year for which loss to be allowed, or up to 2 years after the end of that year if the value is still negligible when claim made.
Events occurring prior to 31 March 1982 to be ignored in computing gains arising after 5 April 1988 (TCGA 1992 s 35 (5), (6) as amended).	First anniversary of 31 January next following year of assessment in which disposal made (capital gains tax) or 2 years after end of accounting period in which disposal made (corporation tax).
Variation or disclaimer of the terms of a will or intestacy, made within two years of the death, to be treated as effected by the deceased (TCGA 1992 s 62(6), (7)).	6 months after instrument of variation or disclaimer effected or such longer time as the Board may allow.
Postponement of charge on deemed disposal of assets where a subsidiary company ceases to be resident in the UK (TCGA 1992 s 187(1)).	2 years from date of ceasing to be resident in UK.

Claim	Time limit
Determination of main residence for principal private residence exemption (TCGA 1992 s 222(5)(a)).	2 years from the beginning of the period for which a determination requires to be made, ie the date of acquisition of a second or further residence, but provided that an initial notice has been given within the time limit it may subsequently be varied at any time and the notice of variation may have effect from up to 2 years prior to the date on which it is made.
Rollover relief on disposal of shares to trustees of qualifying employee share ownership trust (TCGA 1992 s 229(1)).	2 years from date of acquisition of replacement assets.
Losses on certain loans to traders to be allowed as capital losses (TCGA 1992 s 253(3)).	The loss is treated as accruing on the date that the claim is made, or at an earlier date, which is: (a) no more than 2 years before the beginning of the year of assessment in which the claim is made (capital gains tax) or (b) no earlier than the first day of the earliest accounting period ending no more than 2 years before the date of the claim.
Losses arising from payments by guarantor of certain irrecoverable loans to traders to be allowed as capital losses at time of claim or 'earlier time' (TCGA 1992 s 253(4), (4A)).	Fifth anniversary of 31 January next following year of assessment in which payment made (capital gains tax); 6 years after end of accounting period in which the payment was made (corporation tax: TCGA 1992 s 253(4A), FA 1996 s 135(2): accounting periods ending after 30 June 1999).
Tax to be paid by instalments where the consideration is payable over a period and undue hardship would otherwise be suffered (TCGA 1992 s 280).	Date of payment of tax.
Halving of postponed charges, or held over or rolled over gains, on disposals of assets acquired after 31 March 1982 (but before 6 April 1988) from a person who acquired (or is deemed to have acquired) them before 31 March 1982 (TCGA 1992 Sch 4 para 9).	First anniversary of 31 January next following year of assessment in which disposal (or other event) occurred (capital gains tax); 2 years from the end of the accounting period in which the disposal (or other event) occurred, or such longer time as the Board may allow (corporation tax).
Gain on a disposal of an asset held at 6 April 1965 to be computed as if the asset had been acquired on that date. An election once made is irrevocable (TCGA 1992 Sch 2 para 17).	First anniversary of 31 January next following year of assessment in which disposal made (capital gains tax); 2 years from end of accounting period in which disposal made (corporation tax); or such further time as the Board may by notice allow.
Quoted ordinary (and participating preference) shares and units in certain unit trusts held (or deemed to have been held) at 6 April 1965 to be pooled at their 6 April 1965 values for disposals after 5 April 1985 (31 March 1985 for companies) or 19 March 1968, as the case may be (TCGA 1992 s 109(4), (5), Sch 2 paras 4(2), (11) as amended, 5).	First anniversary of 31 January next following year of assessment in which first relevant disposal made (capital gains tax); 2 years from end of accounting period in which first relevant disposal made (corporation tax); or such further time as the Board may allow.
Retirement relief generally. Relief must be claimed unless due by reason of a disposal made by an individual aged 50 or over; reorganisation provisions of TCGA 1992 s 126 et seq not to apply; relief to be given in respect of certain capital distributions; spouse's period of ownership to be aggregated with that of person making the disposal (TCGA 1992 Sch 6 as amended paras 2, 5, 12,16). (To be phased out from 6 April 1999 and not available for disposals after 5 April 2003 (FA 1998 s 140).)	First anniversary of 31 January next following year of assessment.

Exchanges

Recognised stock exchanges

The following is a list of countries with exchanges which have been designated as recognised stock exchanges under TA 1988 s 841. Unless otherwise specified, any stock exchange (or options exchange) in a country listed below is a recognised stock exchange for the purposes of TA 1988 s 841, provided it is recognised under the law of the country concerned relating to stock exchanges.

Country	Effective date
Australia	14 December 1970
Australian Stock Exchange and its stock exchange subsidiaries	22 September 1988
Austria[3]	14 December 1970
Belgium[3]	14 December 1970
EASDAQ	
Brazil	
Rio De Janeiro Stock Exchange	17 August 1995
São Paulo Stock Exchange	20 December 1995
Canada	
Any stock exchange prescribed for the purposes of the Canadian Income Tax Act	14 December 1970
China	
Hong Kong – Any stock exchange recognised under Section 2A(1) of the Hong Kong Companies Ordinance	6 April 1971
Denmark	
Copenhagen Stock Exchange	14 December 1970
Finland	
Helsinki Stock Exchange	14 December 1970
France[3]	14 December 1970
Germany[3]	16 August 1971
Greece	
Athens Stock Exchange	14 June 1993
Irish Republic	14 December 1970
Italy[3]	3 May 1972
Japan[3]	14 December 1970
Korea	10 October 1994
Luxembourg[3]	29 February 1972
Malaysia	
Kuala Lumpur Stock Exchange	10 October 1994
Mexico	10 October 1994
Netherlands[3]	14 December 1970
New Zealand	22 September 1988
Norway[3]	14 December 1970
Portugal[3]	29 February 1972
Singapore	30 June 1977
South Africa	
Johannesburg Stock Exchange	14 December 1970
Spain[3]	16 August 1971
Sri Lanka	
Colombo Stock Exchange	29 February 1972
Sweden	
Stockholm Stock Exchange	16 July 1985
Switzerland	30 June 1977
Thailand	10 October 1994
United Kingdom	6 April 1965
United States	
Any stock exchange registered with the Securities and Exchange Commission as a national securities exchange[1]	14 December 1970
Nasdaq Stock Market[2]	10 March 1992

[1] The term "national securities exchange" does not include any local exchanges registered with the Securities and Exchange Commission.

[2] As maintained through the facilities of the National Association of Securities Dealers Inc and its subsidiaries.

[3] Any stock exchange which is a stock exchange within the meaning of the law of the country concerned relating to stock exchanges.

Recognised futures exchanges

The following is a list of exchanges which have been designated as recognised futures exchanges under TCGA 1992 s 288(6). By concession, those exchanges were recognised futures exchanges for the tax year of recognition onwards.

Country	Tax year of recognition
Australia	
Sydney Futures Exchange	1988–89
Canada	
Montreal Exchange	1987–88
China	
Hong Kong Futures Exchange	1987–88
Sweden	
OM Stockholm	1991–92
United Kingdom	
International Petroleum Exchange of London	1985–86
London Fox	1991–92
London Gold Market	1985–86
London International Financial Futures and Options Exchange (LIFFE)	1991–92
London Metal Exchange	1985–86
London Rubber Market	1985–86
London Silver Market	1985–86
OM London	1991–92
United States	
Chicago Board of Trade	1987–88
Chicago Mercantile Exchange	1986–87
Citrus Associates of the New York Cotton Exchange	1988–89
Coffee, Sugar and Cocoa Exchange, New York	1987–88
Commodity Exchange (COMEX)	1988–89
Mid America Commodity Exchange	1987–88
New York Cotton Exchange	1988–89
New York Mercantile Exchange	1986–87
Philadelphia Board of Trade	1986–87

Recognised clearing systems

The following is a list of systems for clearing quoted Eurobonds or relevant foreign securities which have been designated as recognised clearing systems under TA 1988 s 841A(2) (formerly TA 1988 s 124(6)).

Country	Effective date
Belgium	
Euro-clear	26 July 1984
Luxembourg	
Cedel	26 July 1984
United Kingdom	
Bank of England European Settlements Office	16 August 1993
First Chicago Clearing Centre	14 October 1988
United States	
The Depository Trust Co	18 July 1995

Recognised investment exchanges

The following exchange has been designated as a recognised investment exchange (under the Financial Services Act 1986 s 37(3)) for the purposes of TA 1988 s 841(3).

Country	Effective date
United Kingdom	
London International Financial Futures Exchange (Administration and Management) (LIFFE (A&M))	March 1992

Applications for clearances and approvals

Clearance application	Address
Share exchanges (TCGA 1992 ss 138, 139, 140B, 140D)	Inland Revenue, Capital Gains Clearance Section, Sapphire House, 550 Streetsbrook Road, Solihull, West Midlands B91 1QU
Transfer of long term insurance business (TCGA 1992 s 211, TA 1988 s 444A)	Transferor UK-resident: Financial Institutions Division, Room S16, West Wing, Somerset House, Strand, London WC2R 1LB
	Transferor not UK-resident: Financial Institutions Division, Room S15, West Wing, Somerset House, Strand, London WC2R 1LB
Demergers (TA 1988 s 215)	Inland Revenue, Room 100, New Wing, Somerset House, London WC2R 1LB
Company purchase of own shares (TA 1988 s 225)	Inland Revenue, Central Correspondence Unit, New Wing, Somerset House, London WC2R 1LB
Transactions in securities (TA 1988 s 707)	The S703 Compliance Unit (S1S2), Room 522, 22 Kingsway, London WC2B 6NR
Company migration (FA 1988 s 130	Inland Revenue, International Division (Company Migrations), Room 311, Melbourne House, Aldwych, London WC2B 4LL

Approval application	Address
Pensions (TA 1988 ss 590, 591)	Pension Schemes Office, Inland Revenue, Yorke House, PO Box 62, Castle Meadow Road, Nottingham NG2 1BG
Employee share schemes (TA 1988 Sch 9)	Inland Revenue, Employee Share Schemes, Second Floor, New Wing, Somerset House, London WC2R 1LB
Qualifying life assurance policies (TA 1988 Sch 15)	Insurance Group, Financial Institutions Division, 5th Floor, 22 Kingsway, London WC2B 6NR
Professional bodies (relief for subscriptions) (TA 1988 s 201)	Inland Revenue, Birmingham Victoria, City Centre House, 30 Union Street, Birmingham B2 4AE
Profit-related pay schemes (TA 1988 s 176)	Inland Revenue, Profit-Related Pay Office, St Mungo's Road, Cumbernauld, Glasgow G70 5TR

Inland Revenue explanatory pamphlets

Tax Bulletin: published six times a year. Available only on annual subscription or at the Revenue internet site (below): contact Miss Sue Williams, Room 530, 22 Kingsway, London WC2B 6NR (020 7438 7700).

Copies of the pamphlets listed below are obtainable from the offices of HM Inspectors of Taxes, or from Tax Enquiry Centres, with the exception of

IR67 and CGT reform – the 1998 Finance Act: Inland Revenue Library, Room 28, New Wing, Somerset House, Strand, London WC2R 1LB (IR67: £5.20; CGT reform: £5; cheque/po made payable to 'Inland Revenue')

PRP2: Profit-Related Pay Unit, Inland Revenue Accounts Office, St Mungo's Road, Cumbernauld, Glasgow G67 1YZ (01236 783043, e-mail: wtrenwith.it.smr@gtnet.gov.uk

Inheritance tax: CTO: (England and Wales) Ferrers House, PO Box 38, Castle Meadow Road, Nottingham NG2 1BB (0115 974 2400)

(Scotland) Mulberry House, 16 Picardy Place, Edinburgh EH1 3NB (0131 524 3027)

(Northern Ireland) Dorchester House, 52–58 Great Victoria Street, Belfast BT2 7QL (028 9050 5353)

IR76, IR120 (You and the Pensions Schemes Office), PSO1: Pension Schemes Office, Yorke House, PO Box 62, Castle Meadow Road, Nottingham NG2 1BG (0115 974 1670: supplies line).

IR120: Braille and audio cassette versions must be ordered and will be sent through the post or, together with clear print version, are obtainable from the RNIB on 01345 023153.

The charities publications are available from FICO, Unit 342, Room 313, St. John's House, Merton Road, Bootle, Merseyside L69 9BB (0151 472 6106); CB series is available from FICO (Scotland), Trinity Park House, South Trinity Road, Edinburgh EH5 3SD (0131 551 8127).

Digest of DT agreements is available from FICO, Fitz Roy House, PO Box 46, Nottingham NG2 1BD (0115 974 2000).

Business Economic Notes are obtainable by post from the Inland Revenue Library, Room 28, New Wing, Somerset House, Strand, London WC2R 1LB (price £2.00 per booklet BEN 23-26, £1.50 for earlier booklets – post free) or by calling at the Information Centre (address as above).

The SO series is available from local stamp offices, by phoning 0845 603 0135, or from (England and Wales) The Stamp Office, Room 35, East Block, Barrington Road, Worthing BN12 4SE (01903 508930); (Scotland) Edinburgh Stamp Office, Mulberry House, 16 Picardy Place, Edinburgh EH1 3NF (0131 556 8998); (Northern Ireland) The Stamp Office, Dorchester House, 52-58 Great Victoria Street, Belfast BT2 7QE (02890 505124).

The Collection Series is available from local collection offices. Collection 4 (England and Wales) from Enforcement Office, Durrington Bridge House, Barrington Road, Worthing, West Sussex BN12 4SE; Collection 3 and 4 (Scotland) from Enforcement Section, Elgin House, 20 Haymarket Yards, Edinburgh EH12 5WT; Collection 3 and 4 (N Ireland) from Belfast 2 (Enforcement) 4th Floor, Olivetree House, 23 Fountain Street, Belfast BT1 5ET.

Self-assessment: SAT1 (£7.50) and SAT2 (£5) available from Inland Revenue Library, Room 28, New Wing, Somerset House, Strand, London WC2R 1LB (cheques/po made payable to 'Inland Revenue'). Text also available on 3.5" disks in 'text only' format (same price).

Self-assessment generally: Orderline 0645 000404; fax 0645 000604; e-mail saorderline.ir@gtnet.gov.uk; PO Box 37, St Austell, Cornwall PL25 5YN. (SA/BK5 from Orderline only.) Information also available on the Internet at: www.inlandrevenue.gov.uk/sa and general advice on the Helpline 0845 9000 444.

Guide to corporation tax self-assessment (£15) available from Inland Revenue Library, Room 28, New Wing, Somerset House, Strand, London WC2R 1LB.

Special Compliance Office (COP8, COP9, IR120): Special Compliance Office, Angel Court, 199 Borough High Street, London SE1 1HZ (020 7234 3708).

The AO series is available from The Adjudicator's Office, Haymarket House, 28 Haymarket, London SW1Y 4SP.

Education Service Pack: Pam Humphrey, Publicity Manager, Inland Revenue, Room 12, New Wing, Somerset House, Strand, London WC2R 1 LB (0207 438 6259; fax 0207 438 7428). Education service pages are available at the Revenue internet site (below).

Internet: A number of publications are available on the internet at: www.inlandrevenue.gov.uk

Pamphlet	Date Supp	Title
IR List	1999	Catalogue of leaflets and booklets
IR 1	2000	Extra-statutory concessions
IR 6	1994	Double taxation relief for companies
IR 14/15 (CIS)	1998	Construction industry scheme
IR 16	1997	Share acquisitions by directors and employees – explanatory notes
IR 20	1999	Residents and non-residents – liability to tax in the UK
IR 33	1992	Income tax and school leavers
IR 34	1996	Pay As You Earn
IR 37	1999	Appeals against tax – National Insurance Contributions, SSP and SMP
IR 40 (CIS)	1998	Construction industry Scheme: conditions for getting a subcontractor's tax certificate
IR 41	1999	Income tax and jobseekers
IR 45	1999	What to do about tax when someone dies
IR 46	2000	Clubs, societies and voluntary associations
IR 56/NI39	1999	Employed or self-employed? A guide for tax and national insurance
IR 60	1997	Income tax and students
IR 64	1993	Giving to charity. How businesses can get tax relief
IR 65	1993	Giving to charity. How individuals can get tax relief
IR 67	1986 (1988)	Capital taxation and the national heritage
IR 68	1990	Accrued income scheme. Taxing securities on transfer
IR 69	1999	Expenses payments: forms P11D. How to save yourself work

Pamphlet	Date Supp	Title
IR 72	1995	Investigations: the examination of business accounts
IR 73	1994	Inland Revenue investigations: how settlements are negotiated
IR 75	1987	Tax reliefs for charities
IR 76	1999	Personal pension schemes – Guidance notes
IR 78	1991	Personal pensions: a guide for tax
IR 80	1998	Income tax and married couples
IR 87	1999	Letting and your home. Including the 'Rent a Room' scheme and letting your previous home when you live elsewhere
IR 89	1998	Personal equity plans (PEPs) – a guide for potential investors
IR 90	1999	Tax allowances and reliefs
IR 91	1995	A guide for widows and widowers
IR 93	1997	Separation, divorce and maintenance payments
IR 95	1996	Approved profit-sharing schemes – an outline for employees
IR 96	1996	Approved profit-sharing schemes – explanatory notes
IR 97	1996	Approved SAYE share option schemes – an outline for employees
IR 98	1996	Approved SAYE share option schemes – explanatory notes
IR 101	1996	Approved company share option plans – an outline for employees
IR 102	1996	Approved company share option plans – explanatory notes
IR 109	2000	Employer compliance reviews and negotiations
IR 110	2000	A guide for people with savings
IR 113	1994	Gift aid: A guide for donors and charities
IR 114	1998	TESSA: Tax free interest for taxpayers
IR 115	1992	Tax and childcare
IR 116 (C1S)	1999	Guide for subcontractors with tax certificates
IR 117 (C1S)	1999	Guide for subcontractors with Registration Cards
IR 119	1999	Tax relief for vocational training
IR 120	1999	You and the Inland Revenue (Tax Collection, NICs and Accounts Offices). Versions are available in Bengali, Braille, Chinese, Greek, Gujarati, Hindi, Punjabi, Turkish, Urdu, Vietnamese and Welsh, clear print and audio cassettes
	1995	You and the Inland Revenue (Special Compliance Office)
	1996	You and the Inland Revenue (Financial Intermediaries and Claims Office)
	1998	You and the Inland Revenue (Pension Schemes Office)
	1999	You and the Inland Revenue (Enforcement Office)
	1999	You and the Inland Revenue (Capital Taxes Office)
	1999	You and the Inland Revenue (Tax Credit Office)
IR 121	2000	Income tax and pensioners
IR 122	1997	Volunteer drivers
IR 123	1999	Mortgage interest relief – buying your home
IR 125	1999	Using your own car for work
IR 126	1995	Corporation tax pay and file: a general guide
IR 129	1995	Occupational pension schemes: an introduction
IR 131	2000	Inland Revenue Statements of Practice
IR 134	1997	Income tax and relocation packages
IR 136	1994	Income tax and company vans. A guide for employees and employers
IR 137	1999	The Enterprise Investment Scheme
IR 138	1995	Living or retiring abroad? A guide to UK tax on your UK income and pension
IR 139	1995	Income from abroad? A guide to UK tax on overseas income
IR 140	1999	Non-resident landlords, their agents and tenants
IR 141	1995	Open government
IR 144	1995	Income tax and incapacity benefit
IR 144	1995	Income tax and incapacity benefit; clear print, audio and braille versions
IR 145	1997	Low interest loans provided by employers
IR 148/CA69	1999	Are your workers employed or self-employed? A guide for tax and national insurance for contractors in the construction industry
IR 150	1999	Taxation of rents – a guide to property income
IR 152	1996	Trusts – an introduction
IR 153	1997	Tax exemption for sickness or unemployment insurance payments
IR 155	1999	PAYE settlement agreements
IR 156	1996	Our heritage. Your right to see tax exempt works of art
IR 160	1999	Inland Revenue enquiries under self-assessment
IR 161	1998	Tax relief for employees' business travel. A short guide to the tax treatment of employees' travel expenses from 6 April 1998
IR 162	1999	A better approach to local office enquiry work under self-assessment
IR 163	1998	Millennium Gift Aid
IR 164 (CIS)	1998	Advice to sub-contractors going into deduction under the Construction Industry Scheme
IR 165	1999	The individual savings account (ISA) – a guide for savers
IR 166	1999	The euro
IR 167	1999	Charter for Inland Revenue taxpayers
IR 169	2000	Venture capital trusts (VCTs)—a brief guide
IR 170	1999	Blind person's allowance
IR 171	1999	Income tax: a guide for people with children
IR 172	2000	Income tax and company cars
IR 173	1999	Tax credits: a summary for employers
ISA/1	1999	The answers on ISAs
CS1	1993	Deeds of covenant – guidance for charities
CS2	1998	Trading by charities – guidelines on the tax treatment of trades carried on by charities
—	1994	Fund-raising for charity. What to look out for on tax
CB(1)	1993	Setting up a charity in Scotland
CB(1)	1995	A'cur buidheann carthannais air chois an Alba (Gaelic)
480	1999	Expenses and benefits. A tax guide
490	1998	Employee travel. A tax and NICs guide for employers

Pamphlet	Date Supp	Title
FD/CW	1994	Double taxation relief: intercompany loans and royalties
—	1999	Digest of double taxation agreements
PRP 2	1996	Tax relief for profit-related pay – notes for guidance
PSO1	1995	Occupational pension schemes. A guide for members of tax-approved schemes
CISFACT 5	1998	The new construction industry scheme. A handy guide
CGT 1	1999	Capital gains tax – An introduction
—	1998	Capital gains tax reform – the 1998 Finance Act
IHT 2	1998	Inheritance tax on lifetime gifts
IHT 3	1999	Inheritance tax – an introduction
IHT 8	1995	Alterations to an inheritance following a death. Inheritance tax
IHT 11	1998	Payment of inheritance tax from national savings
IHT 12	1998	Excepted estates procedures
IHT 13	1996	Inheritance tax and penalties
IHT14	2000	Inheritance tax – the personal representatives' responsibilities
IHT15	1996	Inheritance tax – how to calculate the liability
IHT16	1996	Inheritance tax – settled property
IHT17	1996	Inheritance tax – businesses, farms and woodlands
IHT18	1996	Inheritance tax – foreign aspects
IHT 210	2000	How to fill in form IHT 200
IHT 213	2000	How to fill in form IHT (WS)
IHT 215	2000	Practitioners guide (forms IHT 200 and IHT (WS))
SO 1	1999	Stamp duty on buying a freehold house in England, Wales and Northern Ireland
SO 1 (Scotland)	1999	Stamp duty on buying land or buildings in Scotland
SO 2	1997	Stamp Office customer promise and service information
SO 3	1996	If things go wrong. Complaints and lost documents
SO 6	1996	A short history of stamp duties
SO 7	1999	Stamp duty on buying a leasehold domestic property
SO 7 (Scotland)	1999	Stamp duty and leases in Scotland
SO 8	1999	Stamp duty on agreements securing short tenancies
SO 9	1999	A table of ad valorem stamp duties
SO 10	1999	Stamp duty interest and penalties
SO 11	1997	Stamp duty and charities
SO 12	1998	Stamp duty on commercial leases and agreements for leases
SO 13	1998	Code of practice SDRT inspections
Collection 1	1995	Distraint
Collection 1 (Scotland)	1994	Summary Warrant
Collection 1 (N Ireland)	1995	Distraint
Collection 2	1994	Magistrates' Court proceedings
Collection 2 (Scotland)	1994	Sheriff Court proceedings
Collection 2 (N Ireland)	1994	Magistrates' Court proceedings
Collection 3	1995	County Court proceedings
Collection 3 (Scotland)	1994	Court of Session proceedings
Collection 3 (N Ireland)	1995	High Court proceedings
Collection 4	1995	Bankruptcy and winding up
Collection 4 (Scotland)	1995	Sequestration and winding up
Collection 4 (N Ireland)	1995	Bankruptcy and winding up
COP 1	1999	Mistakes by the Inland Revenue
COP 2	1995	Investigations
COP 3	2000	Reviews of employers' and contractors' records
COP 4	1997	Inspection of schemes operated by financial intermediaries
COP 5	1998	Inspection of charities' records
COP 6	1994	Collection of tax
COP 6 (Scotland)	1995	Collection of tax
COP 7	1994	Collection of amounts due from employers and contractors in the construction industry
COP 7 (Scotland)	1994	Collection of amounts due from employers and contractors in the construction industry
COP 8	1997	Special Compliance Office Investigations: cases other than suspected serious fraud
COP 9	1997	Special Compliance Office Investigations: cases of suspected serious fraud
COP 10	1999	Information and advice
COP 11	1996	Enquiries into tax returns by local tax offices
COP 14	1999	Enquiries into Company Tax Returns
COP 17	1999	Enquiries into applications for WFTC and DPTC
AO1	2000	How to complain about the Inland Revenue and the Valuation Office Agency
AO2	1998	How to complain about Customs and Excise
RAO	1994	How to complain about the Inland Revenue – ethnic language versions
—	1999	Guide to corporation tax self assessment
Inst 1	1998	A modem system for corporation tax payments. A guide to quarterly instalment payments
WFTC/BK1	1999	Your guide to working families' tax credit
DPTC/BK1	1999	Your guide to disabled person's tax credit
CTC/BK1	1999	Working families' tax credit and disabled person's tax credit (help with the cost of childcare)
WFTC/FS1	1999	Factsheet—working families' tax credit
DPTC/FS1	1999	Factsheet—disabled person's tax credit
CTC/FS1	1999	Factsheet—working families' tax credit, disabled person's tax credit and childcare
WFTC/AC	1999	If you think a tax credit decision is wrong
WFTC/APN1	1999	If you think a tax credit decision is wrong (Northern Ireland)
WFTC/EG	1999	An employer's guide to tax credits WFTC and DPTC
SA/BK3	1995	Self-assessment – a guide to keeping records for the self-employed
SA/BK4	1997	Self-assessment – a general guide to keeping records

Inland Revenue explanatory pamphlets — continued

Pamphlet	Date	Supp	Title
SA/BK5	1999		Self-assessment – electronic version of the tax return
SA/BK6	1997		Self-assessment – penalties for late returns
SA/BK7	1997		Self-assessment – surcharges for late payment of tax
SA/BK8	1997		Self-assessment – your guide
SAT 1	1995		Self-assessment: the new current year basis of assessment
SAT 2	1995		Self-assessment: the legal framework
SAT 3	1995		Self-assessment: what it will mean for employers
SVD 1	1999		Shares Valuation Division. An introduction
NE 1	1999		First steps as a new employer
CWL 1	1999		Starting your own business? (Published with HM Customs & Excise and Contributions Agency)
CWL 2	1999		NI contributions for self-employed people. Class 2 and Class 4
CWG 1	1999		Employer's quick guide to PAYE and NICs
CWG 2	1999		Employer's further guide to PAYE and NICs
CWG 3	1999		Employer's annual pack orderline guide and order form
—	1999		Education service pack

Business economic notes:

BEN 1	(1990)	Travel agents	BEN 14	(1990)	The pet industry
BEN 2	(1995)	Road haulage	BEN 15	(1990)	Veterinary surgeons
BEN 3	(1990)	The lodging industry	BEN 16	(1990)	Catering—general
BEN 4	(1990)	Hairdressers	BEN 17	(1990)	Catering—restaurants
BEN 5	(1990)	Waste materials reclamation and disposal	BEN 18	(1990)	Catering—fast-foods
			BEN 19	(1993)	Farming—stock valuation for income tax purposes
BEN 6	(1990)	Funeral directors			
BEN 7	(1990)	Dentists	BEN 20	(1994)	Insurance brokers and agents
BEN 8	(1990)	Florists	BEN 21	(1994)	Residential rest and nursing homes
BEN 9	(1988)	Licensed victuallers	BEN 22	(1995)	Dispensing chemists
BEN 10	(1990)	The jewellery trade	BEN 23	(1997)	Driving instructors
BEN 11	(1990)	Electrical retailers	BEN 24	(1997)	Independent fishmongers
BEN 12	(1990)	Antiques and fine art dealers	BEN 25	(1997)	Taxi cabs and private hire vehicles
BEN 13	(1990)	Fish and chip shops	BEN 26	(1997)	Confectioners, tobacconists and newsagents

Internal guidance booklets and manuals: *

Assessed Taxes	Interest Review Unit Guidelines
Assessment Procedures	International Tax Handbook
Banking Manual	Investigation Handbook
Capital Allowances Instructions	Life Assurance Manual
Capital Gains Manual	Movements Manual (PAYE)
Claims Manual	National Audit Group Instructions
Collection Manual	Oil Taxation Office PRT Manual
Company Taxation Manual	Oil Taxation Office Ring Fence CT Manual
Complaints Handbook	Oil Taxation Office Section 830 Manual
Compliance and Investigation Operation Manual	Pay and File Manual (Collection)
(CTO) Advanced Instruction Manual (IHT)	PAYE Instructions (Collection)
(CTO) General Examination Manual (IHT)	PAYE Settlement Agreement Handbook
Double Taxation Relief Manual	Pension Schemes Office Manual
Employee Share Schemes	Personal Contact Manual
Employer Compliance Manual	Profit Related Pay Unit Manual
Employers Section Manual	Property Income Manual
Employment Procedures Manual	Regional Office Manual
Enforcement Manual	Relief
Enforcement Manual (Scotland)	Residence Guide
Enquiry Handbook	Schedule D Compliance
European Economic Interest Groupings	Schedule E Manual
General Insurance Manual	Self Self Assessment Manual
Independent Taxation Manual	Shares Valuation Division Manual
Inheritance Tax Double Taxation Conventions	Small Self Administered Schemes
Insolvency Manual	Stamp Office
Insolvency Manual (Scotland)	Subcontractors in the Construction Industry
Inspector's Manual	Trust Manual

* Copies of the manuals are available on CD-rom, with an updating service, as part of a database, from Butterworths Tolley, Reed Elsevier (UK) Ltd, 2 Addiscombe Road, Croydon, Surrey CR9 5AF: telephone 0181 686 9141; fax 0181 686 3155. Extracts published in looseleaf format as *Simon's Direct Tax Service,* Binders 12 and 13: prices available on application to the publishers.

All internal guidance manuals are available for inspection free of charge in Inland Revenue Tax Enquiry Centres. The inheritance tax manuals may be inspected free of charge at certain Capital Taxes Offices.

National Insurance Contributions Leaflets see page 88.

Capital gains tax

Annual exemption

Individuals, personal representatives[1] and certain trusts[2]

Exempt amount of net gains	1995-96	1996-97	1997-98	1998-99	1999-2000	2000–01
	£6,000	£6,300	£6,500	£6,800	£7,100	£7,200

[1] Year of death and following 2 years (maximum).
[2] Trusts for mentally disabled persons and those in receipt of attendance allowance or disability living allowance. Exemption divided by number of qualifying settlements created (after 9 March 1981) by one settlor, subject to a minimum of one-tenth.

Trusts[1] generally

Exempt amount of net gains	1995-96	1996-97	1997-98	1998-99	1999-2000	2000-01
	£3,000	£3,150	£3,250	£3,400	£3,550	£3,600

[1] Exemption divided by number of qualifying settlements created (after 6 June 1978) by one settlor, subject to a minimum of one-fifth.

Chattel exemption

	Disposals exemption	*Marginal relief: Maximum chargeable gain*
1989-90 to 2000–01	£6,000	$\frac{5}{3}$ excess over £6,000

Rate of tax

2000–01	**Individuals:** gains taxed as top slice of income: 10% to starting rate limit, 20% to basic rate limit, 40% above, subject to tapering in certain cases. **Trusts, personal representatives:** 34%, subject to tapering relief in certain cases
1999–2000	**Individuals:** gains taxed as top slice of income: 20% to basic rate limit, 40% above, subject to tapering in certain cases. **Trusts, personal representatives:** 34%, subject to tapering in certain cases
1998–99	**Individuals:** gains taxed at income tax rates (as top slice of income[1]), subject to tapering in certain cases **Trusts, personal representatives:** 34%, subject to tapering in certain cases
1997–98	**Individuals:** gains taxed at income tax rates (as top slice of income[1]) **Trusts, personal representatives:** 23% (34% for trusts charged to rate applicable to trusts)
1996–97	**Individuals:** gains taxed at income tax rates (as top slice of income[1]) **Trusts, personal representatives:** 24% (34% for trusts charged to rate applicable to trusts))

[1] Adjustment is necessary for savings income (including interest from banks and building societies, interest distributions from authorised unit trusts, interest from gilts and other securities including corporate bonds, purchased life annuities, and discounts). Adjustment is also necessary for dividends or other qualifying distributions from a UK-resident company.

Retirement relief (phased out from 6 April 1999)

Disposals after	*Minimum age*	*100% relief on gains up to*	*50% relief on gains between*	*Maximum relief*
5 April 2003	–	–	–	–
5 April 2002	50	£50,000	£50,000.01–£200,000	£125,000
5 April 2001	50	£100,000	£100,000.01–£400,000	£250,000
5 April 2000	50	£150,000	£150,000.01–£600,000	£375,000
5 April 1999	50	£200,000	£200,000.01–£800,000	£500,000
27 November 1995	50	£250,000	£250,000.01–£1,000,000	£625,000

(% determined by qualifying period. Relief also available where early retirement occurs for reasons of ill-health. Relief given after indexation allowance but before tapering relief.)

Tapering relief

Tapering relief is available for disposals made after 5 April 1998 (TCGA 1992 s 2A inserted by FA 1998 s 121; (2000) SWTI 392). The chargeable gain is reduced according to the length of time for which the asset has been held (counting from 6 April 1998). Non-business assets acquired before 17 March 1998 and business assets acquired before 17 March 1998 and disposed of before 6 April 2000 qualify for an addition of one year to the period for which they are held after 5 April 1998. There is no one-year addition for disposals of business assets after 5 April 2000. The reductions available for gains on business assets are greater than for gains on non-business assets.

Business assets				Non-business assets			
Number of complete yrs after 5.4.98 for which asset held	% of gain chargeable	Equivalent tax rates:		Number of complete yrs after 5.4.98 for which asset held	% of gain chargeable	Equivalent tax rates:	
		Higher rate taxp'r	20% rate taxp'r			Higher rate taxp'r	20% rate taxp'r
Disposals after 5 April 2000				0	100	40	20
0	100	40	20	1	100	40	20
1	87.5	35	17·5	2	100	40	20
2	75	30	15	3	95	38	19
3	50	20	10	4	90	36	18
4 or more	25	10	5	5	85	34	17
				6	80	32	16
Disposals before 6 April 2000				7	75	30	15
0	100	40	20	8	70	28	14
1	92·5	37	18·5	9	65	26	13
2	85	34	17·0	10 or more	60	24	12
3	77·5	31	15·5				

Leases

Depreciation table (TCGA 1992 Sch 8 para 1)

Yrs	%	Yrs	%	Yrs	%	Yrs	%	Yrs	%	Yrs	%	Yrs	%
50 (or more)	100	42	96·593	34	91·156	27	83·816	20	72·770	13	56·167	6	31·195
49	99·657	41	96·041	33	90·280	26	82·496	19	70·791	12	53·191	5	26·722
48	99·289	40	95·457	32	89·354	25	81·100	18	68·697	11	50·038	4	21·983
47	98·902	39	94·842	31	88·371	24	79·622	17	66·470	10	46.695	3	16·959
46	98·490	38	94·189	30	87·330	23	78·055	16	64·116	9	43·154	2	11·629
45	98·059	37	93·497	29	86·226	22	76·399	15	61·617	8	39·399	1	5·983
44	97·595	36	92·761	28	85·053	21	74·635	14	58·971	7	35·414	0	0
43	97·107	35	91·981										

Formula: fraction of expenditure disallowed—

$$\frac{\text{Percentage for duration of lease at acquisition or expenditure} \; \mathbf{minus} \; \text{Percentage for duration of lease at disposal}}{\text{Percentage for duration of lease at acquisition or expenditure}}$$

Fractions of years:
Add one-twelfth of the difference between the percentage for the whole year and the next higher percentage for each additional month. Odd days under 14 are not counted; 14 odd days or more count as a month.

Short leases: premiums treated as rent (TA 1988 s 34, TCGA 1992 Sch 8 para 5)

Part of premium for grant of a short lease which is chargeable to income tax under Schedule A—

$P - (2\% \times (n - 1) \times P)$

Where P = amount of premium
n = number of complete years which lease has to run when granted

Length of Lease (complete years)	Amount chargeable to CGT %	Income tax Sch A %	Length of Lease (complete years)	Amount chargeable to CGT %	Income tax Sch A %	Length of Lease (complete years)	Amount chargeable to CGT %	Income tax Sch A %
Over 50	100	0	34	66	34	17	32	68
50	98	2	33	64	36	16	30	70
49	96	4	32	62	38	15	28	72
48	94	6	31	60	40	14	26	74
47	92	8	30	58	42	13	24	76
46	90	10	29	56	44	12	22	78
45	88	12	28	54	46	11	20	80
44	86	14	27	52	48	10	18	82
43	84	16	26	50	50	9	16	84
42	82	18	25	48	52	8	14	86
41	80	20	24	46	54	7	12	88
40	78	22	23	44	56	6	10	90
39	76	24	22	42	58	5	8	92
38	74	26	21	40	60	4	6	94
37	72	28	20	38	62	3	4	96
36	70	30	19	36	64	2	2	98
35	68	32	18	34	66	1 or less	0	100

Gilt-edged securities exempt from tax on chargeable gains

The following securities have been specified for the purposes of TCGA 1992 Sch 9 and are exempt from capital gains tax. A similar exemption exists for qualifying corporate bonds issued after 13 March 1984. A 1-year qualifying limit applied to disposals before 2 July 1986. The gain accruing on the disposal of an option or contract to acquire or dispose of gilt-edged securities or qualifying corporate bonds after 1 July 1986 is also exempt from capital gains tax. (Securities redeemed before 31 March 2000 do not appear on this list.)

Readers should note that under the loan relationship provisions of FA 1996 Part IV Chapter II, the definition of 'qualifying corporate bond' for the purposes of corporation tax only has been extended (see TCGA 1992 ss 117, 117A, 117B).

* Repaid at latest date shown unless the Treasury give notice of earlier repayment.

Stocks		Redemption dates	Dividend due dates	
13%	Treasury Stock 2000	14 July 2000	14 January	14 July
13%	Treasury Stock 2000 'A'			
8%	Treasury Stock 2000	7 December 2000	7 June	7 December
8%	Treasury Stock 2000 'A'			
10%	Treasury Stock 2001	26 February 2001	26 February	26 August
10%	Treasury Stock 2001 'A'			
10%	Treasury Stock 2001 'B'			
14%	Treasury Stock 1998-2001*	22 May 1998/22 May 2001	22 May	22 November
9½%	Conversion Loan 2001	12 July 2001	12 January	12 July
9¾%	Conversion Stock 2001	10 August 2001	10 February	10 August
2½%	Index-Linked Treasury Stock 2001	24 September 2001	24 March	24 September
7%	Treasury Stock 2001	6 November 2001	6 May	6 November
7%	Treasury Stock 2001 'A'			
10%	Conversion Stock 2002	11 April 2002	11 April	11 October
9½%	Conversion Stock 2002	14 June 2002	14 June	14 December
9¾%	Treasury Stock 2002	27 August 2002	27 February	27 August
9¾%	Treasury Stock 2002 'A'			
9¾%	Treasury Stock 2002 'B'			
9¾%	Treasury Stock 2002 'C'			
9%	Exchequer Stock 2002	19 November 2002	19 May	19 November
9¾%	Conversion Loan 2003	7 May 2003	7 May	7 November
2½%	Index-Linked Treasury Stock 2003	20 May 2003	20 May	20 November
8%	Treasury Stock 2003	10 June 2003	10 June	10 December
8%	Treasury Stock 2003 'A'			
13¾%	Treasury Stock 2000-03*	25 July 2000/25 July 2003	25 January	25 July
13¾%	Treasury Stock 2000-03 'A'			
10%	Treasury Stock 2003	8 September 2003	8 March	8 September
10%	Treasury Stock 2003 'A'			
10%	Treasury Stock 2003 'B'			
11½%	Treasury Stock 2001-04*	19 March 2001/19 March 2004	19 March	19 September
10%	Treasury Stock 2004	18 May 2004	18 May	18 November
3½%	Funding Stock 1999-2004*	14 July 1999/14 July 2004	14 January	14 July
4⅜%	Index-Linked Treasury Stock 2004	21 October 2004	21 April	21 October
9½%	Conversion Stock 2004	25 October 2004	25 April	25 October
9½%	Conversion Stock 2004 'A'			
6¾%	Treasury Stock 2004	26 November 2004	26 May	26 November
6¾%	Treasury Stock 2004 'A'			
5%	Treasury Loan 2004	7 June 2004	7 June	7 December
9½%	Conversion Stock 2005	18 April 2005	18 April	18 October
9½%	Conversion Stock 2005 'A'			
10½%	Exchequer Stock 2005	20 September 2005	20 March	20 September
12½%	Treasury Stock 2003-05*	21 November 2003/ 21 November 2005	21 May	21 November
12½%	Treasury Stock 2003-05* 'A'			
8½%	Treasury Stock 2005	7 December 2005	7 June	7 December
2%	Index-Linked Treasury Stock 2006	19 July 2006	19 January	19 July
7¾%	Treasury Stock 2006	8 September 2006	8 March	8 September
8%	Treasury Loan 2002-06*	5 October 2002/5 October 2006	5 April	5 October
8%	Treasury Loan 2002-06 'A'			
9¾%	Conversion Stock 2006	15 November 2006	15 May	15 November
7½%	Treasury Stock 2006	7 December 2006	7 June	7 December
11¾%	Treasury Stock 2003-07*	22 January 2003/22 January 2007	22 January	22 July
11¾%	Treasury Stock 2003-07 'A'			
7¼%	Treasury Stock 2007	7 June 2007	7 June	7 December
8½%	Treasury Loan 2007	16 July 2007	16 January	16 July
8½%	Treasury Loan 2007 'A'			
8½%	Treasury Loan 2007 'B'			
8½%	Treasury Loan 2007 'C'			
13½%	Treasury Stock 2004-08*	26 March 2004/26 March 2008	26 March	26 September

Gilt-edged securities — continued

Stocks		Redemption dates	Dividend due dates	
9%	Treasury Loan 2008	13 October 2008	13 April	13 October
9%	Treasury Loan 2008 'A'			
9%	Treasury Loan 2008 'B'			
9%	Treasury Loan 2008 'C'			
9%	Treasury Loan 2008 'D'			
2½%	Index-Linked Treasury Stock 2009	20 May 2009	20 May	20 November
8%	Treasury Stock 2009	25 September 2009	25 March	25 September
8%	Treasury Stock 2009 'A'			
6¼%	Treasury Stock 2010	25 November 2010	25 May	25 November
9%	Conversion Loan 2011	12 July 2011	12 January	12 July
9%	Conversion Loan 2011 'A'			
9%	Conversion Loan 2011 'B'			
9%	Conversion Loan 2011 'C'			
9%	Conversion Loan 2011 'D'			
2½%	Index-Linked Treasury Stock 2011	23 August 2011	23 February	23 August
9%	Treasury Stock 2012	6 August 2012	6 February	6 August
9%	Treasury Stock 2012 'A'			
5½%	Treasury Stock 2008-12*	10 September 2008/ 10 September 2012	10 March	10 September
2½%	Index-Linked Treasury Stock 2013	16 August 2013	16 February	16 August
8%	Treasury Stock 2013	27 September 2013	27 March	27 September
7¾%	Treasury Loan 2012-15*	26 January 2012/26 January 2015	26 January	26 July
8%	Treasury Stock 2015	7 December 2015	7 June	7 December
8%	Treasury Stock 2015 'A'			
2½%	Treasury Stock 1986-2016*	15 March 1986/15 March 2016	15 March	15 September
2½%	Index-Linked Treasury Stock 2016	26 July 2016	26 January	26 July
2½%	Index-Linked Treasury Stock 2016 'A'			
8¾%	Treasury Stock 2017	25 August 2017	25 February	25 August
8¾%	Treasury Stock 2017 'A'			
12%	Exchequer Stock 2013-17*	12 December 2013/ 12 December 2017	12 June	12 December
2½%	Index-Linked Treasury Stock 2020	16 April 2020	16 April	16 October
2½%	Index-Linked Treasury Stock 2024	17 July 2024	17 January	17 July
6%	Treasury Stock 2028	7 December 2028	7 June	7 December
4⅛%	Index-Linked Treasury Stock 2030	22 July 2030	22 January	22 July
4%	Consolidated Loan	1 February 1957 or after	1 February	1 August
3½%	War Loan	1 December 1952 or after	1 June	1 December
3½%	Conversion Loan	1 April 1961 or after	1 April	1 October
3%	Treasury Stock	5 April 1966 or after	5 April	5 October
2½%	Consolidated Stock	5 April 1923 or after	5 January, 5 July	5 April, 5 October
2½%	Treasury Stock 1975 or after	1 April 1975 or after	1 April	1 October
2½%	Annuities	5 January 1905 or after	5 January, 5 July	5 April, 5 October
2¾%	Annuities	5 January 1905 or after	5 January, 5 July	5 April, 5 October

Reliefs

The following is a summary of the main reliefs and exemptions for the year 2000-01. The legislation should be referred to for conditions and exceptions.

Charities

Gains accruing to charities which are both applicable and applied for charitable purposes	Exempt

Individuals

Annual exemption (see p 36 for earlier years)	£7,200
Chattel exemption (see p 36 for marginal relief)	£6,000
Compensation (injury to person, profession or vocation)	Exempt
Decorations for valour (acquired otherwise than for money or money's worth)	Gain exempt
Enterprise Investment Scheme (see p 74)	Gain on disposal after relevant five year period exempt to extent full relief given on shares
Foreign currency acquired for personal expenditure	Gain exempt
Gifts for public benefit, works of art, historic buildings etc	No chargeable gain/allowable loss
Gilt-edged stock (see p 38)	No chargeable gain/allowable loss
Married persons living together	No chargeable gain/allowable loss on disposals from one to the other
Motor vehicles	Gain exempt
Principal private residence	Gain exempt
If residence is partly let, exemption for the let part is limited to the smaller of—	(1) exemption on owner-occupied part and (2) £40,000
Qualifying corporate bonds	No chargeable gain (for loans made before 17 March 1998, allowable loss in certain cases if all or part of loss is irrecoverable)
Retirement relief (phased-out over 5 years beginning in 1999-2000: see p 36)	£200,000 plus 50% of gains between £200,000 and £800,000
Hold-over relief for gifts	Restricted to: (1) gifts of business assets (including unquoted shares in trading companies and holding companies of trading groups). Relief is not available on the transfer of shares or securities to a company made after 8 November 1999: (1999) SWTI 1799, (2000) SWTI 344. (2) gifts of heritage property (3) gifts to heritage maintenance funds (4) gifts to political parties, and (5) gifts on which there is an immediate charge to inheritance tax. Where available, transferee's acquisition cost treated as reduced by held-over gain.
Roll-over relief on reinvestment (now forms part of a rationalised Enterprise Investment Scheme). Withdrawn for acquisitions after 5 April 1998.	(See FA 1998, s 74, Sch 13)
Venture capital trusts (see p 75)	Gain on disposal of shares by original investor exempt if company still a venture capital trust.

Reliefs — continued

Businesses

Roll-over relief for replacement of business assets

Qualifying assets:

    Buildings and land both occupied and used for the purposes of the trade
    Fixed plant and machinery
    Ships, aircraft and hovercraft
    Satellites, space stations and spacecraft
    Goodwill
    Milk and potato quotas
    Ewe and suckler cow premium quotas
    Fish quotas (from 29 March 1999)
    UK oil licences (from 1 July 1999)

The "replacement" assets must be acquired within 12 months before or 3 years after the disposal of the old asset. Both assets must be within any of the above classes. Holdover relief is available where the new asset is a depreciating asset (having a predictable useful life not exceeding 60 years).

Personal representatives

Annual exemption

Year of death and following 2 years: (See p 36 for earlier years)	£7,200

Allowable expenses

Expenses allowable for the costs of establishing title in computing chargeable gains on disposal of assets in a deceased person's estate: deaths occurring after 5 April 1993 (SP 8/94). (The Revenue accepts computations based either on the scale or on the actual allowable expenditure incurred.)

Gross value of estate	Allowable expenditure
Up to £40,000	1.75% of the probate value of the assets sold by the personal representatives
Between £40,001 and £70,000	£700, to be divided between all the assets of the estate in proportion to the probate values and allowed in those proportions on assets sold by the personal representatives
Between £70,001 and £300,000	1% of the probate value of the assets sold
Between £300,001 and £400,000	£3,000, to be divided between all the assets of the estate in proportion to the probate values and allowed in those proportions on assets sold by the personal representatives
Between £400,001 and £750,000	0.75% of the probate value of the assets sold
Exceeding £75,000	Negotiable according to the facts of the particular case

Trustees

Annual exemption see p 36.

Allowable expenses

Expenses allowable in computing chargeable gains of corporate trustees in the administration of trusts and estates: acquisition, disposals and deemed disposals after 5 April 1993 (SP 8/94). (The Revenue accepts computations based either on the scale or on the actual allowable expenditure incurred.)

Transfers of assets to beneficiaries etc	
(a) Quoted stocks and shares	
(i) One beneficiary	£20 per holding
(ii) More than one beneficiary	£20 per holding, divided equally between the beneficiaries
(b) Unquoted shares	As (a) above, plus any exceptional expenditure
(c) Other assets	As (a) above, plus any exceptional expenditure
Actual disposals and acquisitions	
(a) Quoted stocks and shares	Investment fee as charged by the trustee (where a comprehensive annual management fee is charged, the investment fee is taken to be £0.25 per £100 of the sale or purchase moneys)
(b) Unquoted shares	As (a) above, plus actual valuation costs
(c) Other assets	Investment fee (as (a) above), subject to a maximum of £60, plus actual valuation costs
Deemed disposals by trustees	
(a) Quoted stocks and shares	£6 per holding
(b) Unquoted shares	Actual valuation costs
(c) Other assets	Actual valuation costs

Indexation allowance

For persons subject to capital gains tax, gains on disposals after 5 April 1998 of assets held on that date are indexed up to April 1998 but not beyond. No indexation allowance is available for assets acquired after 31 March 1998. Tapering relief is available for disposals after 5 April 1998, see p 37. For persons subject to corporation tax, indexation continues to be available as previously, and there is no tapering relief.

The indexation allowance is calculated as follows: allowable expenditure (or MV at 31.3.82) $\times \dfrac{RD - RI}{RI}$

RD = Retail prices index figure for month of disposal
RI = Retail prices index figure for base month (ie the month in which the allowable expenditure was incurred, or March 1982 if later).

The following indexed rise can be used when calculating the allowance—

RD—Month of disposal

1982	1995 Apr	May	June	July	Aug	Sept	Oct	Nov	Dec	1996 Jan	Feb	Mar	Apr	May	June	July	Aug	Sept	Oct	Nov	Dec	1997 Jan	Feb	Mar	Apr	May	June	July	Aug	Sept
Mar	·876	·883	·886	·877	·887	·896	·886	·886	·897	·891	·899	·907	·921	·925	·926	·918	·927	·936	·936	·937	·944	·944	·951	·956	·967	·975	·983	·983	·995	1·005
Apr	·839	·846	·848	·840	·850	·858	·848	·848	·860	·853	·862	·869	·883	·887	·888	·881	·889	·898	·898	·899	·905	·905	·913	·918	·929	·936	·944	·944	·956	·966
May	·825	·833	·835	·827	·837	·845	·835	·835	·846	·840	·849	·856	·870	·873	·874	·867	·876	·884	·884	·886	·992	·892	·899	·904	·915	·922	·930	·930	·942	·952
June	·820	·828	·830	·822	·831	·840	·830	·830	·841	·835	·844	·851	·864	·868	·869	·862	·870	·879	·879	·880	·886	·886	·894	·899	·910	·917	·924	·924	·936	·946
July	·820	·827	·830	·821	·839	·830	·830	·830	·841	·834	·843	·850	·864	·867	·869	·861	·870	·878	·878	·880	·886	·886	·893	·898	·909	·916	·924	·924	·936	·946
Aug	·819	·827	·829	·820	·830	·839	·829	·829	·840	·834	·842	·850	·863	·867	·868	·861	·869	·878	·878	·879	·885	·885	·893	·897	·908	·916	·923	·923	·935	·945
Sept	·820	·820	·828	·830	·822	·831	·840	·830	·830	·841	·835	·844	·851	·864	·868	·869	·862	·870	·878	·880	·886	·886	·884	·899	·910	·917	·924	·924	·936	·946
Oct	·811	·819	·821	·813	·822	·831	·821	·821	·832	·826	·835	·842	·855	·859	·860	·853	·861	·870	·870	·871	·877	·877	·874	·889	·900	·907	·915	·915	·927	·937
Nov	·803	·810	·812	·804	·813	·822	·812	·812	·823	·817	·826	·833	·846	·850	·851	·844	·852	·861	·861	·862	·868	·868	·875	·880	·891	·898	·905	·905	·917	·927
Dec	·806	·813	·816	·807	·817	·825	·816	·816	·826	·820	·829	·836	·849	·853	·854	·847	·856	·864	·864	·865	·871	·871	·879	·833	·894	·902	·909	·909	·921	·931
1983 Jan	·804	·811	·813	·805	·815	·823	·813	·813	·824	·818	·827	·834	·847	·851	·852	·845	·853	·862	·862	·863	·869	·869	·876	·881	·892	·899	·907	·907	·919	·928
Feb	·796	·803	·806	·797	·807	·815	·806	·806	·816	·810	·819	·826	·839	·843	·844	·837	·845	·854	·854	·855	·861	·861	·868	·873	·884	·891	·898	·898	·910	·920
Mar	·793	·800	·802	·794	·803	·812	·802	·802	·813	·807	·815	·823	·836	·840	·841	·834	·842	·850	·850	·852	·858	·858	·865	·870	·880	·888	·895	·895	·907	·917
Apr	·768	·775	·777	·769	·779	·787	·777	·777	·788	·782	·790	·797	·811	·814	·815	·808	·816	·825	·825	·826	·832	·832	·839	·844	·854	·862	·869	·869	·881	·890
May	·760	·768	·779	·762	·771	·779	·770	·770	·781	·775	·783	·790	·803	·807	·808	·801	·809	·817	·817	·818	·824	·824	·821	·836	·847	·854	·861	·861	·873	·882
June	·756	·763	·766	·757	·767	·775	·766	·766	·776	·770	·779	·786	·799	·802	·803	·796	·805	·813	·813	·814	·820	·820	·827	·832	·842	·849	·856	·856	·868	·878
July	·747	·754	·756	·748	·757	·766	·756	·756	·767	·761	·769	·776	·789	·793	·794	·787	·795	·803	·803	·804	·810	·810	·817	·822	·839	·846	·846	·846	·858	·868
Aug	·739	·746	·748	·740	·750	·758	·748	·748	·759	·753	·761	·768	·781	·785	·786	·779	·787	·795	·795	·796	·802	·802	·809	·814	·824	·831	·838	·838	·850	·859
Sept	·731	·738	·741	·733	·742	·750	·741	·741	·751	·745	·753	·760	·773	·777	·778	·771	·779	·787	·787	·788	·794	·794	·801	·806	·816	·823	·830	·830	·842	·851
Oct	·725	·732	·735	·726	·736	·744	·735	·735	·745	·739	·747	·754	·767	·770	·772	·765	·773	·781	·781	·782	·788	·788	·795	·799	·810	·817	·824	·824	·835	·845
Nov	·719	·726	·728	·720	·730	·738	·728	·728	·739	·733	·741	·748	·761	·764	·765	·758	·767	·775	·775	·776	·782	·782	·788	·793	·803	·810	·817	·817	·829	·838
Dec	·715	·722	·724	·716	·725	·733	·724	·724	·734	·729	·737	·743	·756	·760	·761	·754	·762	·770	·770	·771	·777	·777	·784	·788	·799	·806	·813	·813	·824	·833
1984 Jan	·716	·723	·725	·717	·726	·734	·725	·725	·735	·730	·738	·745	·757	·761	·762	·755	·763	·771	·771	·772	·778	·778	·785	·789	·800	·807	·814	·814	·825	·834
Feb	·709	·716	·718	·710	·719	·727	·718	·718	·728	·722	·731	·737	·750	·753	·755	·748	·756	·764	·764	·765	·771	·771	·778	·782	·792	·799	·806	·806	·818	·827
Mar	·703	·710	·712	·704	·714	·722	·712	·712	·723	·717	·725	·732	·744	·748	·749	·742	·750	·758	·758	·759	·765	·765	·772	·776	·787	·794	·800	·800	·812	·821
Apr	·681	·688	·690	·682	·691	·699	·690	·690	·700	·694	·702	·709	·721	·725	·726	·719	·727	·735	·735	·736	·742	·742	·749	·753	·763	·770	·777	·777	·788	·797
May	·675	·681	·684	·676	·685	·693	·684	·684	·694	·688	·696	·703	·715	·718	·720	·713	·721	·729	·729	·730	·735	·735	·742	·747	·757	·763	·770	·770	·781	·790
June	·670	·677	·679	·671	·680	·688	·679	·679	·689	·684	·692	·698	·711	·714	·715	·708	·716	·724	·724	·725	·731	·731	·738	·742	·752	·759	·766	·766	·777	·786
July	·672	·679	·681	·673	·682	·690	·681	·681	·691	·686	·694	·700	·713	·716	·717	·710	·718	·726	·726	·727	·733	·733	·740	·744	·754	·761	·768	·768	·779	·788
Aug	·657	·663	·666	·658	·667	·675	·666	·666	·676	·670	·678	·685	·697	·700	·701	·695	·702	·710	·710	·711	·717	·717	·723	·728	·738	·745	·751	·751	·762	·771
Sept	·653	·660	·662	·655	·663	·671	·662	·662	·672	·667	·675	·681	·693	·697	·698	·691	·699	·707	·707	·708	·713	·713	·720	·724	·734	·741	·748	·748	·759	·768
Oct	·643	·650	·652	·644	·653	·661	·652	·652	·662	·657	·664	·671	·683	·686	·687	·681	·689	·696	·696	·697	·703	·703	·709	·714	·724	·730	·737	·737	·748	·757
Nov	·638	·645	·647	·639	·648	·656	·647	·647	·657	·651	·659	·666	·678	·681	·682	·676	·683	·691	·691	·692	·698	·698	·704	·709	·719	·725	·732	·732	·743	·752
Dec	·640	·646	·648	·641	·650	·657	·648	·648	·658	·653	·661	·667	·679	·683	·684	·677	·685	·692	·692	·694	·699	·699	·705	·710	·720	·727	·733	·733	·744	·753
1985 Jan	·634	·640	·642	·635	·644	·651	·642	·642	·652	·647	·655	·661	·673	·676	·678	·671	·679	·686	·686	·687	·693	·693	·699	·704	·714	·720	·727	·727	·738	·747
Feb	·621	·627	·629	·622	·630	·638	·629	·629	·639	·634	·641	·648	·660	·663	·664	·658	·665	·673	·673	·674	·679	·679	·686	·690	·700	·707	·713	·713	·724	·733
Mar	·606	·612	·614	·607	·615	·623	·614	·614	·624	·619	·626	·633	·644	·648	·649	·642	·650	·657	·657	·658	·664	·664	·670	·675	·784	·691	·697	·697	·708	·717
Apr	·572	·578	·581	·573	·582	·589	·581	·581	·590	·585	·592	·598	·610	·613	·614	·608	·615	·623	·623	·624	·629	·629	·635	·640	·649	·655	·662	·662	·672	·681
May	·565	·571	·573	·566	·574	·582	·573	·573	·583	·577	·585	·591	·603	·606	·607	·601	·608	·615	·615	·616	·622	·622	·628	·632	·642	·648	·654	·654	·665	·673
June	·562	·568	·570	·563	·571	·578	·570	·570	·579	·574	·582	·588	·599	·603	·604	·597	·605	·612	·612	·613	·618	·618	·625	·629	·638	·644	·651	·651	·661	·670
July	·565	·571	·573	·566	·574	·581	·573	·573	·582	·577	·585	·591	·602	·606	·607	·600	·608	·615	·615	·616	·621	·621	·628	·632	·641	·684	·654	·654	·664	·673
Aug	·560	·567	·569	·561	·570	·577	·569	·569	·578	·573	·580	·587	·598	·601	·602	·596	·603	·611	·611	·612	·617	·617	·623	·627	·637	·643	·649	·649	·660	·668
Sept	·561	·568	·570	·562	·571	·578	·570	·570	·579	·574	·581	·587	·599	·602	·603	·597	·604	·612	·612	·613	·618	·618	·624	·628	·638	·644	·650	·650	·661	·669
Oct	·559	·565	·567	·560	·568	·575	·567	·567	·577	·571	·579	·585	·596	·600	·601	·594	·602	·609	·609	·610	·615	·615	·622	·626	·635	·641	·648	·648	·658	·667
Nov	·553	·560	·562	·554	·563	·570	·562	·562	·571	·566	·573	·579	·591	·594	·595	·589	·596	·603	·603	·604	·610	·610	·616	·620	·630	·636	·642	·642	·652	·661
Dec	·551	·558	·560	·552	·561	·568	·560	·560	·569	·564	·571	·577	·589	·592	·593	·587	·594	·601	·601	·602	·608	·608	·614	·618	·627	·634	·640	·640	·650	·659

Indexation allowance — continued

RD—Month of disposal

1982	1997			1998												1999												2000			
	Oct	Nov	Dec	Jan	Feb	Mar	Apr	May	June	July	Aug	Sept	Oct	Nov	Dec	Jan	Feb	Mar	Apr	May	June	July	Aug	Sept	Oct	Nov	Dec	Jan	Feb	Mar	Apr
Mar	1·008	1·009	1·014	1·008	1·018	1·024	1·047	1·058	1·057	1·052	1·061	1·069	1·071	1·069	1·069	1·057	1·061	1·066	1·079	1·085	1·085	1·078	1·083	1·092	1·096	1·098	1·106	1·097	1·108		
Apr	·968	·969	·974	·968	·978	·984	1·006	1·018	1·016	1·011	1·020	1·029	1·030	1·029	1·029	1·016	1·020	1·025	1·039	1·043	1·043	1·037	1·042	1·051	1·055	1·057	1·064	1·056	1·067		
May	·954	·955	·960	·954	·964	·970	·992	1·003	1·002	·997	1·006	1·014	1·015	1·014	1·014	1·002	1·006	1·010	1·024	1·029	1·029	1·023	1·028	1·036	1·040	1·042	1·050	1·041	1·052		
June	·949	·950	·955	·949	·958	·965	·987	·998	·996	·991	1·000	1·009	1·010	1·009	1·009	·996	1·000	1·005	1·018	1·023	1·023	1·017	1·022	1·031	1·034	1·037	1·044	1·035	1·046		
July	·948	·949	·954	·948	·958	·964	·986	·997	·996	·991	·999	1·008	1·009	1·008	1·008	·996	·999	1·004	1·018	1·023	1·023	1·016	1·021	1·030	1·034	1·036	1·043	1·035	1·046		
Aug	·947	·949	·954	·947	·957	·963	·985	·996	·995	·990	·999	1·007	1·009	1·007	1·007	·995	·999	1·004	1·017	1·022	1·022	1·016	1·021	1·030	1·033	1·035	1·043	1·034	1·045		
Sept	·949	·950	·955	·949	·958	·965	·987	·998	·996	·991	1·000	1·009	1·010	1·009	1·009	·996	1·000	1·005	1·018	1·023	1·023	1·017	1·022	1·031	1·034	1·037	1·044	1·035	1·046		
Oct	·939	·940	·945	·939	·949	·955	·977	·988	·986	·982	·990	·999	1·000	·999	·999	·986	·990	·995	1·008	1·013	1·013	1·007	1·012	1·021	1·024	1·027	1·034	1·025	1·036		
Nov	·930	·931	·936	·930	·939	·945	·967	·978	·977	·972	·980	·989	·990	·989	·989	·977	·980	·985	·999	1·003	1·003	·997	1·002	1·011	1·014	1·017	1·024	1·015	1·026		
Dec	·933	·934	·939	·933	·943	·949	·971	·982	·980	·976	·984	·992	·994	·992	·992	·980	·984	·989	1·002	1·007	1·007	1·001	1·006	1·014	1·018	1·020	1·028	1·019	1·030		

1983																															
Jan	·931	·932	·937	·931	·940	·946	·968	·979	·978	·973	·982	·990	·991	·990	·990	·978	·982	·986	1·000	1·005	1·005	·999	1·003	1·012	1·015	1·018	1·025	1·017	1·028		
Feb	·922	·924	·929	·922	·932	·938	·960	·971	·969	·965	·973	·982	·983	·982	·982	·969	·973	·978	·991	·996	·996	·990	·995	1·003	1·007	1·009	1·016	1·008	1·019		
Mar	·919	·920	·925	·919	·929	·935	·956	·967	·966	·961	·969	·978	·979	·978	·978	·966	·969	·974	·988	·992	·992	·986	·991	1·000	1·003	1·006	1·013	1·004	1·015		
Apr	·892	·894	·898	·892	·902	·908	·929	·940	·939	·934	·942	·951	·952	·951	·951	·939	·942	·947	·960	·965	·965	·959	·964	·972	·975	·978	·985	·977	·987		
May	·884	·886	·890	·884	·894	·900	·921	·932	·931	·926	·934	·942	·944	·942	·942	·931	·934	·939	·952	·957	·957	·951	·955	·964	·967	·970	·977	·968	·979		
June	·880	·881	·886	·880	·889	·895	·917	·927	·926	·921	·929	·938	·939	·938	·938	·926	·929	·934	·947	·952	·952	·946	·951	·959	·962	·965	·972	·964	·974		
July	·870	·871	·876	·870	·879	·885	·906	·917	·916	·911	·919	·927	·929	·927	·927	·916	·919	·924	·937	·941	·941	·936	·940	·948	·952	·954	·961	·953	·964		
Aug	·862	·863	·867	·862	·871	·877	·898	·908	·907	·902	·911	·919	·920	·919	·919	·907	·911	·915	·928	·933	·933	·927	·932	·940	·943	·946	·953	·944	·955		
Sept	·853	·855	·859	·853	·863	·869	·889	·900	·899	·894	·902	·910	·911	·910	·910	·899	·902	·907	·920	·924	·924	·918	·923	·931	·935	·937	·944	·936	·946		
Oct	·847	·848	·853	·847	·856	·862	·883	·893	·892	·887	·895	·904	·905	·904	·904	·892	·895	·900	·913	·917	·917	·912	·916	·924	·928	·930	·937	·929	·939		
Nov	·840	·842	·846	·840	·850	·855	·876	·887	·885	·881	·889	·897	·898	·897	·897	·885	·889	·893	·906	·911	·911	·905	·910	·918	·921	·923	·930	·922	·933		
Dec	·836	·837	·841	·836	·845	·851	·871	·882	·880	·876	·884	·892	·893	·892	·892	·880	·884	·888	·901	·906	·906	·900	·905	·913	·916	·918	·925	·917	·928		

1984																															
Jan	·837	·838	·842	·837	·846	·852	·872	·883	·882	·877	·885	·893	·894	·893	·893	·882	·885	·890	·902	·907	·907	·901	·906	·914	·917	·920	·926	·918	·929		
Feb	·829	·830	·835	·829	·838	·844	·865	·875	·874	·869	·877	·885	·885	·885	·885	·874	·877	·882	·895	·899	·899	·893	·898	·906	·909	·912	·919	·911	·921		
Mar	·823	·824	·829	·823	·832	·838	·859	·869	·868	·863	·871	·879	·880	·879	·879	·868	·871	·876	·888	·893	·893	·887	·892	·900	·903	·906	·912	·904	·915		
Apr	·799	·800	·805	·799	·808	·814	·834	·844	·843	·839	·847	·855	·856	·855	·855	·843	·847	·851	·864	·868	·868	·863	·867	·875	·878	·881	·887	·879	·890		
May	·793	·794	·798	·793	·802	·807	·828	·838	·837	·832	·840	·848	·849	·848	·848	·837	·840	·844	·857	·861	·861	·856	·860	·868	·871	·874	·880	·872	·883		
June	·788	·789	·794	·788	·797	·803	·823	·833	·832	·827	·835	·843	·844	·843	·843	·832	·835	·840	·852	·856	·856	·851	·855	·863	·867	·869	·876	·868	·878		
July	·790	·791	·796	·790	·799	·805	·825	·835	·834	·829	·837	·845	·846	·845	·845	·834	·837	·842	·854	·859	·859	·853	·857	·865	·869	·871	·878	·870	·880		
Aug	·773	·775	·779	·773	·782	·788	·808	·818	·817	·812	·820	·828	·829	·828	·828	·817	·820	·825	·837	·841	·841	·836	·840	·848	·851	·854	·860	·852	·862		
Sept	·770	·771	·776	·770	·779	·784	·804	·814	·813	·809	·817	·824	·825	·824	·824	·813	·817	·821	·833	·838	·838	·832	·837	·844	·848	·850	·857	·849	·859		
Oct	·759	·760	·765	·759	·768	·773	·793	·803	·802	·798	·805	·813	·814	·813	·813	·802	·805	·810	·822	·826	·826	·821	·825	·833	·836	·839	·845	·837	·847		
Nov	·754	·755	·759	·754	·762	·768	·788	·798	·797	·792	·800	·808	·809	·808	·808	·797	·800	·804	·816	·821	·821	·815	·820	·827	·831	·833	·839	·832	·842		
Dec	·755	·756	·761	·755	·764	·769	·789	·799	·798	·794	·801	·809	·810	·809	·809	·798	·801	·806	·818	·822	·822	·817	·821	·829	·832	·834	·841	·833	·843		

1985																															
Jan	·749	·750	·754	·749	·758	·763	·783	·793	·792	·787	·795	·803	·804	·803	·803	·792	·795	·799	·811	·816	·816	·810	·815	·822	·826	·828	·834	·827	·837		
Feb	·735	·736	·740	·735	·744	·749	·769	·778	·777	·773	·781	·788	·789	·788	·788	·777	·781	·785	·797	·801	·801	·796	·800	·808	·811	·813	·820	·812	·822		
Mar	·719	·720	·724	·719	·727	·733	·752	·762	·761	·756	·764	·772	·773	·772	·772	·761	·764	·768	·780	·784	·784	·779	·783	·791	·794	·796	·803	·795	·805		
Apr	·683	·684	·688	·683	·691	·697	·716	·725	·724	·720	·727	·735	·736	·735	·735	·724	·727	·731	·743	·747	·747	·742	·746	·754	·757	·759	·765	·758	·767		
May	·675	·676	·681	·675	·684	·689	·708	·717	·716	·712	·719	·727	·728	·727	·727	·716	·719	·724	·735	·739	·739	·734	·738	·746	·749	·751	·757	·750	·759		
June	·672	·673	·677	·672	·680	·685	·704	·714	·713	·708	·716	·723	·724	·723	·723	·713	·716	·720	·731	·736	·736	·730	·735	·742	·745	·747	·753	·746	·756		
July	·675	·676	·680	·675	·683	·688	·707	·717	·716	·712	·719	·727	·726	·727	·726	·716	·719	·723	·735	·739	·739	·734	·738	·745	·748	·750	·757	·749	·759		
Aug	·670	·671	·676	·670	·679	·684	·703	·712	·711	·707	·714	·722	·723	·722	·722	·711	·714	·719	·730	·734	·734	·729	·733	·741	·744	·746	·752	·745	·754		
Sept	·671	·672	·676	·671	·680	·685	·704	·713	·712	·708	·715	·723	·724	·723	·723	·712	·715	·719	·731	0·735	·735	·730	·734	·741	·745	·747	·753	·746	·755		
Oct	·669	·670	·674	·669	·677	·682	·701	·710	·709	·705	·713	·720	·721	·720	·720	·709	·713	·717	·728	·732	·732	·727	·731	·739	·742	·744	·750	·743	·752		
Nov	·663	·664	·668	·663	·671	·676	·695	·705	·704	·699	·707	·714	·715	·714	·714	·704	·707	·711	·722	·726	·726	·721	·725	·733	·736	·738	·744	·737	·746		
Dec	·661	·662	·666	·661	·669	·674	·693	·702	·701	·697	·704	·712	·713	·712	·712	·701	·704	·709	·720	·724	·724	·719	·723	·730	·734	·736	·742	·735	·744		

RD—Month of disposal

RI Base month ↓

1986	1995 Apr	May	Jun	Jul	Aug	Sep	Oct	Nov	Dec	1996 Jan	Feb	Mar	Apr	May	Jun	Jul	Aug	Sep	Oct	Nov	Dec	1997 Jan	Feb	Mar	Apr	May	Jun	Jul	Aug	Sep
Jan	·548	·554	·556	·549	·557	·565	·556	·556	·566	·561	·568	·574	·585	·589	·590	·583	·591	·598	·598	·599	·604	·604	·610	·615	·624	·630	·636	·636	·647	·655
Feb	·542	·549	·551	·543	·552	·559	·551	·551	·560	·555	·562	·568	·580	·583	·584	·578	·585	·592	·592	·593	·598	·598	·605	·609	·618	·624	·630	·630	·641	·649
Mar	·540	·547	·549	·541	·550	·557	·549	·549	·558	·553	·560	·566	·578	·581	·582	·576	·583	·590	·590	·591	·596	·596	·602	·607	·616	·622	·628	·628	·639	·647
Apr	·526	·532	·534	·527	·535	·542	·534	·534	·543	·538	·545	·551	·562	·566	·567	·560	·568	·575	·575	·576	·581	·581	·587	·591	·600	·606	·613	·613	·623	·631
May	·523	·529	·531	·524	·532	·539	·531	·531	·540	·535	·542	·548	·560	·563	·564	·558	·565	·572	·572	·573	·578	·578	·584	·588	·597	·604	·610	·610	·620	·628
June	·524	·530	·532	·525	·533	·540	·532	·532	·541	·536	·543	·549	·560	·563	·565	·558	·566	·573	·573	·574	·579	·579	·585	·589	·598	·604	·611	·611	·621	·629
July	·528	·534	·536	·529	·537	·544	·536	·536	·545	·540	·547	·554	·565	·568	·569	·563	·570	·577	·577	·578	·583	·583	·589	·594	·603	·609	·615	·615	·625	·634
Aug	·523	·529	·531	·524	·532	·540	·531	·531	·541	·535	·543	·549	·560	·563	·564	·558	·565	·572	·572	·573	·578	·578	·585	·589	·598	·604	·610	·620	·629	·631
Sept	·516	·522	·524	·517	·525	·532	·524	·524	·533	·528	·535	·541	·552	·555	·556	·550	·557	·565	·565	·566	·571	·571	·577	·581	·590	·596	·602	·602	·612	·621
Oct	·513	·519	·522	·514	·523	·530	·522	·522	·531	·526	·533	·539	·550	·553	·554	·548	·555	·562	·562	·563	·568	·568	·574	·578	·588	·594	·600	·600	·610	·618
Nov	·501	·507	·509	·502	·510	·517	·509	·509	·518	·513	·520	·526	·537	·540	·541	·535	·542	·549	·549	·550	·555	·555	·561	·565	·574	·580	·586	·586	·596	·604
Dec	·496	·502	·504	·497	·505	·512	·504	·504	·513	·508	·515	·521	·532	·535	·536	·530	·537	·544	·544	·545	·550	·550	·556	·556	·569	·575	·581	·581	·591	·599
1987																														
Jan	·490	·496	·498	·491	·499	·506	·498	·498	·507	·502	·509	·515	·526	·529	·530	·524	·531	·538	·538	·539	·544	·544	·550	·554	·563	·569	·575	·575	·585	·593
Feb	·484	·490	·492	·485	·493	·500	·492	·492	·501	·496	·503	·509	·520	·523	·524	·518	·525	·532	·532	·533	·538	·538	·544	·548	·557	·563	·569	·569	·579	·587
Mar	·481	·487	·489	·482	·490	·497	·489	·489	·498	·493	·500	·506	·517	·520	·521	·515	·522	·529	·529	·530	·535	·535	·541	·545	·554	·560	·566	·576	·583	·585
Apr	·464	·470	·472	·465	·472	·479	·472	·472	·480	·475	·482	·488	·499	·502	·503	·497	·504	·511	·511	·512	·517	·517	·523	·527	·535	·541	·547	·547	·557	·565
May	·462	·468	·470	·463	·471	·478	·470	·470	·479	·474	·481	·487	·498	·500	·501	·496	·502	·509	·509	·510	·515	·515	·521	·525	·534	·540	·546	·546	·555	·563
Jun	·462	·468	·470	·463	·471	·478	·470	·470	·479	·474	·481	·487	·498	·500	·501	·496	·502	·509	·509	·510	·515	·515	·521	·525	·534	·540	·546	·546	·555	·563
Jul	·464	·470	·472	·465	·472	·479	·472	·472	·480	·475	·482	·488	·499	·502	·503	·497	·504	·511	·511	·512	·517	·517	·523	·527	·535	·541	·547	·547	·557	·565
Aug	·459	·465	·467	·460	·468	·475	·467	·467	·476	·471	·478	·484	·495	·498	·499	·493	·500	·506	·506	·507	·512	·512	·518	·522	·531	·537	·543	·543	·552	·560
Sep	·455	·461	·463	·456	·464	·471	·463	·463	·472	·467	·474	·479	·490	·493	·494	·488	·495	·502	·502	·503	·508	·508	·514	·518	·526	·532	·538	·538	·548	·556
Oct	·448	·454	·456	·449	·457	·464	·456	·456	·465	·460	·466	·472	·483	·486	·487	·481	·488	·495	·495	·496	·500	·500	·506	·510	·519	·525	·531	·531	·540	·548
Nov	·441	·447	·449	·442	·450	·456	·449	·449	·457	·453	·459	·465	·476	·479	·480	·474	·481	·487	·487	·488	·493	·493	·499	·503	·512	·517	·523	·523	·533	·541
Dec	·442	·448	·450	·443	·451	·458	·450	·450	·459	·454	·461	·467	·477	·480	·481	·475	·482	·489	·489	·490	·495	·495	·500	·504	·513	·519	·525	·525	·534	·542
1988																														
Jan	·442	·448	·450	·443	·451	·458	·450	·450	·459	·454	·461	·467	·477	·480	·481	·475	·482	·489	·489	·490	·495	·495	·500	·504	·513	·519	·525	·525	·534	·542
Feb	·437	·443	·445	·438	·446	·452	·445	·445	·453	·448	·455	·461	·472	·474	·475	·470	·476	·483	·483	·484	·489	·489	·495	·499	·507	·513	·519	·519	·528	·536
Mar	·431	·437	·439	·432	·440	·447	·439	·439	·448	·443	·450	·455	·466	·469	·470	·464	·471	·477	·477	·478	·483	·483	·489	·493	·501	·507	·513	·513	·523	·530
Apr	·408	·414	·416	·409	·417	·423	·416	·416	·424	·420	·426	·432	·442	·445	·446	·440	·447	·454	·454	·455	·459	·459	·465	·469	·477	·483	·489	·498	·506	·508
May	·403	·409	·411	·404	·411	·418	·411	·411	·419	·414	·421	·427	·437	·440	·441	·435	·442	·448	·448	·449	·454	·454	·460	·463	·472	·477	·483	·493	·492	·500
Jun	·398	·403	·405	·399	·406	·413	·405	·405	·414	·409	·416	·421	·432	·434	·435	·430	·436	·443	·443	·444	·448	·448	·454	·458	·466	·472	·477	·477	·487	·494
Jul	·396	·402	·404	·397	·405	·411	·404	·404	·412	·408	·414	·420	·430	·433	·434	·428	·435	·441	·441	·442	·447	·447	·453	·456	·465	·470	·476	·476	·485	·493
Aug	·381	·386	·388	·382	·389	·396	·388	·388	·397	·392	·399	·404	·414	·417	·418	·412	·419	·425	·425	·426	·431	·431	·437	·440	·449	·454	·460	·460	·469	·470
Sep	·375	·380	·382	·375	·383	·389	·382	·382	·390	·386	·392	·398	·408	·411	·411	·406	·412	·419	·419	·420	·424	·424	·430	·434	·442	·447	·453	·453	·462	·470
Oct	·361	·366	·368	·362	·369	·375	·368	·368	·376	·372	·378	·384	·394	·396	·397	·392	·398	·405	·405	·405	·410	·410	·416	·419	·427	·433	·438	·438	·447	·455
Nov	·355	·360	·362	·355	·363	·369	·362	·362	·370	·365	·372	·377	·387	·390	·391	·385	·392	·398	·398	·399	·404	·404	·409	·413	·421	·426	·432	·432	·441	·448
Dec	·351	·356	·358	·352	·359	·365	·358	·358	·366	·362	·368	·374	·383	·386	·387	·382	·388	·394	·394	·395	·400	·400	·405	·409	·417	·422	·428	·428	·437	·444
1989																														
Jan	·342	·348	·350	·343	·350	·357	·350	·350	·358	·353	·359	·365	·375	·377	·378	·373	·379	·386	·386	·386	·391	·391	·396	·400	·408	·414	·419	·419	·428	·435
Feb	·333	·338	·340	·334	·341	·347	·340	·340	·348	·343	·350	·355	·365	·368	·369	·363	·369	·376	·376	·377	·381	·381	·386	·390	·398	·403	·409	·409	·418	·425
Mar	·327	·332	·334	·328	·335	·341	·334	·334	·342	·337	·344	·349	·359	·362	·362	·357	·363	·370	·370	·370	·375	·375	·380	·384	·392	·397	·402	·402	·411	·419
Apr	·304	·309	·311	·304	·311	·318	·311	·311	·318	·314	·320	·325	·335	·338	·339	·333	·339	·346	·346	·346	·351	·351	·356	·360	·367	·373	·378	·378	·387	·394
May	·296	·301	·303	·297	·303	·310	·303	·303	·310	·306	·312	·317	·327	·330	·330	·325	·331	·337	·337	·338	·343	·343	·348	·351	·359	·364	·370	·370	·378	·386
Jun	·291	·296	·298	·292	·299	·305	·298	·298	·306	·302	·308	·313	·322	·325	·326	·321	·327	·333	·333	·334	·338	·338	·343	·347	·354	·360	·365	·365	·373	·380
Jul	·290	·295	·297	·291	·298	·304	·297	·297	·305	·300	·306	·312	·321	·324	·325	·319	·326	·332	·332	·332	·337	·337	·342	·345	·353	·358	·364	·364	·372	·379
Aug	·287	·292	·294	·288	·294	·301	·294	·294	·301	·297	·303	·308	·318	·320	·321	·316	·322	·328	·328	·328	·333	·333	·339	·342	·350	·355	·360	·360	·369	·376
Sep	·278	·283	·285	·279	·286	·292	·285	·285	·292	·288	·294	·299	·309	·311	·312	·307	·313	·319	·319	·320	·324	·324	·329	·333	·340	·346	·351	·351	·359	·366
Oct	·268	·273	·275	·269	·276	·282	·275	·275	·283	·278	·284	·289	·299	·301	·302	·297	·303	·309	·309	·310	·314	·314	·319	·323	·330	·335	·340	·340	·349	·356
Nov	·257	·262	·264	·258	·265	·271	·264	·264	·272	·268	·273	·278	·288	·290	·291	·286	·292	·298	·298	·299	·303	·303	·308	·311	·319	·324	·329	·329	·338	·344
Dec	·254	·259	·261	·255	·262	·268	·261	·261	·269	·264	·270	·275	·285	·287	·288	·283	·289	·295	·295	·295	·300	·300	·305	·308	·316	·321	·326	·326	·334	·341
1990																														
Jan	·247	·252	·254	·248	·254	·260	·254	·254	·261	·257	·263	·268	·277	·279	·280	·275	·281	·287	·287	·288	·292	·292	·297	·300	·308	·313	·318	·318	·326	·333
Feb	·240	·245	·246	·240	·247	·253	·246	·246	·254	·250	·255	·260	·270	·272	·273	·268	·274	·280	·280	·280	·285	·285	·290	·293	·300	·305	·310	·310	·319	·325
Mar	·227	·232	·234	·228	·235	·241	·234	·234	·241	·237	·243	·248	·257	·259	·260	·255	·261	·267	·267	·268	·272	·272	·277	·280	·287	·292	·297	·297	·306	·312
Apr	·191	·196	·197	·192	·198	·204	·197	·197	·205	·201	·206	·211	·220	·222	·223	·218	·224	·229	·229	·230	·234	·234	·239	·242	·249	·254	·259	·259	·267	·273
May	·181	·185	·187	·181	·188	·193	·187	·187	·194	·190	·196	·200	·209	·212	·212	·208	·213	·219	·219	·219	·223	·223	·228	·231	·239	·243	·248	·248	·256	·262
Jun	·176	·181	·182	·177	·183	·189	·182	·182	·189	·185	·191	·196	·204	·207	·208	·203	·208	·214	·214	·215	·219	·219	·223	·227	·234	·238	·243	·243	·251	·257
Jul	·175	·180	·181	·176	·182	·188	·181	·181	·188	·185	·190	·195	·203	·206	·207	·202	·207	·213	·213	·214	·218	·218	·222	·226	·233	·237	·242	·242	·250	·256
Aug	·163	·168	·169	·164	·170	·176	·169	·169	·176	·173	·178	·183	·191	·194	·194	·190	·195	·201	·201	·201	·205	·205	·210	·213	·220	·225	·230	·230	·237	·244
Sep	·152	·157	·159	·153	·159	·165	·159	·159	·166	·162	·167	·172	·180	·183	·183	·179	·184	·189	·189	·190	·194	·194	·199	·202	·209	·213	·218	·218	·226	·232
Oct	·144	·148	·150	·144	·150	·156	·150	·150	·157	·153	·158	·163	·171	·173	·174	·170	·175	·180	·180	·181	·185	·185	·190	·193	·200	·204	·209	·209	·216	·223
Nov	·146	·151	·152	·147	·153	·158	·152	·152	·159	·155	·161	·165	·174	·176	·177	·172	·178	·183	·183	·184	·188	·188	·192	·195	·202	·207	·212	·212	·219	·225
Dec	·147	·152	·153	·148	·154	·159	·153	·153	·160	·156	·162	·166	·175	·177	·178	·173	·179	·184	·184	·185	·189	·189	·193	·196	·203	·208	·212	·212	·220	·226

Indexation allowance — continued

RD—Month of disposal

RI Base month

RI Base month	1997			1998												1999												2000			
	Oct	Nov	Dec	Jan	Feb	Mar	Apr	May	June	July	Aug	Sept	Oct	Nov	Dec	Jan	Feb	Mar	Apr	May	June	July	Aug	Sept	Oct	Nov	Dec	Jan	Feb	Mar	Apr
1986																															
Jan	·657	·658	·662	·657	·665	·671	·689	·699	·698	·694	·701	·708	·709	·708	·708	·698	·701	·705	·716	·721	·721	·715	·720	·727	·730	·732	·738	·731	·740		
Feb	·651	·652	·656	·651	·659	·665	·683	·692	·691	·687	·695	·702	·703	·702	·702	·691	·695	·699	·710	·714	·714	·709	·713	·720	·724	·726	·732	·725	·734		
Mar	·649	·650	·654	·649	·657	·662	·681	·690	·689	·685	·692	·700	·701	·700	·700	·689	·692	·696	·708	·712	·712	·707	·711	·718	·721	·723	·730	·722	·732		
Apr	·633	·634	·638	·633	·641	·646	·665	·674	·673	·669	·676	·683	·684	·683	·683	·673	·676	·680	·691	·696	·696	·690	·695	·702	·705	·707	·713	·706	·715		
May	·630	·631	·635	·630	·638	·643	·662	·671	·670	·666	·673	·680	·681	·680	·680	·670	·673	·677	·688	·692	·692	·687	·691	·699	·702	·704	·710	·703	·712		
June	·631	·632	·636	·631	·639	·644	·663	·672	·671	·667	·674	·681	·682	·681	·681	·671	·674	·678	·689	·693	·693	·688	·692	·699	·703	·705	·711	·704	·713		
July	·636	·637	·641	·636	·644	·649	·667	·677	·676	·672	·679	·686	·687	·686	·686	·676	·679	·683	·694	·698	·698	·693	·697	·704	·707	·709	·716	·708	·718		
Aug	·632	·636	·631	·639	·644	·662	·671	·670	·666	·673	·681	·682	·681	·682	·681	·670	·673	·678	·689	·693	·693	·688	·692	·699	·702	·704	·710	·703	·712		
Sept	·623	·624	·628	·623	·631	·636	·654	·663	·662	·658	·665	·672	·673	·672	·672	·662	·665	·669	·681	·685	·685	·680	·684	·691	·694	·696	·702	·695	·704		
Oct	·620	·621	·625	·620	·628	·633	·652	·661	·660	·656	·663	·670	·671	·670	·670	·660	·663	·667	·678	·682	·682	·677	·681	·688	·691	·693	·699	·692	·701		
Nov	·606	·607	·611	·606	·614	·619	·638	·647	·646	·642	·649	·656	·657	·656	·656	·646	·649	·653	·664	·668	·668	·663	·667	·674	·677	·679	·685	·678	·687		
Dec	·601	·602	·606	·601	·609	·614	·632	·641	·640	·636	·643	·650	·651	·650	·650	·640	·643	·647	·658	·662	·662	·657	·661	·668	·671	·673	·679	·672	·681		
1987																															
Jan	·595	·596	·600	·595	·603	·608	·626	·635	·634	·630	·637	·644	·645	·644	·644	·634	·637	·641	·652	·656	·656	·651	·655	·662	·665	·667	·673	·666	·675		
Feb	·589	·590	·594	·589	·597	·602	·620	·628	·627	·624	·630	·637	·638	·637	·637	·627	·630	·634	·645	·649	·649	·644	·648	·655	·658	·660	·666	·659	·668		
Mar	·586	·590	·585	·593	·593	·598	·616	·625	·624	·620	·627	·634	·635	·634	·634	·624	·627	·631	·642	·646	·646	·641	·645	·652	·655	·657	·663	·656	·665		
Apr	·567	·568	·572	·567	·575	·580	·597	·606	·605	·601	·608	·615	·616	·615	·615	·605	·608	·612	·623	·627	·627	·622	·626	·633	·636	·638	·643	·637	·645		
May	·565	·566	·570	·565	·573	·578	·596	·605	·604	·600	·606	·613	·614	·613	·613	·604	·606	·610	·621	·625	·625	·620	·624	·631	·634	·636	·642	·635	·644		
June	·565	·566	·570	·565	·573	·578	·596	·605	·604	·600	·606	·613	·614	·613	·613	·604	·606	·610	·621	·625	·625	·620	·624	·631	·634	·636	·642	·635	·644		
July	·567	·568	·572	·567	·575	·580	·597	·606	·605	·601	·608	·615	·616	·615	·615	·605	·608	·612	·623	·627	·627	·622	·626	·633	·636	·638	·643	·637	·645		
Aug	·562	·563	·567	·562	·570	·575	·593	·601	·600	·596	·603	·610	·611	·610	·610	·600	·603	·607	·618	·622	·622	·617	·621	·628	·631	·633	·639	·632	·641		
Sept	·558	·559	·563	·558	·565	·570	·588	·597	·596	·592	·599	·605	·606	·605	·605	·596	·599	·603	·613	·617	·617	·612	·616	·623	·626	·628	·634	·627	·636		
Oct	·550	·551	·555	·550	·558	·563	·580	·589	·588	·584	·591	·598	·599	·598	·598	·589	·591	·595	·605	·609	·609	·604	·608	·615	·618	·620	·626	·619	·628		
Nov	·543	·544	·547	·543	·550	·555	·573	·581	·580	·576	·583	·590	·591	·590	·590	·580	·583	·587	·598	·602	·602	·597	·601	·607	·610	·612	·618	·611	·620		
Dec	·544	·545	·549	·544	·552	·557	·574	·583	·582	·578	·585	·591	·592	·591	·591	·582	·585	·589	·599	·603	·603	·598	·602	·609	·612	·614	·620	·613	·621		
1988																															
Jan	·544	·545	·549	·544	·552	·557	·574	·583	·582	·578	·585	·591	·592	·591	·591	·582	·585	·589	·599	·603	·603	·598	·602	·609	·612	·614	·620	·613	·621		
Feb	·538	·539	·543	·538	·546	·551	·568	·577	·576	·572	·579	·585	·586	·585	·585	·576	·579	·582	·593	·597	·597	·592	·596	·603	·606	·608	·613	·607	·615		
Mar	·532	·533	·537	·532	·540	·545	·562	·571	·570	·566	·573	·579	·580	·579	·579	·570	·573	·576	·587	·591	·591	·586	·590	·597	·599	·601	·607	·600	·609		
Apr	·509	·512	·508	·515	·520	·537	·545	·544	·541	·547	·554	·554	·555	·554	·554	·548	·551	·561	·565	·565	·560	·564	·571	·574	·576	·581		·575	·583		
May	·502	·503	·507	·502	·509	·514	·531	·540	·539	·535	·541	·548	·548	·549	·548	·548	·541	·545	·556	·559	·559	·555	·558	·565	·568	·570	·575	·569	·577		
June	·496	·497	·501	·496	·504	·508	·525	·534	·533	·529	·536	·542	·543	·542	·542	·533	·536	·539	·550	·553	·553	·549	·553	·559	·562	·564	·569	·563	·571		
July	·495	·496	·500	·495	·502	·507	·524	·532	·531	·528	·534	·541	·542	·541	·541	·531	·534	·538	·548	·552	·552	·547	·551	·558	·560	·562	·568	·561	·570		
Aug	·478	·479	·483	·478	·486	·490	·507	·515	·514	·511	·517	·524	·525	·524	·524	·514	·517	·521	·531	·535	·535	·530	·534	·540	·543	·545	·551	·544	·552		
Sept	·471	·472	·476	·471	·479	·483	·500	·508	·507	·504	·510	·517	·518	·517	·517	·507	·510	·514	·524	·528	·528	·523	·527	·533	·536	·538	·543	·537	·545		
Oct	·457	·458	·461	·457	·464	·468	·485	·493	·492	·489	·495	·501	·502	·501	·501	·492	·495	·499	·509	·512	·512	·508	·511	·518	·521	·522	·528	·521	·530		
Nov	·450	·451	·455	·450	·457	·462	·478	·486	·485	·482	·488	·495	·495	·495	·495	·485	·488	·492	·502	·505	·505	·501	·505	·511	·514	·515	·521	·515	·523		
Dec	·446	·447	·451	·446	·453	·458	·474	·482	·481	·478	·484	·490	·491	·490	·490	·481	·484	·488	·498	·501	·501	·497	·500	·507	·510	·511	·517	·510	·519		
1989																															
Jan	·437	·438	·441	·437	·444	·449	·465	·473	·472	·468	·475	·481	·482	·481	·481	·472	·475	·478	·488	·492	·492	·487	·491	·497	·500	·502	·507	·501	·509		
Feb	·427	·428	·431	·427	·434	·438	·454	·462	·462	·458	·464	·470	·471	·470	·470	·462	·464	·468	·478	·481	·481	·477	·480	·487	·489	·491	·496	·490	·498		
Mar	·420	·421	·425	·420	·427	·432	·448	·456	·455	·451	·458	·464	·465	·464	·464	·455	·458	·461	·471	·475	·475	·470	·474	·480	·483	·484	·490	·484	·492		
Apr	·395	·396	·400	·395	·402	·407	·423	·430	·430	·426	·432	·438	·439	·438	·438	·430	·432	·436	·445	·449	·449	·444	·448	·454	·457	·458	·464	·457	·465		
May	·387	·388	·391	·387	·394	·398	·414	·422	·421	·417	·423	·430	·430	·430	·430	·421	·423	·427	·437	·440	·440	·436	·439	·445	·448	·450	·455	·449	·457		
June	·382	·383	·386	·382	·389	·393	·409	·417	·416	·412	·419	·425	·425	·425	·425	·416	·419	·422	·432	·435	·435	·431	·434	·440	·443	·445	·450	·444	·451		
July	·381	·382	·385	·381	·388	·392	·408	·416	·415	·411	·417	·423	·424	·423	·423	·415	·417	·421	·430	·434	·434	·429	·433	·439	·442	·443	·448	·442	·450		
Aug	·377	·378	·382	·377	·384	·389	·404	·412	·411	·408	·414	·420	·421	·420	·420	·411	·414	·417	·427	·430	·430	·426	·429	·435	·438	·440	·445	·439	·446		
Sept	·368	·369	·372	·368	·375	·379	·395	·402	·401	·398	·404	·410	·411	·410	·410	·401	·404	·407	·416	·419	·419	·415	·419	·425	·428	·430	·435	·429	·437		
Oct	·357	·358	·362	·357	·364	·369	·384	·391	·391	·387	·393	·399	·400	·399	·399	·391	·393	·397	·406	·409	·409	·405	·408	·414	·417	·419	·424	·418	·426		
Nov	·346	·347	·350	·346	·353	·357	·372	·380	·379	·376	·381	·387	·388	·387	·387	·379	·381	·385	·394	·397	·397	·393	·397	·403	·405	·407	·412	·406	·414		
Dec	·343	·343	·347	·343	·349	·354	·369	·376	·375	·372	·378	·384	·385	·384	·384	·375	·378	·381	·391	·394	·394	·390	·393	·399	·402	·403	·408	·402	·410		
1990																															
Jan	·335	·336	·339	·335	·341	·346	·361	·368	·367	·364	·370	·376	·377	·376	·376	·367	·370	·373	·382	·386	·386	·382	·385	·391	·393	·395	·400	·394	·402		
Feb	·327	·328	·331	·327	·334	·338	·353	·360	·359	·356	·362	·368	·369	·368	·368	·359	·362	·365	·374	·378	·378	·374	·377	·383	·385	·387	·392	·386	·394		
Mar	·314	·315	·318	·314	·320	·325	·339	·347	·346	·343	·348	·354	·355	·354	·354	·346	·348	·352	·361	·364	·364	·360	·363	·369	·371	·373	·378	·372	·380		
Apr	·275	·276	·279	·275	·281	·285	·300	·307	·306	·303	·309	·314	·315	·314	·314	·306	·309	·312	·321	·324	·324	·320	·323	·329	·331	·333	·337	·332	·339		
May	·264	·265	·268	·264	·270	·274	·288	·296	·295	·292	·297	·303	·303	·303	·303	·295	·297	·300	·309	·312	·312	·308	·311	·317	·319	·321	·326	·320	·327		
June	·259	·260	·263	·259	·265	·269	·283	·290	·290	·287	·292	·298	·298	·298	·298	·290	·292	·295	·304	·307	·307	·303	·306	·312	·314	·316	·320	·315	·322		
July	·258	·259	·262	·258	·264	·268	·282	·289	·289	·285	·291	·297	·297	·297	·297	·289	·291	·294	·303	·306	·306	·302	·305	·311	·313	·315	·319	·314	·321		
Aug	·245	·246	·249	·245	·251	·255	·269	·276	·276	·272	·278	·283	·284	·283	·283	·276	·278	·281	·290	·293	·293	·289	·292	·297	·300	·301	·306	·301	·308		
Sept	·234	·234	·237	·234	·240	·244	·258	·265	·264	·261	·266	·271	·272	·271	·271	·264	·266	·269	·277	·280	·280	·277	·280	·285	·288	·289	·294	·289	·295		
Oct	·224	·225	·228	·224	·230	·234	·248	·255	·254	·251	·256	·262	·262	·262	·262	·254	·256	·259	·268	·271	·271	·267	·270	·276	·278	·279	·284	·279	·285		
Nov	·227	·228	·231	·227	·233	·237	·251	·258	·257	·254	·259	·265	·265	·265	·265	·257	·259	·262	·271	·274	·274	·270	·273	·278	·281	·282	·287	·282	·288		
Dec	·228	·229	·232	·228	·234	·238	·252	·259	·258	·255	·260	·266	·266	·266	·266	·258	·260	·263	·272	·275	·275	·271	·274	·279	·282	·283	·288	·283	·289		

45

RD—Month of disposal

RI Base month

Base month	1995 Apr	May	Jun	Jul	Aug	Sep	Oct	Nov	Dec	1996 Jan	Feb	Mar	Apr	May	Jun	Jul	Aug	Sep	Oct	Nov	Dec	1997 Jan	Feb	Mar	Apr	May	Jun	Jul	Aug	Sep
1991																														
Jan	144	149	151	145	151	157	151	151	157	154	159	164	172	174	175	171	176	181	181	182	186	186	190	194	200	205	210	210	217	224
Feb	138	143	144	139	145	150	144	144	151	147	153	157	166	168	169	164	170	175	175	176	180	180	184	187	194	199	203	203	211	217
Mar	134	139	140	135	141	146	140	140	147	143	148	153	161	164	160	165	170	170	170	171	175	175	180	183	189	194	199	199	206	212
Apr	119	124	125	120	126	131	125	125	132	128	134	138	147	149	150	145	150	156	156	156	160	160	165	168	174	179	183	183	191	197
May	116	121	122	117	123	128	122	122	129	125	130	135	143	145	146	142	147	152	152	153	157	157	161	164	171	175	180	180	187	193
Jun	111	116	117	112	118	123	117	117	124	120	125	130	138	140	141	136	142	147	147	148	151	151	156	159	166	170	174	174	182	188
Jul	114	118	120	114	120	126	120	120	126	123	128	132	141	143	143	139	144	149	149	150	154	154	158	161	168	173	177	177	185	191
Aug	111	116	117	112	118	123	117	117	124	120	125	130	138	140	141	136	142	147	147	148	151	151	156	159	166	170	174	174	182	188
Sep	107	111	113	108	114	119	113	113	120	116	121	126	134	136	137	132	137	143	143	143	147	147	152	155	161	166	170	170	178	184
Oct	103	107	109	104	110	115	109	109	115	112	117	121	130	132	132	128	133	138	138	139	143	143	147	150	157	161	166	166	173	179
Nov	099	103	105	100	105	111	105	105	111	108	113	117	125	128	128	124	129	134	134	135	139	139	143	146	153	157	162	162	169	175
Dec	098	102	104	099	105	110	104	104	111	107	112	116	125	127	127	123	128	133	133	134	138	138	142	145	152	156	161	161	168	174
1992																														
Jan	099	103	105	100	105	111	105	105	111	108	113	117	125	128	128	124	129	134	134	135	139	139	143	146	153	157	162	162	169	175
Feb	093	098	099	094	100	105	099	099	106	102	107	112	120	122	123	118	123	128	128	129	133	133	140	147	151	156	156	156	163	169
Mar	090	094	096	091	097	102	096	096	102	099	104	108	116	119	119	115	120	125	125	126	129	129	134	137	143	148	152	152	159	165
Apr	073	078	079	074	080	085	079	079	086	082	087	091	099	102	102	098	103	108	108	109	112	112	117	120	126	130	135	135	142	148
May	070	074	075	070	076	081	075	075	082	078	083	088	095	098	098	094	099	104	104	105	108	108	113	116	122	126	131	131	138	144
June	070	074	075	070	076	081	075	075	082	078	083	088	095	098	098	094	099	104	104	105	108	108	113	122	126	131	131	131	138	144
July	073	078	079	074	080	085	079	079	086	082	087	091	099	102	102	098	103	108	108	109	112	112	117	120	126	130	135	135	142	148
Aug	073	077	078	073	079	084	078	078	085	081	086	091	099	101	102	097	102	107	107	108	112	112	116	119	125	130	134	134	141	147
Sept	069	073	075	070	075	080	075	075	081	077	082	087	095	097	098	093	098	103	103	104	108	108	112	115	121	126	130	130	137	143
Oct	065	069	071	066	071	076	071	071	077	074	079	083	091	093	094	089	094	099	099	100	104	104	108	111	117	122	126	126	133	139
Nov	067	071	072	067	073	078	072	072	079	075	080	084	092	094	095	091	096	101	101	102	105	105	110	112	119	123	127	127	135	140
Dec	070	075	076	071	077	082	076	076	083	079	084	088	096	098	099	095	100	105	105	106	109	109	114	116	123	127	131	131	139	144
1993																														
Jan	080	085	086	081	087	092	086	086	093	089	094	099	107	109	109	105	110	115	115	116	120	120	124	127	133	138	142	142	149	155
Feb	073	078	079	074	080	085	079	079	086	082	087	091	099	102	102	098	103	108	108	109	112	112	117	120	126	130	135	135	142	148
Mar	070	074	075	070	076	081	075	075	082	078	083	088	095	098	098	094	099	104	104	105	108	108	113	116	122	126	131	131	138	144
Apr	060	064	065	060	066	071	065	065	072	068	073	078	085	087	088	084	089	094	094	095	098	098	102	105	112	116	120	120	127	133
May	056	060	062	057	062	067	062	062	068	064	069	074	082	084	084	080	085	090	090	091	094	094	099	101	108	112	116	116	123	129
June	057	061	062	057	063	068	062	062	069	065	070	074	082	084	084	081	086	091	091	091	095	095	099	102	109	113	117	117	124	130
July	059	063	065	060	065	070	065	065	071	068	072	077	085	087	087	083	088	093	093	094	097	097	102	104	111	115	119	119	127	132
Aug	054	059	060	055	061	066	060	060	067	063	068	072	080	082	083	079	084	088	088	089	093	093	097	100	106	110	115	115	122	127
Sept	050	054	056	051	056	061	056	056	062	058	063	068	075	078	078	074	079	084	084	085	088	088	092	095	101	106	110	110	117	123
Oct	051	055	056	051	057	062	056	056	063	059	064	068	076	078	079	075	080	085	085	085	089	089	093	096	102	106	111	111	118	123
Nov	052	056	058	053	059	064	058	058	064	061	066	070	078	080	081	076	081	086	086	087	090	090	095	097	104	108	112	112	119	125
Dec	050	054	056	051	056	061	056	056	062	058	063	068	075	078	078	074	079	084	084	085	088	088	092	095	101	106	110	110	117	123
1994																														
Jan	054	059	060	055	061	066	060	060	067	063	068	072	080	082	083	079	084	088	088	089	093	093	097	100	106	110	115	115	122	127
Feb	049	053	054	049	055	060	054	054	061	057	062	066	074	076	077	072	077	082	082	083	087	087	091	094	100	104	108	108	115	121
Mar	046	050	051	046	052	057	051	051	058	054	059	063	071	073	074	069	074	079	079	080	084	084	088	091	097	101	105	105	112	118
Apr	033	037	039	034	040	044	039	039	045	042	046	051	058	060	061	057	062	067	067	067	071	071	075	078	084	088	092	092	099	105
May	030	034	035	030	036	041	035	035	041	038	043	047	055	057	057	053	058	063	063	063	067	067	071	074	080	084	088	088	095	101
June	030	034	035	030	036	041	035	035	041	038	043	047	055	057	057	053	058	063	063	064	067	067	071	074	080	084	088	088	095	101
July	035	039	040	035	041	046	040	040	047	043	048	052	060	062	063	058	063	068	068	069	072	072	076	079	085	090	094	094	101	106
Aug	030	034	035	030	036	041	035	035	041	038	043	047	055	057	057	053	058	063	063	064	067	067	071	074	080	084	088	088	095	101
Sept	028	032	034	029	034	039	033	033	039	036	041	045	052	054	055	051	056	061	061	061	065	065	069	072	078	082	086	086	093	099
Oct	026	030	032	027	032	037	032	032	038	034	039	043	051	053	054	049	054	059	059	060	063	063	067	070	076	081	085	085	092	097
Nov	025	030	031	026	032	036	031	031	037	034	039	043	050	052	053	049	054	058	058	059	063	063	067	070	076	080	084	084	091	096
Dec	021	025	026	021	027	032	026	026	032	029	034	038	045	047	048	044	049	053	053	054	058	058	062	064	071	075	079	079	086	091
1995																														
Jan	021	025	026	021	027	032	026	026	032	029	034	038	045	047	048	044	049	053	053	054	058	058	062	064	071	075	079	079	086	091
Feb	014	018	020	015	020	025	020	020	026	022	027	031	039	041	042	037	042	047	047	048	051	051	055	058	064	068	072	072	079	084
Mar	010	014	016	011	016	021	016	016	022	018	023	027	035	037	037	033	038	043	043	043	047	047	051	054	060	064	068	068	075	080
Apr	—	004	005	001	006	011	005	005	011	008	013	017	024	026	027	023	028	032	032	033	036	036	040	043	049	053	057	057	064	069
May	—	—	001	000	002	007	001	001	007	004	009	013	020	022	023	019	023	028	028	029	032	032	036	039	045	049	053	053	059	065
June	—	—	—	000	001	005	000	000	006	003	007	011	019	021	021	017	022	027	027	027	031	031	035	037	043	047	051	051	058	063
July	—	—	—	—	005	010	005	005	011	007	012	016	023	025	026	022	027	032	032	032	036	036	040	042	048	052	056	056	063	068
Aug	—	—	—	—	—	005	000	000	006	002	007	011	018	020	021	017	021	026	026	027	030	030	034	037	043	047	051	051	058	063
Sept	—	—	—	—	—	—	000	000	001	000	002	006	013	015	016	012	017	021	021	022	025	025	029	032	038	042	046	046	052	058
Oct	—	—	—	—	—	—	—	000	006	003	007	011	019	021	021	017	022	027	027	027	031	031	035	037	043	047	051	051	058	063
Nov	—	—	—	—	—	—	—	—	006	003	007	011	019	021	021	017	022	027	027	027	031	031	035	037	043	047	051	051	058	063
Dec	—	—	—	—	—	—	—	—	—	000	001	005	013	015	015	011	016	021	021	021	025	025	029	031	037	041	045	045	052	057

RD—Month of disposal

RI Base month

	1997			1998												1999												2000			
	Oct	Nov	Dec	Jan	Feb	Mar	Apr	May	Jun	Jul	Aug	Sep	Oct	Nov	Dec	Jan	Feb	Mar	Apr	May	Jun	Jul	Aug	Sep	Oct	Nov	Dec	Jan	Feb	Mar	Apr
1991																															
Jan	·225	·226	·229	·225	·231	·235	·249	·256	·255	·252	·257	·263	·263	·263	·263	·255	·257	·260	·269	·272	·272	·268	·271	·276	·279	·280	·285	·280	·286		
Feb	·218	·219	·222	·218	·225	·228	·242	·249	·248	·245	·251	·256	·257	·256	·256	·248	·251	·254	·262	·265	·265	·261	·264	·270	·272	·273	·278	·273	·280		
Mar	·214	·215	·218	·214	·220	·224	·237	·244	·244	·240	·246	·251	·252	·251	·251	·244	·246	·249	·257	·260	·260	·256	·260	·265	·267	·269	·273	·268	·275		
Apr	·198	·199	·202	·198	·204	·208	·222	·228	·228	·225	·230	·235	·236	·235	·235	·228	·230	·233	·241	·244	·244	·240	·243	·249	·251	·252	·257	·252	·258		
May	·195	·196	·199	·195	·201	·204	·218	·225	·224	·221	·226	·231	·232	·231	·231	·224	·226	·229	·237	·240	·240	·237	·240	·245	·247	·249	·253	·248	·255		
June	·189	·190	·193	·189	·195	·199	·213	·219	·218	·216	·221	·226	·227	·226	·226	·218	·221	·224	·232	·235	·235	·231	·234	·239	·242	·243	·248	·242	·249		
July	·192	·193	·196	·192	·198	·202	·215	·222	·221	·218	·223	·229	·229	·229	·229	·221	·223	·226	·235	·238	·238	·234	·237	·242	·244	·246	·250	·245	·252		
Aug	·189	·190	·193	·189	·195	·199	·213	·219	·218	·216	·221	·226	·227	·226	·226	·218	·221	·224	·232	·235	·235	·231	·234	·239	·242	·243	·248	·242	·249		
Sept	·185	·186	·189	·185	·191	·195	·208	·215	·214	·211	·216	·221	·222	·221	·221	·214	·216	·219	·227	·230	·230	·227	·230	·235	·237	·238	·243	·238	·244		
Oct	·181	·181	·184	·181	·187	·190	·204	·210	·209	·207	·212	·217	·218	·217	·217	·209	·212	·215	·223	·226	·226	·222	·225	·230	·232	·234	·238	·233	·240		
Nov	·176	·177	·180	·176	·182	·186	·199	·206	·205	·202	·207	·212	·213	·212	·212	·205	·207	·210	·218	·221	·221	·218	·221	·226	·228	·229	·234	·229	·235		
Dec	·175	·176	·179	·175	·181	·185	·198	·205	·204	·201	·206	·211	·212	·211	·211	·204	·206	·209	·217	·220	·220	·217	·220	·225	·227	·228	·233	·228	·234		
1992																															
Jan	·176	·177	·180	·176	·182	·186	·199	·206	·205	·202	·207	·212	·213	·212	·212	·205	·207	·210	·218	·221	·221	·218	·221	·226	·228	·229	·234	·229	·235		
Feb	·170	·171	·174	·170	·176	·180	·193	·200	·199	·196	·201	·206	·207	·206	·206	·199	·201	·204	·212	·215	·215	·211	·214	·219	·222	·223	·227	·222	·229		
Mar	·167	·168	·170	·167	·173	·176	·189	·196	·195	·192	·198	·203	·203	·203	·203	·195	·198	·200	·208	·211	·211	·208	·211	·216	·218	·219	·224	·219	·225		
Apr	·149	·150	·153	·149	·155	·159	·171	·178	·177	·174	·179	·184	·185	·184	·184	·177	·179	·182	·190	·193	·193	·189	·192	·197	·200	·201	·205	·200	·207		
May	·145	·146	·149	·145	·151	·154	·167	·174	·173	·170	·175	·180	·181	·180	·180	·173	·175	·178	·186	·189	·189	·185	·188	·193	·195	·197	·201	·196	·202		
Jun	·145	·146	·149	·145	·151	·154	·167	·174	·173	·170	·175	·180	·181	·180	·180	·173	·175	·178	·186	·189	·189	·185	·188	·193	·195	·197	·201	·196	·202		
Jul	·149	·150	·153	·149	·155	·159	·171	·178	·177	·174	·179	·184	·185	·184	·184	·177	·179	·182	·190	·193	·193	·189	·192	·197	·200	·201	·205	·200	·207		
Aug	·148	·149	·152	·148	·154	·158	·171	·177	·176	·174	·179	·184	·184	·184	·184	·176	·179	·181	·189	·192	·192	·189	·192	·197	·199	·200	·204	·199	·206		
Sep	·144	·145	·148	·144	·150	·154	·166	·173	·172	·169	·174	·179	·180	·179	·179	·172	·174	·177	·185	·188	·188	·184	·187	·192	·194	·196	·200	·195	·202		
Oct	·140	·141	·144	·140	·146	·149	·162	·169	·168	·165	·170	·175	·176	·175	·175	·168	·170	·173	·181	·184	·184	·180	·183	·188	·190	·192	·196	·191	·197		
Nov	·142	·142	·145	·142	·147	·151	·164	·170	·170	·167	·172	·177	·178	·177	·177	·170	·172	·175	·183	·185	·185	·182	·185	·190	·192	·193	·198	·193	·199		
Dec	·146	·147	·149	·146	·152	·155	·168	·175	·174	·171	·176	·181	·182	·181	·181	·174	·176	·179	·187	·190	·190	·186	·189	·194	·196	·198	·202	·197	·203		
1993																															
Jan	·157	·157	·160	·157	·162	·166	·179	·186	·185	·182	·187	·192	·193	·192	·192	·185	·187	·190	·198	·201	·201	·197	·200	·205	·207	·209	·213	·208	·215		
Feb	·149	·150	·153	·149	·155	·159	·171	·178	·177	·174	·179	·184	·185	·184	·184	·177	·179	·182	·190	·193	·193	·189	·192	·197	·200	·201	·205	·200	·207		
Mar	·145	·146	·149	·145	·151	·154	·167	·174	·173	·170	·175	·180	·181	·180	·180	·173	·175	·178	·186	·189	·189	·185	·188	·193	·195	·197	·201	·196	·202		
Apr	·134	·135	·138	·134	·140	·144	·156	·163	·162	·159	·164	·169	·170	·169	·169	·162	·164	·167	·175	·178	·178	·174	·177	·182	·184	·186	·190	·185	·191		
May	·130	·131	·134	·130	·136	·140	·152	·159	·158	·155	·160	·165	·166	·165	·165	·159	·161	·164	·172	·174	·174	·171	·174	·179	·181	·182	·187	·182	·188		
Jun	·131	·132	·135	·131	·137	·140	·153	·160	·159	·156	·161	·166	·167	·166	·166	·159	·161	·164	·172	·174	·174	·171	·174	·179	·181	·182	·187	·182	·188		
Jul	·134	·134	·137	·134	·139	·143	·156	·162	·161	·158	·168	·169	·168	·169	·168	·168	·163	·166	·174	·177	·177	·173	·176	·181	·183	·185	·189	·184	·190		
Aug	·129	·130	·132	·129	·134	·138	·151	·157	·156	·154	·159	·163	·164	·163	·163	·156	·159	·161	·169	·172	·172	·168	·171	·176	·178	·180	·184	·179	·185		
Sep	·124	·125	·128	·124	·130	·133	·146	·152	·152	·149	·154	·159	·159	·159	·159	·152	·154	·156	·164	·167	·167	·163	·166	·171	·173	·175	·179	·174	·180		
Oct	·125	·126	·128	·125	·130	·134	·147	·153	·152	·150	·154	·159	·160	·159	·159	·152	·154	·157	·165	·168	·168	·164	·167	·172	·174	·176	·180	·175	·181		
Nov	·126	·127	·130	·126	·132	·136	·148	·155	·154	·151	·156	·161	·162	·161	·161	·154	·156	·159	·167	·169	·169	·166	·169	·174	·176	·177	·181	·177	·183		
Dec	·124	·125	·128	·124	·130	·133	·146	·152	·152	·149	·154	·159	·159	·159	·159	·152	·154	·156	·164	·167	·167	·163	·166	·171	·173	·175	·179	·174	·180		
1994																															
Jan	·129	·130	·132	·129	·134	·138	·151	·157	·156	·154	·159	·163	·164	·163	·163	·156	·159	·161	·169	·172	·172	·168	·171	·176	·178	·180	·184	·179	·185		
Feb	·122	·123	·126	·122	·128	·132	·144	·151	·150	·147	·152	·157	·158	·157	·157	·150	·152	·155	·163	·165	·165	·162	·165	·170	·172	·173	·177	·172	·179		
Mar	·119	·120	·123	·119	·125	·128	·141	·147	·147	·144	·149	·154	·154	·154	·154	·147	·149	·152	·159	·162	·162	·159	·161	·166	·168	·170	·174	·169	·175		
Apr	·106	·107	·110	·106	·112	·115	·128	·134	·133	·130	·135	·140	·141	·140	·140	·133	·135	·138	·146	·148	·148	·145	·148	·153	·155	·156	·160	·155	·162		
May	·102	·103	·106	·102	·108	·111	·124	·130	·129	·126	·131	·136	·137	·136	·136	·129	·131	·134	·142	·144	·144	·141	·144	·149	·151	·152	·156	·151	·158		
Jun	·102	·103	·106	·102	·108	·111	·124	·130	·129	·126	·131	·136	·137	·136	·136	·129	·131	·134	·142	·144	·144	·141	·144	·149	·151	·152	·156	·151	·158		
Jul	·108	·108	·111	·108	·113	·117	·129	·135	·135	·132	·137	·142	·142	·142	·142	·135	·137	·140	·147	·150	·150	·147	·149	·154	·156	·158	·162	·157	·163		
Aug	·102	·103	·106	·102	·108	·111	·124	·130	·129	·126	·131	·136	·137	·136	·136	·129	·131	·134	·142	·144	·144	·141	·144	·149	·151	·152	·156	·151	·158		
Sep	·100	·101	·103	·100	·106	·109	·121	·128	·127	·124	·129	·133	·134	·134	·134	·127	·129	·132	·139	·142	·142	·139	·141	·146	·149	·150	·154	·149	·155		
Oct	·098	·099	·102	·098	·104	·107	·120	·126	·125	·123	·127	·132	·133	·132	·132	·125	·127	·130	·138	·140	·140	·137	·140	·145	·147	·148	·152	·147	·154		
Nov	·098	·098	·101	·098	·103	·107	·119	·125	·125	·122	·127	·131	·132	·131	·131	·125	·127	·130	·137	·140	·140	·136	·139	·144	·146	·147	·151	·147	·153		
Dec	·092	·093	·096	·092	·098	·101	·114	·120	·119	·116	·121	·126	·127	·126	·126	·119	·121	·124	·132	·134	·134	·131	·134	·138	·140	·142	·146	·141	·147		
1995																															
Jan	·092	·093	·096	·092	·098	·101	·114	·120	·119	·116	·121	·126	·127	·126	·126	·119	·121	·124	·132	·134	·134	·131	·134	·138	·140	·142	·146	·141	·147		
Feb	·086	·086	·089	·086	·091	·095	·107	·113	·112	·110	·114	·119	·120	·119	·119	·112	·114	·117	·125	·127	·127	·124	·127	·131	·133	·135	·139	·134	·140		
Mar	·081	·082	·085	·081	·087	·090	·102	·108	·108	·105	·110	·115	·115	·115	·115	·108	·110	·113	·120	·123	·123	·119	·122	·127	·129	·130	·134	·129	·136		
Apr	·070	·071	·074	·070	·076	·079	·091	·097	·097	·094	·099	·103	·104	·103	·103	·097	·099	·101	·109	·111	·111	·108	·111	·115	·117	·119	·123	·118	·124		
May	·066	·067	·070	·066	·072	·075	·087	·093	·092	·090	·094	·099	·100	·099	·099	·092	·094	·097	·104	·107	·107	·104	·106	·111	·113	·114	·118	·114	·120		
Jun	·065	·065	·068	·065	·070	·073	·085	·091	·091	·088	·093	·097	·098	·097	·097	·091	·093	·095	·103	·105	·105	·102	·105	·109	·111	·113	·117	·112	·118		
Jul	·070	·070	·073	·070	·075	·078	·091	·097	·096	·093	·098	·103	·103	·103	·103	·096	·098	·101	·108	·111	·111	·107	·110	·115	·117	·118	·122	·117	·123		
Aug	·064	·065	·067	·064	·069	·073	·085	·091	·090	·087	·092	·097	·097	·097	·097	·090	·092	·095	·102	·105	·105	·101	·104	·109	·111	·112	·116	·111	·117		
Sep	·059	·060	·062	·059	·064	·068	·080	·086	·085	·082	·087	·092	·092	·092	·092	·085	·087	·090	·097	·100	·100	·096	·099	·104	·106	·107	·111	·106	·112		
Oct	·065	·065	·068	·065	·070	·073	·085	·091	·091	·088	·093	·097	·098	·097	·091	·091	·093	·095	·103	·105	·105	·102	·105	·109	·111	·113	·117	·112	·118		
Nov	·065	·065	·068	·065	·070	·073	·085	·091	·091	·088	·093	·097	·098	·097	·091	·091	·093	·093	·103	·105	·105	·102	·105	·109	·111	·113	·117	·112	·118		
Dec	·058	·059	·062	·058	·064	·067	·079	·085	·084	·082	·086	·091	·092	·091	·091	·084	·086	·089	·096	·099	·099	·096	·098	·103	·105	·106	·110	·106	·111		

RD—Month of disposal

RI Base month

Base	1995 Apr	May	Jun	Jul	Aug	Sep	Oct	Nov	Dec	1996 Jan	Feb	Mar	Apr	May	Jun	Jul	Aug	Sep	Oct	Nov	Dec	1997 Jan	Feb	Mar	Apr	May	Jun	Jul	Aug	Sep
1996																														
Jan	—	—	—	—	—	—	—	—	—	—	·005	·009	·016	·018	·019	·015	·019	·024	·024	·025	·028	·028	·032	·035	·041	·045	·049	·049	·055	·061
Feb	—	—	—	—	—	—	—	—	—	—	—	·004	·011	·013	·014	·010	·015	·019	·019	·020	·023	·023	·027	·030	·036	·040	·044	·044	·050	·056
Mar	—	—	—	—	—	—	—	—	—	—	—	—	·007	·009	·010	·006	·011	·015	·015	·016	·019	·019	·023	·026	·032	·036	·040	·040	·046	·051
Apr	—	—	—	—	—	—	—	—	—	—	—	—	—	·002	·003	·000	·003	·008	·008	·009	·012	·012	·016	·018	·024	·028	·032	·032	·039	·044
May	—	—	—	—	—	—	—	—	—	—	—	—	—	—	·001	·000	·001	·006	·006	·007	·010	·010	·014	·016	·022	·026	·030	·030	·037	·042
June	—	—	—	—	—	—	—	—	—	—	—	—	—	—	—	·000	·001	·005	·005	·006	·009	·009	·013	·016	·022	·025	·029	·029	·036	·041
July	—	—	—	—	—	—	—	—	—	—	—	—	—	—	—	—	·005	·009	·009	·010	·013	·013	·017	·020	·026	·030	·033	·033	·040	·045
Aug	—	—	—	—	—	—	—	—	—	—	—	—	—	—	—	—	—	·005	·005	·005	·008	·008	·012	·015	·021	·025	·029	·029	·035	·040
Sept	—	—	—	—	—	—	—	—	—	—	—	—	—	—	—	—	—	—	·000	·001	·004	·004	·008	·010	·016	·020	·024	·024	·031	·036
Oct	—	—	—	—	—	—	—	—	—	—	—	—	—	—	—	—	—	—	—	·001	·004	·004	·008	·010	·016	·020	·024	·024	·031	·036
Nov	—	—	—	—	—	—	—	—	—	—	—	—	—	—	—	—	—	—	—	—	·003	·003	·007	·010	·016	·019	·023	·023	·030	·035
Dec	—	—	—	—	—	—	—	—	—	—	—	—	—	—	—	—	—	—	—	—	—	·000	·004	·006	·012	·016	·020	·020	·027	·032
1997																														
Jan	—	—	—	—	—	—	—	—	—	—	—	—	—	—	—	—	—	—	—	—	—	—	·004	·006	·012	·016	·020	·020	·027	·032
Feb	—	—	—	—	—	—	—	—	—	—	—	—	—	—	—	—	—	—	—	—	—	—	—	·003	·008	·012	·016	·016	·023	·028
Mar	—	—	—	—	—	—	—	—	—	—	—	—	—	—	—	—	—	—	—	—	—	—	—	—	·006	·010	·014	·014	·020	·025
Apr	—	—	—	—	—	—	—	—	—	—	—	—	—	—	—	—	—	—	—	—	—	—	—	—	—	·004	·008	·008	·014	·019
May	—	—	—	—	—	—	—	—	—	—	—	—	—	—	—	—	—	—	—	—	—	—	—	—	—	—	·004	·004	·010	·015
Jun	—	—	—	—	—	—	—	—	—	—	—	—	—	—	—	—	—	—	—	—	—	—	—	—	—	—	—	—	·006	·011
Jul	—	—	—	—	—	—	—	—	—	—	—	—	—	—	—	—	—	—	—	—	—	—	—	—	—	—	—	—	·006	·011
Aug	—	—	—	—	—	—	—	—	—	—	—	—	—	—	—	—	—	—	—	—	—	—	—	—	—	—	—	—	—	·005
Sep	—	—	—	—	—	—	—	—	—	—	—	—	—	—	—	—	—	—	—	—	—	—	—	—	—	—	—	—	—	—
Oct	—	—	—	—	—	—	—	—	—	—	—	—	—	—	—	—	—	—	—	—	—	—	—	—	—	—	—	—	—	—
Nov	—	—	—	—	—	—	—	—	—	—	—	—	—	—	—	—	—	—	—	—	—	—	—	—	—	—	—	—	—	—
Dec	—	—	—	—	—	—	—	—	—	—	—	—	—	—	—	—	—	—	—	—	—	—	—	—	—	—	—	—	—	—
1998																														
Jan	—	—	—	—	—	—	—	—	—	—	—	—	—	—	—	—	—	—	—	—	—	—	—	—	—	—	—	—	—	—
Feb	—	—	—	—	—	—	—	—	—	—	—	—	—	—	—	—	—	—	—	—	—	—	—	—	—	—	—	—	—	—
Mar	—	—	—	—	—	—	—	—	—	—	—	—	—	—	—	—	—	—	—	—	—	—	—	—	—	—	—	—	—	—
Apr	—	—	—	—	—	—	—	—	—	—	—	—	—	—	—	—	—	—	—	—	—	—	—	—	—	—	—	—	—	—
May	—	—	—	—	—	—	—	—	—	—	—	—	—	—	—	—	—	—	—	—	—	—	—	—	—	—	—	—	—	—
Jun	—	—	—	—	—	—	—	—	—	—	—	—	—	—	—	—	—	—	—	—	—	—	—	—	—	—	—	—	—	—
Jul	—	—	—	—	—	—	—	—	—	—	—	—	—	—	—	—	—	—	—	—	—	—	—	—	—	—	—	—	—	—
Aug	—	—	—	—	—	—	—	—	—	—	—	—	—	—	—	—	—	—	—	—	—	—	—	—	—	—	—	—	—	—
Sep	—	—	—	—	—	—	—	—	—	—	—	—	—	—	—	—	—	—	—	—	—	—	—	—	—	—	—	—	—	—
Oct	—	—	—	—	—	—	—	—	—	—	—	—	—	—	—	—	—	—	—	—	—	—	—	—	—	—	—	—	—	—
Nov	—	—	—	—	—	—	—	—	—	—	—	—	—	—	—	—	—	—	—	—	—	—	—	—	—	—	—	—	—	—
Dec	—	—	—	—	—	—	—	—	—	—	—	—	—	—	—	—	—	—	—	—	—	—	—	—	—	—	—	—	—	—
1999																														
Jan	—	—	—	—	—	—	—	—	—	—	—	—	—	—	—	—	—	—	—	—	—	—	—	—	—	—	—	—	—	—
Feb	—	—	—	—	—	—	—	—	—	—	—	—	—	—	—	—	—	—	—	—	—	—	—	—	—	—	—	—	—	—
Mar	—	—	—	—	—	—	—	—	—	—	—	—	—	—	—	—	—	—	—	—	—	—	—	—	—	—	—	—	—	—
Apr	—	—	—	—	—	—	—	—	—	—	—	—	—	—	—	—	—	—	—	—	—	—	—	—	—	—	—	—	—	—
May	—	—	—	—	—	—	—	—	—	—	—	—	—	—	—	—	—	—	—	—	—	—	—	—	—	—	—	—	—	—
Jun	—	—	—	—	—	—	—	—	—	—	—	—	—	—	—	—	—	—	—	—	—	—	—	—	—	—	—	—	—	—
Jul	—	—	—	—	—	—	—	—	—	—	—	—	—	—	—	—	—	—	—	—	—	—	—	—	—	—	—	—	—	—
Aug	—	—	—	—	—	—	—	—	—	—	—	—	—	—	—	—	—	—	—	—	—	—	—	—	—	—	—	—	—	—
Sep	—	—	—	—	—	—	—	—	—	—	—	—	—	—	—	—	—	—	—	—	—	—	—	—	—	—	—	—	—	—
Oct	—	—	—	—	—	—	—	—	—	—	—	—	—	—	—	—	—	—	—	—	—	—	—	—	—	—	—	—	—	—
Nov	—	—	—	—	—	—	—	—	—	—	—	—	—	—	—	—	—	—	—	—	—	—	—	—	—	—	—	—	—	—
Dec	—	—	—	—	—	—	—	—	—	—	·005	—	—	—	—	—	—	—	—	—	—	—	—	—	—	—	—	—	—	—

Indexation allowance — continued

RD—Month of disposal

RI Base month	1997			1998												1999												2000			
	Oct	Nov	Dec	Jan	Feb	Mar	Apr	May	June	July	Aug	Sept	Oct	Nov	Dec	Jan	Feb	Mar	Apr	May	June	July	Aug	Sept	Oct	Nov	Dec	Jan	Feb	Mar	Apr
1996 Jan	·062	·063	·065	·062	·067	·071	·083	·089	·088	·085	·090	·095	·095	·095	·095	·088	·090	·093	·100	·103	·103	·099	·102	·107	·109	·110	·114	·109	·115		
Feb	·057	·058	·060	·057	·062	·066	·078	·083	·083	·080	·085	·089	·090	·089	·089	·083	·085	·087	·095	·097	·097	·094	·097	·101	·103	·105	·109	·104	·110		
Mar	·053	·053	·056	·053	·058	·061	·073	·079	·079	·076	·081	·085	·086	·085	·085	·079	·081	·087	·090	·093	·093	·090	·092	·097	·099	·100	·104	·100	·106		
Apr	·045	·046	·048	·045	·050	·054	·066	·071	·071	·068	·073	·077	·078	·077	·077	·071	·073	·075	·083	·085	·085	·082	·085	·089	·091	·092	·096	·092	·098		
May	·043	·044	·046	·043	·048	·052	·063	·069	·069	·066	·071	·075	·076	·075	·075	·069	·071	·073	·080	·083	·083	·080	·082	·087	·089	·090	·094	·090	·095		
Jun	·042	·043	·046	·042	·048	·051	·063	·069	·068	·065	·070	·075	·075	·075	·075	·068	·070	·073	·080	·082	·082	·079	·082	·086	·088	·090	·093	·089	·095		
Jul	·047	·047	·050	·047	·052	·055	·067	·073	·072	·070	·074	·079	·079	·079	·079	·072	·074	·077	·084	·087	·087	·083	·086	·091	·093	·094	·098	·093	·099		
Aug	·042	·042	·045	·042	·047	·050	·062	·068	·067	·065	·069	·074	·074	·074	·074	·067	·069	·072	·079	·082	·082	·078	·081	·086	·088	·089	·093	·088	·094		
Sep	·037	·038	·040	·037	·042	·046	·057	·063	·062	·060	·064	·069	·070	·069	·069	·062	·064	·067	·074	·077	·077	·073	·076	·081	·083	·084	·088	·083	·089		
Oct	·037	·038	·040	·037	·042	·046	·057	·063	·062	·060	·064	·069	·070	·069	·069	·062	·064	·067	·074	·077	·077	·073	·076	·081	·083	·084	·088	·083	·089		
Nov	·036	·037	·040	·036	·042	·045	·057	·062	·062	·059	·064	·068	·069	·068	·068	·062	·064	·066	·073	·076	·076	·073	·075	·080	·082	·083	·087	·083	·088		
Dec	·033	·034	·036	·033	·038	·041	·053	·059	·058	·056	·060	·065	·065	·065	·065	·058	·060	·063	·070	·073	·073	·069	·072	·076	·078	·080	·084	·079	·085		
1997 Jan	·033	·034	·036	·033	·038	·041	·053	·059	·058	·056	·060	·065	·065	·065	·065	·058	·060	·063	·070	·073	·073	·069	·072	·076	·078	·080	·084	·079	·085		
Feb	·029	·030	·032	·029	·034	·037	·049	·055	·054	·052	·056	·061	·061	·061	·061	·054	·056	·059	·066	·068	·068	·065	·068	·072	·074	·075	·079	·075	·081		
Mar	·025	·027	·030	·026	·032	·035	·046	·052	·051	·049	·053	·058	·059	·058	·058	·051	·053	·056	·063	·066	·066	·062	·065	·069	·071	·073	·077	·072	·078		
Apr	·020	·021	·024	·020	·026	·029	·040	·046	·045	·043	·047	·052	·052	·052	·052	·045	·047	·050	·057	·060	·060	·056	·059	·063	·065	·067	·070	·066	·072		
May	·017	·017	·020	·017	·022	·025	·036	·042	·041	·039	·043	·048	·048	·048	·048	·041	·043	·046	·053	·055	·055	·052	·055	·059	·061	·062	·066	·062	·068		
Jun	·013	·013	·016	·013	·018	·021	·032	·038	·037	·035	·039	·044	·044	·044	·044	·037	·039	·042	·049	·051	·051	·048	·051	·055	·057	·058	·062	·058	·063		
Jul	·013	·013	·016	·013	·018	·021	·032	·038	·037	·035	·039	·044	·044	·044	·044	·037	·039	·042	·049	·051	·051	·048	·051	·055	·057	·058	·062	·058	·063		
Aug	·006	·007	·009	·006	·011	·015	·026	·032	·031	·028	·033	·037	·038	·037	·037	·031	·033	·035	·042	·045	·045	·042	·044	·049	·050	·052	·056	·051	·057		
Sep	·001	·002	·004	·001	·006	·009	·021	·026	·026	·023	·028	·032	·033	·032	·032	·026	·028	·030	·037	·040	·040	·036	·039	·043	·045	·046	·050	·046	·051		
Oct	—	·001	·003	·000	·005	·008	·019	·025	·024	·022	·026	·031	·031	·031	·031	·024	·026	·029	·036	·038	·038	·035	·038	·042	·044	·045	·049	·045	·050		
Nov	—	—	·003	·000	·004	·008	·019	·024	·024	·021	·026	·030	·031	·030	·030	·024	·026	·028	·035	·038	·038	·034	·037	·041	·043	·044	·048	·044	·049		
Dec	—	—	—	·000	·002	·005	·016	·022	·021	·019	·023	·028	·028	·028	·028	·021	·023	·026	·032	·035	·035	·032	·034	·039	·041	·042	·046	·041	·047		
1998 Jan	—	—	—	—	·005	·008	·019	·025	·024	·022	·026	·031	·031	·031	·031	·024	·026	·029	·036	·038	·038	·035	·038	·042	·044	·045	·049	·045	·050		
Feb	—	—	—	—	—	·003	·014	·020	·019	·017	·021	·026	·026	·026	·026	·019	·021	·024	·031	·033	·033	·030	·032	·037	·039	·040	·044	·039	·045		
Mar	—	—	—	—	—	—	·011	·017	·016	·014	·018	·022	·023	·022	·022	·016	·018	·021	·027	·030	·030	·027	·029	·034	·035	·037	·040	·036	·042		
Apr	—	—	—	—	—	—	—	·006	·005	·002	·007	·011	·012	·011	·011	·005	·007	·009	·016	·018	·018	·015	·018	·022	·024	·025	·029	·025	·030		
May	—	—	—	—	—	—	—	—	·000	·001	·006	·006	·006	·006	·006	·000	·001	·004	·010	·013	·013	·010	·012	·017	·018	·020	·023	·019	·024		
Jun	—	—	—	—	—	—	—	—	—	·000	·002	·006	·007	·006	·006	·000	·002	·004	·011	·013	·013	·010	·013	·017	·019	·020	·024	·020	·025		
Jul	—	—	—	—	—	—	—	—	—	—	·004	·009	·009	·009	·009	·002	·004	·007	·013	·016	·016	·013	·015	·020	·021	·023	·026	·022	·028		
Aug	—	—	—	—	—	—	—	—	—	—	—	·004	·005	·004	·004	·000	·000	·002	·009	·012	·012	·009	·011	·015	·017	·018	·022	·018	·023		
Sep	—	—	—	—	—	—	—	—	—	—	—	—	·001	·000	·000	·000	·000	·000	·005	·007	·007	·004	·007	·011	·013	·014	·018	·013	·019		
Oct	—	—	—	—	—	—	—	—	—	—	—	—	—	·000	·000	·000	·000	·000	·004	·007	·007	·004	·006	·010	·012	·013	·017	·013	·018		
Nov	—	—	—	—	—	—	—	—	—	—	—	—	—	—	·000	·000	·000	·000	·005	·007	·007	·004	·007	·011	·013	·014	·018	·013	·019		
Dec	—	—	—	—	—	—	—	—	—	—	—	—	—	—	—	·000	·000	·000	·005	·007	·007	·004	·007	·011	·013	·014	·018	·013	·019		
1999 Jan	—	—	—	—	—	—	—	—	—	—	—	—	—	—	—	—	·002	·004	·011	·013	·013	·010	·013	·017	·019	·020	·024	·020	·025		
Feb	—	—	—	—	—	—	—	—	—	—	—	—	—	—	—	—	—	·002	·009	·012	·012	·009	·011	·015	·017	·018	·022	·018	·023		
Mar	—	—	—	—	—	—	—	—	—	—	—	—	—	—	—	—	—	—	·007	·009	·009	·006	·009	·013	·015	·016	·020	·015	·021		
Apr	—	—	—	—	—	—	—	—	—	—	—	—	—	—	—	—	—	—	—	·002	·002	·000	·002	·006	·008	·009	·013	·008	·014		
May	—	—	—	—	—	—	—	—	—	—	—	—	—	—	—	—	—	—	—	—	·000	·000	·004	·005	·007	·007	·010	·006	·011		
Jun	—	—	—	—	—	—	—	—	—	—	—	—	—	—	—	—	—	—	—	—	—	·000	·000	·004	·005	·007	·010	·006	·011		
Jul	—	—	—	—	—	—	—	—	—	—	—	—	—	—	—	—	—	—	—	—	—	—	·002	·007	·008	·010	·013	·009	·015		
Aug	—	—	—	—	—	—	—	—	—	—	—	—	—	—	—	—	—	—	—	—	—	—	—	·004	·006	·007	·011	·007	·012		
Sep	—	—	—	—	—	—	—	—	—	—	—	—	—	—	—	—	—	—	—	—	—	—	—	—	·002	·003	·007	·002	·008		
Oct	—	—	—	—	—	—	—	—	—	—	—	—	—	—	—	—	—	—	—	—	—	—	—	—	—	·001	·005	·001	·006		
Nov	—	—	—	—	—	—	—	—	—	—	—	—	—	—	—	—	—	—	—	—	—	—	—	—	—	—	·004	·000	·005		
Dec	—	—	—	—	—	—	—	—	—	—	—	—	—	—	—	—	—	—	—	—	—	—	—	—	—	—	—	·000	·001		
2000 Jan	—	—	—	—	—	—	—	—	—	—	—	—	—	—	—	—	—	—	—	—	—	—	—	—	—	—	—	—	·005	—	—
Feb	—	—	—	—	—	—	—	—	—	—	—	—	—	—	—	—	—	—	—	—	—	—	—	—	—	—	—	—	—	—	—
Mar	—	—	—	—	—	—	—	—	—	—	—	—	—	—	—	—	—	—	—	—	—	—	—	—	—	—	—	—	—	—	—

Retail prices index

	Jan	Feb	Mar	Apr	May	June	July	Aug	Sept	Oct	Nov	Dec
1947	–	–	–	–	–	7·33	7·40	7·33	7·40	7·40	7·55	7·63
1948	7·63	7·78	7·78	8·33	8·33	8·49	8·33	8·33	8·33	8·33	8·41	8·41
1949	8·41	8·41	8·41	8·41	8·57	8·57	8·57	8·57	8·65	8·65	8·65	8·73
1950	8·73	8·73	8·73	8·81	8·81	8·81	8·81	8·73	8·81	8·89	8·97	8·97
1951	9·03	9·11	9·19	9·35	9·59	9·67	9·72	9·80	9·88	9·96	9·96	10·04
1952	10·20	10·28	10·28	10·44	10·44	10·65	10·65	10·04	9·96	10·11	10·11	10·11
1953	10·11	10·19	10·67	10·34	10·27	10·34	10·34	10·27	10·27	10·27	10·27	10·27
1954	10·27	10·27	10·34	10·42	10·34	10·42	10·62	10·57	10·49	10·57	10·62	10·62
1955	10·70	10·70	10·70	10·77	10·77	11·00	11·00	10·93	11·00	11·15	11·28	11·28
1956	11·25	11·25	11·38	11·56	11·53	11·51	11·48	11·51	11·48	11·56	11·58	11·63
1957	11·74	11·74	11·71	11·76	11·76	11·89	11·99	11·96	11·94	12·04	12·12	12·17
1958	12·17	12·09	12·19	12·32	12·29	12·40	12·19	12·19	12·19	12·29	12·34	12·40
1959	12·42	12·40	12·40	12·32	12·27	12·29	12·27	12·29	12·22	12·29	12·37	12·40
1960	12·37	12·37	12·34	12·40	12·40	12·47	12·50	12·42	12·42	12·52	12·60	12·62
1961	12·62	12·62	12·67	12·75	12·78	12·90	12·90	13·00	13·00	13·00	13·16	13·18
1962	13·21	13·23	13·28	13·46	13·51	13·59	13·54	13·43	13·41	13·41	13·46	13·51
1963	13·56	13·69	13·71	13·74	13·74	13·74	13·66	13·61	13·66	13·71	13·74	13·76
1964	13·84	13·84	13·89	14·02	14·14	14·20	14·20	14·25	14·25	14·27	14·37	14·42
1965	14·47	14·47	14·52	14·80	14·85	14·90	14·90	14·93	14·93	14·96	15·01	15·08
1966	15·11	15·11	15·13	15·34	15·44	15·49	15·41	15·51	15·49	15·51	15·61	15·64
1967	15·67	15·67	15·67	15·79	15·79	15·84	15·74	15·72	15·69	15·86	15·92	16·02
1968	16·07	16·15	16·20	16·50	16·50	16·58	16·58	16·60	16·63	16·70	16·76	16·96
1969	17·06	17·16	17·21	17·41	17·39	17·47	17·47	17·41	17·47	17·59	17·64	17·77
1970	17·90	18·00	18·10	18·38	18·43	18·48	18·63	18·61	18·71	18·91	19·04	19·16
1971	19·42	19·54	19·70	20·13	20·25	20·38	20·51	20·53	20·56	20·66	20·79	20·89
1972	21·01	21·12	21·19	21·39	21·50	21·62	21·70	21·88	22·00	22·31	22·38	22·48
1973	22·64	22·79	22·92	23·35	23·52	23·65	23·75	23·83	24·03	24·51	24·69	24·87
1974	25·35	25·78	26·01	26·89	27·28	27·55	27·81	27·83	28·14	28·69	29·20	29·63
1975	30·39	30·90	31·51	32·72	34·09	34·75	35·11	35·31	35·61	36·12	36·55	37·01
1976	37·49	37·97	38·17	38·91	39·34	39·54	39·62	40·18	40·71	41·44	42·03	42·59
1977	43·70	44·24	44·56	45·70	46·06	46·54	46·59	46·82	47·07	47·28	47·50	47·76
1978	48·04	48·31	48·62	49·33	49·61	49·99	50·22	50·54	50·75	50·98	51·33	51·76
1979	52·52	52·95	53·38	54·30	54·73	55·67	58·07	58·53	59·11	59·72	60·25	60·68
1980	62·18	63·07	63·93	66·11	66·72	67·35	67·91	68·06	68·49	68·92	69·48	69·86
1981	70·29	70·93	71·99	74·07	74·55	74·98	75·31	75·87	76·30	76·98	77·78	78·28
1982	78·73	78·76	79·44	81·04	81·62	81·85	81·88	81·90	81·85	82·26	82·66	82·51
1983	82·61	82·97	83·12	84·28	84·64	84·84	85·30	85·68	86·06	86·36	86·67	86·89
1984	86·84	87·20	87·48	88·64	88·97	89·20	89·10	89·94	90·11	90·67	90·95	90·87
1985	91·20	91·94	92·80	94·78	95·21	95·41	95·23	95·49	95·44	95·59	95·92	96·05
1986	96·25	96·60	96·73	97·67	97·85	97·79	97·52	97·82	98·30	98·45	99·29	99·62
1987	100·00	100·40	100·60	101·80	101·90	101·90	101·80	102·10	102·40	102·90	103·40	103·30
1988	103·30	103·70	104·10	105·80	106·20	106·60	106·70	107·90	108·40	109·50	110·00	110·30
1989	111·00	111·80	112·30	114·30	115·00	115·40	115·50	115·80	116·60	117·50	118·50	118·80
1990	119·50	120·20	121·40	125·10	126·20	126·70	126·80	128·10	129·30	130·30	130·00	129·90
1991	130·20	130·90	131·40	133·10	133·50	134·10	133·80	134·10	134·60	135·10	135·60	135·70
1992	135·60	136·30	136·70	138·80	139·30	139·30	138·80	138·90	139·40	139·90	139·70	139·20
1993	137·90	138·80	139·30	140·60	141·10	141·00	140·70	141·30	141·90	141·80	141·60	141·90
1994	141·30	142·10	142·50	144·20	144·70	144·70	144·00	144·70	145·00	145·20	145·30	146·00
1995	146·00	146·90	147·50	149·00	149·60	149·80	149·10	149·90	150·60	149·80	149·80	150·70
1996	150·20	150·90	151·50	152·60	152·90	153·00	152·40	153·10	153·80	153·80	153·90	154·40
1997	154·40	155·00	155·40	156·30	156·90	157·50	157·50	158·50	159·30	159·50	159·60	160·00
1998	159·50	160·30	160·80	162·60	163·50	163·40	163·00	163·70	164·40	164·50	164·40	164·40
1999	163·40	163·70	164·10	165·20	165·60	165·60	165·10	165·50	166·20	166·50	166·70	167·30
2000	166·60	167·50										

Corporation tax

Rates of corporation tax and advance corporation tax

Financial year	1991	1992	1993	1994	1995	1996	1997	1998	1999	2000
Corporation tax (full rate)	33%	33%	33%	33%	33%	33%	31%	31%	30%	30%
Advance corporation tax: from 6 April	$\frac{1}{3}$	$\frac{1}{3}$	$\frac{9}{31}$	$\frac{1}{4}$	$\frac{1}{4}$	$\frac{1}{4}$	$\frac{1}{4}$	$\frac{1}{4}$	—*	—*
Tax credit: from 6 April	25%	25%	20%†	20%†	20%†	20%†	20%†	20%†	10%†	10%†

It has been announced that the full rate of corporation tax will remain at 30% for the financial year beginning on 1 April 2001: (2000) SWTI 381.

* Advance corporation tax is abolished from 6 April 1999. ACT remains at ¼ for distributions on 1 April to 5 April 1999.

† Individual shareholders not subject to tax at the higher rate will have no further tax to pay.
In the case of charities, the reduced tax credit was phased in over four years, 1993–94 to 1996–97. In general, trustees of discretionary trusts are taxed at a flat rate on dividend income from 6 April 1993 (35% before 6 April 1996; 34% from 6 April 1996).

Starting and small companies rates (TA 1988 ss 13, 13AA)

Financial year:	1994	1995	1996	1997	1998	1999	2000
Starting rate	—	—	—	—	—	—	10%
first relevant amount*	—	—	—	—	—	—	£10,000
second relevant amount*	—	—	—	—	—	—	£50,000
marginal relief fraction	—	—	—	—	—	—	$\frac{1}{40}$
Small companies rate	25%	25%	24%	21%	21%	20%	20%
lower relevant amount*	£300,000	£300,000	£300,000	£300,000	£300,000	£300,000	£3000,000
upper relevant amount*	£1,500,000	£1,500,000	£1,500,000	£1,500,000	£1,500,000	£1,500,000	£1,500,000
marginal relief fraction	$\frac{1}{50}$	$\frac{1}{50}$	$\frac{9}{400}$	$\frac{1}{40}$	$\frac{1}{40}$	$\frac{1}{40}$	$\frac{1}{40}$

* Reduced proportionally for accounting periods of less than 12 months. Associated companies: divide limits by total number of associated companies (including the company in question).
1) The starting and the small companies rate apply to *basic profits* ("I") where *profits* ("P") do not exceed the first (in the case of the starting rate) and lower (small companies rate) relevant amounts.
2) Where *profits* ("P") exceed the first or lower relevant amounts but not the second or upper relevant amounts, corporation tax on *basic profits* ("I") is reduced by—

(second or upper relevant amount–P) x $\dfrac{I}{P}$ x fraction

For the purposes of 1) and 2) above—

P = profits as finally computed for corporation tax purposes *plus* franked investment income *excluding* franked investment income from UK companies in the same group or from UK companies owned by a consortium of which the recipient is a member (TA 1988 s 13(7) amended by FA 1998 Sch 3 para 7 for distributions made after 5 April 1999).
I = profits on which corporation tax is actually borne (income plus chargeable gains).

Capital gains

A company's chargeable gains are taxed without adjustment (other than indexation for post-1982 gains) at the rate of corporation tax applying to the company's other profits. The reform of capital gains tax for individuals, trustees and personal representatives provided in the Finance Act 1998 does not extend to the capital gains of companies.

Close investment-holding companies

Charged at full rate of corporation tax (see above).

Corporate venturing scheme

From **1 April 2000** ((1999) SWTI 1808; (2000) SWTI 437)

Rate of corporation tax relief*	20%
Minimum percentage of investee company's ordinary share capital held by individuals	20%
Investing company's maximum stake in investee company	30%
Minimum investment period	3 years
Companies can obtain corporation tax relief on amounts invested in new ordinary unquoted shares in small higher-risk trading companies.	

Research and development expenditure

From **1 April 2000** ((1999) SWTI 1806)

Rate of corporation tax relief	150%
Minimum threshold on spending	£25,000
Maximum turnover limit	£25 million
Companies not yet in profit or which have not yet started to trade can claim the relief up front.	

See also the 100% capital allowance for scientific research, p 54

Capital allowances

Rates

Agricultural and forestry land

	Expenditure incurred after	% Rate
Initial allowance	11 April 1978	20
	31 March 1986	Nil
	31 October 1992[1]	20
	31 October 1993	Nil
Writing-down allowance	5 April 1946	10
	31 March 1986	4

Note:
[1] Buildings or works constructed under a contract entered into between 1 November 1992 and 31 October 1993, and brought into use for the purposes of the farming trade by 31 December 1994.

Dredging

	Expenditure incurred after	% Rate
Initial allowance	16 January 1966	15
	31 March 1986	Nil
Writing-down allowance	5 November 1962	4

Industrial buildings and structures

	Expenditure[1] incurred after	% Rate
Initial allowance	12 November 1974[2]	50
	10 March 1981[2-6]	75
	13 March 1984[2/4-8]	50
	31 March 1985[2/5-8]	25
	31 March 1986[2/5-8]	Nil
	31 October 1992[2/5/10]	20
	31 October 1993[5]	Nil
Writing-down allowance	5 November 1962[9]	4

Notes:
[1] The amount qualifying for allowance is the price paid for the relevant interest *minus* (i) the value of the land element and (ii) any value attributable to elements over and above those which would feature in a normal commercial lease negotiated in the open market: FA 1995 s 100 confirming previous practice.
[2] Qualifying hotels: expenditure incurred after 11 April 1978 and before 1 April 1986, or between 1 November 1992 and 31 October 1993 – 20% initial allowance. No initial allowance after 31 March 1986 except under certain pre-14 March 1984 contracts and as above.
[3] Small industrial workshops: expenditure incurred after 26 March 1980 and before 27 March 1983 – 100% initial allowance.
[4] Very small workshops: expenditure incurred after 26 March 1980 and before 27 March 1985 – 100% initial allowance.
[5] Enterprise zones: expenditure incurred not more than 10 years after the site was first included in the zone – 100% initial allowance. (See p 52 for list of enterprise zones.)
[6] Rates and transitional relief apply also to dwelling houses let on assured tenancies: 10 March 1982 – 31 March 1987.
[7] Expenditure qualifying for a regional development grant (where a written offer of financial assistance was made between 1 April 1980–13 March 1984) – 75%.
[8] Payments made after 13 March 1984 but before 1 April 1987 under a contract agreed before 14 March 1984 – 75%.
[9] Small industrial workshops: expenditure incurred after 26 March 1980 and before 27 March 1983 – 25% writing-down allowance.
   Very small workshops: expenditure incurred after 26 March 1980 and before 27 March 1985 – 25% writing-down allowance.
   Enterprise zones: expenditure incurred not more than 10 years after the site was first included in the zone (including qualifying hotels in an enterprise zone) – 25% writing-down allowance.
   Qualifying hotels (other than in an enterprise zone) – 4% writing-down allowance.
   Toll roads: for accounting periods or basis periods ending after 5 April 1991 4% writing-down allowance for expenditure on construction of toll roads.
[10] Building constructed under, or bought unused under, a contract entered into after 31 October 1992 and before 1 November 1993, and brought into use in qualifying trade by 31 December 1994. Balance of relief by 4% pa writing-down allowance. All or part of the initial allowance may be disclaimed. See FA 1993 s 113.

Know-how

Writing-down allowance
Expenditure incurred before 1 April 1986 spread equally over 6 years on straight line basis, ie 16⅔% pa (if not otherwise deductible as trading expense).
Expenditure incurred after 31 March 1986: annual 25% writing down allowance (reducing balance basis).

Machinery and plant Expenditure incurred after		% Rate
First-year allowance[1]	31 October 1993	Nil
	1 July 1997[2]	50
	11 May 1998 (Northern Ireland)[4]	100
	1 July 1998[3]	40
	31 March 2000[6]	100
Writing-down allowance	26 October 1970	25[1]
First-year allowance: long-life assets[5]	25 November 1996	Nil
	1 July 1997[2]	12
	1 July 1998	Nil
Writing-down allowance: long-life assets	25 November 1996	6

Notes:

[1] Special provisions apply to enable expenditure on ships to be set off at will.

[2] (See F(No2)A 1997 ss 42, 43.) Qualifying expenditure incurred by qualifying businesses during the year ended 1 July 1998 attracts a first-year allowance of 50% rather than the normal writing-down allowance of 25%. This does not apply to certain expenditure including that on machinery and plant for leasing, motor cars, ships or railway assets. For qualifying expenditure incurred in that year where the 6% rate of writing-down allowance – see note (6) below – would otherwise apply (ie. in the case of long-life assets), the rate of the first-year allowance is restricted to 12%. After the first year, allowances revert to the normal writing-down rate of 25%/6%. Qualifying businesses are, broadly, those which satisfy any two of the following conditions:
(a) turnover £11,200,000 or less (b) assets £5,600,000 or less (c) not more than 250 employees.

[3] (See FA 1998 s 84.) The conditions for relief during the year ending 1 July 1999 are similar to those outlined in footnote 5 above, but long-life assets do not qualify. In the 1999 Budget it was announced that the relief would be extended to expenditure incurred in the year ending 1 July 2000 and in the 2000 Budget that the relief would be made permanent (2000 Budget Resolution 39; (2000) SWTI 333).

[4] (See FA 1998 s 83; FA 1999, s 78.) Qualifying expenditure on plant and machinery for use in Northern Ireland incurred during the four year period from 12 May 1998 to 11 May 2002 by qualifying businesses attracts a first-year allowance of 100% rather than the normal 25% writing-down allowance. Claims can be made from 22 July 1999. The conditions for relief are similar to those outlined in footnote 5 above, but long-life assets and transport assets used in freight haulage businesses do not qualify.

[5] (See CAA 1990 ss 38A-38H.) On reducing balance basis. Applies to machinery or plant with an expected working life, when new, of 25 years or more. Applies where expenditure on long-life assets in a year is £100,000 or more in the case of individuals and of partnerships made up of individuals (where the individual or at least half the partners devotes substantially the whole of their time to carrying on the business). In this case of companies the de minimis limit is £100,000 divided by one plus the number of associated companies.
Transitional provisions apply to maintain a 25% allowance for expenditure incurred before 1 January 2001 under a contract entered into before 26 November 1996 and to expenditure on second-hand plant or machinery if old rules applied to vendor (CAA 1990 s 38H).
25% allowance for machinery or plant in building used wholly or mainly as, or for purposes ancillary to, a dwelling-house, retail shop, showroom, hotel or office, and for sea-going ships and railway assets bought before 1 January 2011. Motor cars are excluded from the new provisions.

[6] It was announced in the 2000 Budget that small businesses buying computers or investing in e-commerce and new information technology will be able to write off in the first year 100% of the investment until 2003: (2000) SWTI 327, 337.
Cars: Threshold for restriction on capital allowances for expenditure on business cars £12,000 for cars leased or purchased after 10 March 1992; £8,000 from 13 June 1979 to 10 March 1992; £5,000 from 6 April 1976 to 12 June 1979; £4,000 from 26 October 1970 to 5 April 1976. The requirement that expenditure on cars costing less than £12,000 goes into a separate pool will be removed from the start of the chargeable period which includes 1 April 2000 (corporation tax) or 6 April 2000 (income tax) or the start of the chargeable period which includes 1 (or 6) April 2001 at the option of the taxpayer: (2000) SWTI 418.
Leased assets: subject to transitional provisions, a first-year allowance was generally not available for expenditure after 31 May 1980 on the provision of leased plant or machinery unless it was used for a qualifying purpose. Writing-down allowances are available.
(a) Teletext and viewdata receivers and adaptors: transitional provisions were extended – reduced first-year allowance from 1 June 1980 to 31 May 1986.
(b) Leasing to non-residents: from 10 March 1982 writing-down allowance reduced from 25% to 10%.
(c) Ships and aircraft: first-year allowance was available for overseas leasing by UK resident responsible for management etc UNLESS main purpose is to obtain first year allowance, when only 10% writing-down allowance available.
Films: from 10 March 1982 expenditure on production and purchase of film etc is treated as revenue expenditure except for certain British-made films which continue to qualify for capital allowances. From 10 March 1992, pre-production expenditure on films produced with sufficient EC content is relieved as it occurs. 100% write-off is available for expenditure incurred after 1 July 1997 and before 2 July 2000 on a qualifying British film completed after 1 July 1997. See F(No 2)A 1992 ss 41–43, F (No 2)A 1997 s 48, Statement of Practice SP1/98.

Mines, oil wells etc

Expenditure incurred after		% Rate
Initial allowance	16 January 1966	40
	31 March 1986	Nil

Amount of writing-down allowance
Expenditure incurred before 1 April 1986—

Greater of: 1) $\dfrac{A}{A+B}$ x residue of expenditure

where A = output from source in chargeable period or its basis period,
and B = total potential future output of source, estimated as at the end of that chargeable period or its basis period.

2) 5% residue of expenditure for full year.

Expenditure incurred after 31 March 1986: annual writing-down allowance on reducing balance basis— 10% for certain pre-trading expenditure and expenditure on the acquisition of a mineral asset, otherwise 25%.

Note: Transitional provisions for expenditure incurred before 31 March 1987 under contract entered into before 16 July 1985.

Patent rights

Writing-down allowance
Expenditure incurred before 1 April 1986 spread equally over 17 years or, if less
(a) the period for which the rights are acquired, or
(b) 17 years less the number of complete years from the commencement of the patent to the acquisition.

Expenditure incurred after 31 March 1986: annual 25% writing-down allowance (reducing balance basis).

Scientific research*

Expenditure incurred after		% Rate
Allowance in year 1	5 November 1962	100

Note: Land and houses are excluded from 1 April 1985.
*See also corporation tax relief, p. 51.

Enterprise zones

The following areas have been designated as enterprise zones. The designation applies for 10 years from the commencement date. Previous enterprise zones, the designation of which has lapsed, are not shown.

Area	Commencement date
Sunderland (Castletown and Doxford Park)	27 April 1990
Sunderland (Hylton Riverside and Southwick)	27 April 1990
Lanarkshire (Hamilton)	1 February 1993
Lanarkshire (Motherwell)	1 February 1993
Lanarkshire (Monklands)	1 February 1993
Dearne Valley	3 November 1995
East Midlands (North East Derbyshire)	3 November 1995
East Midlands (Bassetlaw)	16 November 1995
East Midlands (Ashfield)	21 November 1995
East Durham	29 November 1995
Tyne Riverside (North Tyneside)	19 February 1996
Tyne Riverside (North Tyneside and South Tyneside)	21 October 1996

Time limits for capital allowances claims see p 25.

Income tax

Lower, basic and higher rates and rate applicable to trusts

2000-01 *Band of taxable income*

Exceeding £	Not exceeding £	Band £	Rate %	Tax on full band £	Cumulative tax £
0	1,520	1,520	10	152·00	152·00
1,520	28,400	26,880	22	5,913·60	6,065·60
28,400	—	—	40	—	—

1999-2000 *Band of taxable income*

Exceeding £	Not exceeding £	Band £	Rate %	Tax on full band £	Cumulative tax £
0	1,500	1,500	10	150	150
1,500	28,000	26,500	23	6,095	6,245
28,000	—	—	40	—	—

1998-99 *Band of taxable income*

Exceeding £	Not exceeding £	Band £	Rate %	Tax on full band £	Cumulative tax £
0	4,300	4,300	20	860	860
4,300	27,100	22,800	23	5,244	6,104
27,100	—	—	40	—	—

1997-98 *Band of taxable income*

Exceeding £	Not exceeding £	Band £	Rate %	Tax on full band £	Cumulative tax £
0	4,100	4,100	20	820	820
4,100	26,100	22,000	23	5,060	5,880
26,100	—	—	40	—	—

1996-97 *Band of taxable income*

Exceeding £	Not exceeding £	Band £	Rate %	Tax on full band £	Cumulative tax £
0	3,900	3,900	20	780	780
3,900	25,500	21,600	24	5,184	5,964
25,500	—	—	40	—	—

1995-96 *Band of taxable income*

Exceeding £	Not exceeding £	Band £	Rate %	Tax on full band £	Cumulative tax £
0	3,200	3,200	20	640	640
3,200	24,300	21,100	25	5,275	5,915
24,300	—	—	40	—	—

1994-95 *Band of taxable income*

Exceeding £	Not exceeding £	Band £	Rate %	Tax on full band £	Cumulative tax £
0	3,000	3,000	20	600	600
3,000	23,700	20,700	25	5,175	5,775
23,700	—	—	40	—	—

Taxation of savings: From 6 April 1999, savings income is chargeable at the rates of 10%, 20% and 40% (TA 1988 s1A; 2000 Budget Resolution 22 which deems the 10% starting rate to apply from that date). From 6 April 1996 to 5 April 1999, savings income was chargeable at the rates of 20% and 40%. Savings income includes interest from banks and building societies, interest distributions from authorised unit trusts, interest on gilts and other securities including corporate bonds, purchased life annuities and discounts. Where income falls within the basic rate limit, there will be no further tax to pay on savings income from which the 20% tax rate has been deducted. Higher rate taxpayers are liable to pay tax at 40% on that part of their savings income falling above the higher rate limit. From 6 April 1999, savings income is treated as the second top slice of income behind dividends. Non-taxpayers may apply to have interest paid without deduction of tax. Taxpayers who are entitled to a refund of tax deducted from interest can claim the refund using form R40. The Revenue are launching a *Taxback* website page ((2000) SWTI 410) to simplify repayments: www.inlandrevenue.gov.uk/taxback.

Taxation of dividends: UK and foreign dividends (except those foreign dividends taxed under the remittance basis) form the top slice of taxable income. From 6 April 1999, special rates apply to dividend income following the reduction of the tax credit to 10%. Where income falls within the basic rate limit the rate is 10% so that the liability is met by the tax credit. Higher rate taxpayers are liable to pay tax at 32.5% on that part of their dividend income falling above the higher rate limit. From 6 April 1993 to 5 April 1999, dividend income was chargeable at the 20% and 40% rates as for savings income above. See FA 1999, s 22; TA 1988, s 1A.

Rate applicable to trusts: 1997–98 to 1999–2000: 34%; Schedule F trust rate: 1999–2000 and 2000-01: 25%.

Additional rate: not charged on investment income of individuals. Additional rate on income arising to trustees of discretionary trusts: 1988–89 to 1996–97: 10%.

Table of income tax reliefs

	2000-01	1999-2000
Personal allowance (under 65)	£4,385	£4,335
Married couple's allowance[1] (from 6 April 2000 available only where either spouse is aged 65 or over at 5 April 2000, see Age allowance below) Monthly reduction in year of marriage	— —	£1,970[2] £164·16
Age allowance Abatement of relief by £1 for every £2 income over.. Personal allowance (under 75) .... Not beneficial if individual's total income exceeds .... Married couple's allowance (elder spouse under 75 but born before 6 April 1935)......... Minimum married couples allowance where income exceeds limit... Not beneficial if husband: under 65 and his total income exceeds...................... 65-74 and his total income exceeds............................ Personal allowance (75 and over).. Not beneficial if individual's total income exceeds .... Married couple's allowance (elder spouse 75 or over) .... Minimum married couples allowance where income exceeds limit... Not beneficial if husband: under 65 and his total income exceeds...................... 65-74 and his total income exceeds............................ 75 or over and his total income exceeds.......................	 £17,000 £5,790 £19,810 £5,185[2] £2,000 — £26,180 £6,050 £20,330 £5,255[2] £2,000 — £26,320 £26,840	 £16,800 £5,720 £19,570 £5,125[2] £1,970 £23,110 £25,880 £5,980 £20,090 £5,195[2] £1,970 £23,250 £26,020 £26,540
Widow's bereavement allowance[1] (available only where the death occurred before 6 April 2000 and the wife had not remarried before that date)	£2,000[2]	£1,970[2]
Additional relief for children[1]	—	£1,970[2]
Blind person (each)	£1,400	£1,380
Mortgage interest relief Limit on amount available for relief... Relief restricted to	 — —	 £30,000 10%
Life assurance relief For contracts made before 14 March 1984 *only*, given by deduction	 12·5%	 12·5%
NI Class 2 Small earnings exception	£3,825	£3,770
NI Class 4 *Band* *Maximum payable*	£4,385–£27,820 £23,435 @ 7% £1,640·45	£7,530-£26,000 £18,470 @ 6% £1,108·20
Lower rate of tax *Band*	10% £1,520	10% £1,500
Basic rate of tax *Band*	22% £26,880	23% £26,500

[1] **From 6 April 2001:** The children's tax credit, relief on which will be given at 10%, will be introduced for families with children (FA 1999, s 30, Sch 3; (2000)SWTI 383). The amount of the relief will be £4,420, withdrawn at the rate of £2 for every £3 of income chargeable to income tax at the higher rate.

[2] Relief is restricted to 10% from 1999–2000, 15% from 1995–96 to 1998–99 and 20% for 1994–95 and is given as a reduction in tax liability.

1998-99	1997-98	1996-97	1995-96	1994-95
£4,195	£4,045	£3,765	£3,525[3]	£3,445[3]
£1,900[2] £158·33	£1,830[2] £152·50	£1,790[2] £149·17	£1,720[2] £143·33	£1,720[2] £143·33
£16,200 £5,410	£15,600 £5,220	£15,200 £4,910	£14,600 £4,630	£14,200 £4,200
£18,630	£17,950	£17,490	£16,810	£15,710
£3,305[2]	£3,185[2]	£3,115[2]	£2,995[2]	£2,665[2]
£1,900	£1,830	£1,790	£1,720	£1,720
£19,010 £21,440 £5,600	£18,310 £20,660 £5,400	£17,850 £20,140 £5,090	£17,150 £19,360 £4,800	£16,090 £17,600 £4,370
£19,010	£18,310	£17,850	£17,150	£16,050
£3,345[2]	£3,225[2]	£3,155[2]	£3,035[2]	£2,705[2]
£1,900	£1,830	£1,790	£1,720	£1,720
£19,090 £21,520 £21,900	£18,390 £20,740 £21,100	£17,930 £20,220 £20,580	—[4] £19,440 £19,780	—[4] £17,680 £18,020
£1,900[2]	£1,830[2]	£1,790[2]	£1,720[2]	£1,720[2]
£1,900[2]	£1,830[2]	£1,790[2]	£1,720[2]	£1,720[2]
£1,330	£1,280	£1,250	£1,200	£1,200
£30,000 10%	£30,000 15%	£30,000 15%	£30,000 15%	£30,000 20%
12·5%	12·5%	12·5%	12·5%	12·5%
£3,590	£3,480	£3,430	£3,260	£3,200
£7,310-£25,220 £17,910 @ 6% £1,074·60	£7,010-£24,180 £17,170 @ 6% £1,030·20	£6,860-£23,660 £16,800 @ 6% £1,008	£6,640-£22,880 £16,240 @ 7·3% £1,185·52[5]	£6,490-£22,360 £15,870 @ 7·3% £1,158·51[5]
20% £4,300	20% £4,100	20% £3,900	20% £3,200	20% £3,000
23% £22,800	23% £22,000	24% £21,600	25% £21,100	25% £20,700

[3] Transitional relief: a married man under 65 may in certain circumstances claim a £3,540 personal allowance if his wife was 75 or over on 5 April 1990 (subject to abatement if his total income exceeds £14,200 in 1994-95 or £14,600 in 1995-96).

[4] Varies depending on personal allowance: see above and note[3].

[5] Before 6 April 1996 50% of class 4 contribution paid is deductible from total income.

Car benefits

PRIVATE USE

Basic cash equivalent 1999–2000 and 2000–01*

List price of car plus extra qualifying accessories[1] *less* capital contributions[2] by employee[3,4].

Multiplied by –
35% where business mileage is under 2,500[5] miles.
25% where business mileage is at least 2,500[5] but less than 18,000[5] miles.
15% where business mileage is 18,000[5] miles or more[6].

Adjustments
1 Reduce cash equivalent by –
¼ where car is 4 years old or more at end of year of assessment.
2 Reduce adjusted cash equivalent in **1** proportionately where car is not available throughout year of assessment.
3 Reduce adjusted cash equivalent in **2** by amount of payments by employee for private use.

Basic cash equivalent 1994–95 to 1998–99*

35% x (list price of car plus extra qualifying accessories[1] *less* capital contributions[2] by employee[3])[4].

Adjustments
1 Reduce *basic cash equivalent* by –
1/3 where business mileage is at least 2,500[5] but less than 18,000[5] miles
2/3 where business mileage is 18,000[5] miles or more[6].
2 Reduce *adjusted cash equivalent* in **1** by –
1/3 where car is 4 years old or more at end of year of assessment.
3 Reduce *adjusted cash equivalent* in **2** proportionately where car is not available throughout year of assessment.
4 Reduce *adjusted cash equivalent* in **3** by amount of payments by employee for private use.

[1] Excluding an accessory provided after car was made available if it was provided before 1 August 1993 or its list price was less than £100. From 6 April 1995 accessories designed for use only by disabled people are also excluded. From 1998–99 where a car is manufactured so as to be capable of running on road fuel gas, its price is proportionately reduced by so much of that price as is reasonably attributable to it being manufactured in that way. Where a new car is converted to run on road fuel gas, the equipment is not regarded as an accessory.
[2] Up to £5,000.
[3] List price as adjusted capped at £80,000.
[4] Classic cars (aged 15 years or more and with a market value of £15,000 or more at end of year of assessment): substitute market value at end of year of assessment if this is higher than adjusted list price. £80,000 cap and reduction for capital contributions apply.
[5] Mileage figures are reduced proportionately where car is not available for whole year.
[6] For second and subsequent cars there is no reduction if business mileage is under 18,000 miles; **from 1999-2000** reduce basic cash equivalent to 25% if business mileage is 18,000 miles or more (from 1994-95 to 1998-1999 the basic cash equivalent was reduced by 1/3).

From 6 April 2002: The existing income tax charge based on 35% of the car's price (subject to certain reductions) is to be abolished (1999 Budget). It will be replaced by a charge on a percentage of the car's price graduated according to the level of the car's carbon dioxide emissions measured in grams per kilometre (g/km) and rounded down to the nearest 5 g/km: (2000) SWTI 399. The following table shows how it is proposed that cars will be taxed in the first three years from 2002–03:

CO_2 emissions in grams per kilometre			Percentage of car's price taxed	CO_2 emissions in grams per kilometre			Percentage of car's price taxed
2002–03	2003–04	2004–05		2002–03	2003–04	2004-05	
165	155	145	15[1]	220	210	200	26[1]
170	160	150	16[1]	225	215	205	27[1]
175	165	155	17[1]	230	220	210	28[1]
180	170	160	18[1]	235	225	215	29[1]
185	175	165	19[1]	240	230	220	30[1]
190	180	170	20[1]	245	235	225	31[1]
195	185	175	21[1]	250	240	230	32[1]
200	190	180	22[1]	255	245	235	33[1]
205	195	185	23[1]	260	250	240	34[1]
210	200	190	24[1]	265	255	245	35[1]
215	205	195	25[1]				

Supplement if car runs solely on diesel:
[1]Add 3%. [2]Add 2%. [3]Add 1%. [4]Maximum charge and so no diesel supplement.
The benefit will be reduced for employee contributions up to £5,000 and where the car is unavailable for part of the year. Further details are available on the internet at www.inlandrevenue.gov.uk/cars.
*This formula is also used to calculate the national insurance contributions payable by employers on the benefit of cars they provide for the private use of their employees, see p 87.

FUEL		(For VAT on fuel, see p 94)
2000-01		
Cylinder capacity: (non-diesel cars)	1,400 cc or less Over 1,400 cc up to 2,000 cc Over 2,000 cc	£1,700 £2,170 £3,200
Cylinder capacity: (diesel cars)	2,000 cc or less Over 2,000 cc	£2,170 £3,200
No internal combustion engine		£3,200
1999-2000		
Cylinder capacity: (non-diesel cars)	1,400 cc or less Over 1,400 cc up to 2,000 cc Over 2,000 cc	£1,210 £1,540 £2,270
Cylinder capacity: (diesel cars)	2,000 cc or less Over 2,000 cc	£1,540 £2,270
No internal combustion engine		£2,270
1998-99		
Cylinder capacity: (non-diesel cars)	1,400 cc or less Over 1,400 cc up to 2,000 cc Over 2,000 cc	£1,010 £1,280 £1,890
Cylinder capacity: (diesel cars)	2,000 cc or less Over 2,000 cc	£1,280 £1,890
No internal combustion engine		£1,890
1997-98		
Cylinder capacity: (non-diesel cars)	1,400 cc or less Over 1,400 cc up to 2,000 cc Over 2,000 cc	£800 £1,010 £1,490
Cylinder capacity: (diesel cars)	2,000 cc or less Over 2,000 cc	£740 £940
No internal combustion engine		£1,490
1996-97		
Cylinder capacity: (non-diesel cars)	1,400 cc or less Over 1,400 cc up to 2,000 cc Over 2,000 cc	£710 £890 £1,320
Cylinder capacity: (diesel cars)	2,000 cc or less Over 2,000 cc	£640 £820
No internal combustion engine		£1,320
1995-96:		
Cylinder capacity: (non-diesel cars)	1,400 cc or less Over 1,400 cc up to 2,000 cc Over 2,000 cc	£670 £850 £1,260
Cylinder capacity: (diesel cars)	2,000 cc or less Over 2,000 cc	£605 £780
No internal combustion engine		£1,260
1994-95:		
Cylinder capacity: (non-diesel cars)	1,400 cc or less Over 1,400 cc up to 2,000 cc Over 2,000 cc	£640 £810 £1,200
Cylinder capacity: (diesel cars)	2,000 cc or less Over 2,000 cc	£580 £750
No Internal combustion engine		£1,200

Fuel benefit reduced to *nil* if the employee is required to make good whole cost of private fuel.

Note: From 6 April 1991 this table is also used to calculate the national insurance contributions payable by employers on the benefit of free fuel they provide for the private use of employees, see p 87.

Car benefits — continued

VANS: PRIVATE USE INCLUDING FUEL		
	Under 4 years old[1]	4 years old or more[1]
1993-94 onwards: Vehicle design weight: up to 3.5 tonnes over 3.5 tonnes	£500 —	£350 —

[1] At the end of the relevant year of assessment.

Fixed profit car scheme: tax-free allowances for business travel[1]

Business mileage	Engine size Up to 1,000cc	1,001– 1,500cc	1,501– 2,000cc	Over 2,000cc	One rate[2]
1997-98 to 2000-01:[3,4] Up to 4,000 miles Excess over 4,000 miles	28p 17p	35p 20p	45p 25p	63p 36p	40p 22·5p
1996-97:[3] Up to 4,000 miles Excess over 4,000 miles	27p 16p	34p 19p	43p 23p	61p 33p	38.5p 21p
1995-96:[3] Up to 4,000 miles Excess over 4,000 miles	27p 15p	34p 19p	43p 23p	60p 32p	38.5p 21p
1994-95:[3] Up to 4,000 miles Excess over 4,000 miles	27p 15p	33p 19p	41p 23p	56p 31p	37p 21p
1993-94:[3] Up to 4,000 miles Excess over 4,000 miles	26p 15p	32p 18p	40p 22p	54p 30p	36p 20p
1992-93:[3] Up to 4,000 miles Excess over 4,000 miles	25p 14p	30p 17p	38p 21p	51p 27p	34p 19p

[1] From 1996–97, employees using their own car may claim these rates as a tax-free allowance or as a deduction whether or not their employer operates the scheme (1995) SWTI 1879.

[2] One rate paid irrespective of engine size.

[3] Subject to transitional relief.

[4] The rates remain unchanged for 1998-99 to 2000-01 (IR Press Release of 8 December 1997 (1997) SWTI 1583, 7 December 1998 (1998) SWTI 1692 and 14 December 1999 (2000) SWTI 7).

Pedal cycles: From 6 April 1999, employees using their bicycle for business cycling are allowed to receive a tax-free mileage rate of up to 12p per mile. Where the employee is not paid by the employer for business cycling, the employee is able to claim tax relief on 12p per business mile (or on the balance up to 12p per mile if the employer pays less than this rate (1999) SWTI 430, (2000) SWTI 7).

Motorcycles: From 6 April 2000, employees using their motorcycle for business travel are allowed to receive a tax-free mileage allowance at up to 24p per mile. Where the employee is not paid by the employer for using the motorcycle, the employee is able to claim tax relief on 24p per business mile (or on the balance up to 24p per mile if the employer pays less than this rate (2000) SWTI 7).

Bus services

From 6 April 1999 onwards: No taxable benefit in respect of the provision of works buses with a seating capacity of 12 or more, provided to employees (or their children) to travel to and from work (TA 1988 s 197AA; FA 1999 s 48).

Cycles and cyclist's safety equipment

From 6 April 1999 onwards: No taxable benefit in respect of the provision to employees of bicycles or cycling safety equipment for travel to and from work (TA 1988 s 197AC; FA 1999 s 50).

Parking facilities

No taxable benefit for work place provision of car parking spaces, or, from 6 April 1999, parking for bicycles or motorcycles (TA 1988 ss 141, 142, 155, 197A; FA 1999 s 49).

Mobile telephones

From

6 April 1999 onwards: no taxable benefit

Cash equivalent of benefit from 6 April 1991 to 5 April 1999 £200

Expensive cars: restricted allowances

Writing-down allowances
(CAA 1990 s 34)

From 11 March 1992
Cars costing more than £12,000 and bought outright, on hire purchase or by way of a lease with option to purchase: writing-down allowance limited to £3,000 per annum.

Before 11 March 1992
Cars costing more than £8,000 and bought outright, on hire purchase or by way of a lease with option to purchase: writing-down allowance limited to £2,000 per annum.

Restriction on deduction for hire charge
(CAA 1990 s 35)

From 11 March 1992
If a car costing more than £12,000 is acquired under a rental lease the maximum allowable deduction in computing Schedule D Case I or II profits is —

$$\frac{£12{,}000 + \tfrac{1}{2}(P - £12{,}000)}{P} \times R$$

Before 11 March 1992
If a car costing more than £8,000 was acquired under a rental lease the maximum allowable deduction in computing Schedule D Case I or II profits was —

$$\frac{£8{,}000 + \tfrac{1}{2}(P - £8{,}000)}{P} \times R$$

P = retail price of car when new
R = annual rental

Working families' and disabled person's tax credits

The Working Families Tax Credit (WFTC) and the Disabled Person's Tax Credit (DPTC) were introduced in October 1999 to replace Family Credit and Disability Working Allowance. The tax credits have been payable to working families depending on their circumstances from 5 October 1999 and from April 2000, will be administered by employers and paid through the PAYE system. The credits do not form part of taxable income and normally last for 26 weeks.

Working families' tax credit	Weekly 5.10.99– 10.4.00	Weekly 11.4.00 onwards
	£	£
Adult credit – basic	52.30	53.15
– working 30 hours	11.05	11.25
Child credit – from birth[1]	19.85	21.25
– from Sept after 11th birthday[1]	20.90	21.25
Child credit – from Sept after 16th birthday	25.95	26.35
Childcare credit (70% of eligible costs) – 1 child (max)	100.00	100.00
– 2 or more children (max)	150.00	150.00
Earnings at which credit is reduced by 55%	90,00	91.45
Capital – upper limit	8,000	8,000
– amount disregarded	3,000	3,000

Disabled person's tax credit	Weekly 5.10.99– 10.4.00	Weekly 11.4.00 onwards
	£	£
Adult credit – single	54.30	55.15
– couples/lone parents	83.55	84.90
– working 30 hours	11.05	11.25
Child credit – from birth[1]	19.85	21.25
– from Sept after 11th birthday[1]	20.90	21.25
Child credit – from Sept after 16th birthday	25.95	26.35
Childcare credit (70% of eligible costs) – 1 child (max)	100.00	100.00
– 2 or more children (max)	150.00	150.00
Earnings at which credit is reduced by 55% – single	70.00	71.10
– couples/lone parents	90.00	91.45
– disabled child[2]	21.90	22.25
Capital – upper limit	16,000	16,000
– amount disregarded	3,000	3,000

[1]The tax credits for children under 16 will increase from June 2000 by £4.35 a week.
[2]The additional credit for a disabled child will be extended to WFTC from October 2000.

Flat rate expenses

For most classes of industry flat rate allowances for the upkeep of tools and special clothing have been agreed between the Revenue and the trade unions concerned. Alternatively, the individual employee may claim as a deduction his or her actual expenses (Concession A1). Rates for healthcare and fire service employees have been introduced (see (1999) SWTI 353). They were added to Concession A1 in the 2000 edition of IR1.

Industry code	Industry	Occupation	Deduction from 1991–92 to 1994–95	Deduction from 1995–96
10	Agriculture	All workers	60	70
100	Aluminium	(a) Continual casting operators, process operators, de-dimplers, driers, drill punchers, dross unloaders, firemen, furnace operators and their helpers, leaders, mouldmen, pourers, remelt department labourers, roll flatteners	110	130
		(b) Cable hands, case makers, labourers, mates, truck drivers and measurers, storekeepers	50	60
		(c) Apprentices	40	45
		(d) All other workers	85	100
330	Banks	Uniformed bank employees	30	40
90	Brass and Copper	All workers	85	100
270	Building	(a) Joiners and carpenters	95	105
		(b) Cement works and roofing felt and asphalt labourers	45	55
		(c) Labourers and navvies	30	40
		(d) All other workers	70	85
250	Building Materials	(a) Stone-masons	70	85
		(b) Tilemakers and labourers	30	40
		(c) All other workers	45	55
190	Clothing	(a) Lacemakers, hosiery bleachers, dyers, scourers and knitters, knitwear bleachers and dyers	40	45
		(b) All other workers	25	30
150	Constructional Engineering	(a) Blacksmiths and their strikers, burners, caulkers, chippers, drillers, erectors, fitters, holders up, markers off, platers, riggers, riveters, rivet heaters, scaffolders, sheeters, template workers, turners, welders	95	115
		(b) Banksmen, labourers, shop-helpers, slewers, straighteners	50	60
		(c) Apprentices and storekeepers	40	45
		(d) All other workers	65	75
170	Electrical and Electricity Supply	(a) Those workers incurring laundry costs only (generally CEGB employees)	20	25
		(b) All other workers	75	90
110	Engineering	(a) Pattern makers	105	120
		(b) Labourers, supervisory and unskilled workers	50	60
		(c) Apprentices and storekeepers	40	45
		(d) Motor mechanics in garage repair shops	85	100
		(e) All other workers	85	100
Not known	Fire service (see above)	Uniformed fire fighters and fire officers	45	60
220	Food	All workers	30	40
20	Forestry	All workers	60	70
240	Glass	All workers	50	60
Not known	Healthcare (see above)	(a) Ambulance staff on active service	95	110
		(b) Nurses and midwives, chiropodists, dental nurses, occupational, speech and other therapists, phlebotomists, physiotherapists, radiographers.	60	70
		(c) Plaster room orderlies, hospital porters, ward clerks, sterile supply workers, hospital domestics, hospital catering staff	50	60
		(d) Laboratory staff, pharmacists, pharmacy assistants	40	45
		(e) Uniformed ancillary staff maintenance workers, grounds staff, drivers, parking attendants and security guards, receptionists and other uniformed staff		45
280	Heating	(a) Pipe fitters and plumbers	90	100
		(b) Coverers, laggers, domestic glaziers, heating engineers and their mates	75	90
		(c) All gas workers, all other workers	60	70

Flat rate expenses — continued

Industry code	Industry	Occupation	Deduction from 1991–92 to 1994–95	Deduction from 1995–96
50	Iron Mining	(a) Fillers, miners and underground workers	85	100
		(b) All other workers	65	75
70	Iron and Steel	(a) Day labourers, general labourers, stockmen, time keepers, warehouse staff and weighmen	50	60
		(b) Apprentices	40	45
		(c) All other workers	105	120
210	Leather	(a) Curriers (wet workers), fellmongering workers, tanning operatives (wet)	45	55
		(b) All other workers	30	40
140	Particular Engineering	(a) Pattern makers	105	120
		(b) All chainmakers; cleaners, galvanisers, tinners and wire drawers in the wire drawing industry; tool-makers in the lock making industry	85	100
		(c) Apprentices and storekeepers	40	45
		(d) All other workers	50	60
355	Police Force	Uniformed police officers (ranks up to and including Chief Inspector)	45	55
160	Precious Metals	All workers	60	70
230	Printing	(a) Letterpress Section Electrical engineers (rotary presses), electrotypers, ink and roller makers, machine minders (rotary), maintenance engineers (rotary presses) and stereotypers	90	105
		(b) Bench hands (P & B), compositors (Lp), readers (Lp), T & E Section wire room operators, warehousemen (Ppr box)	25	30
		(c) All other workers	60	70
320	Prisons	Uniformed prison officers	45	55
300	Public Service	(i) Dock and Inland Waterways		
		(a) Dockers, dredger drivers, hopper steerers	45	55
		(b) All other workers	30	40
		(ii) Public Transport		
		(a) Garage hands (including cleaners)	45	55
		(b) Conductors and drivers	30	40
60	Quarrying	All workers	60	70
290	Railways	(See the appropriate category for craftsmen, e.g. engineers, vehicle builders etc.) All other workers	60	70
30	Seamen	(a) Carpenters (Seamen) Passenger liners	140	165
		(b) Carpenters (Seamen) Cargo vessels, tankers, coasters and ferries	110	130
		(c) Other seamen Passenger liners	nil	nil
		(d) Other seamen Cargo vessels, tankers, coasters and ferries	nil	nil
120	Shipyards	(a) Blacksmiths and their strikers, boilermakers, burners, carpenters, caulkers, drillers, furnacemen (platers), holders up, fitters, platers, plumbers, riveters, sheet iron workers, shipwrights, tubers, welders	95	115
		(b) Labourers	50	60
		(c) Apprentices and storekeepers	40	45
		(d) All other workers	65	75
200	Textile Prints	All workers	50	60
180	Textiles	(a) Carders, carding engineers, overlookers (all), technicians in spinning mills	70	85
		(b) All other workers	50	60
130	Vehicles	(a) Builders, railway wagon etc. repairers, and railway wagon lifters	90	105
		(b) Railway vehicle painters and letterers, railway wagon etc. builders' and repairers' assistants	50	60
		(c) All other workers	30	40
260	Wood & Furniture	(a) Carpenters, cabinet makers, joiners, wood carvers and woodcutting machinists	95	115
		(b) Artificial limb makers (other than in wood), organ builders and packing case makers	75	90
		(c) Coopers not providing own tools, labourers, polishers and upholsterers	40	45
		(d) All other workers	65	75

1) 'Industry code' is an industry identification term used for Inland Revenue computer purposes.
2) The expressions 'all workers' and 'all other workers' refer only to manual workers who have to bear the cost of upkeep of tools and special clothing. They do not extend to other employees such as office staff.

Loan benefits and official rate of interest

A director, or an employee earning £8,500 or more a year, who receives a loan by reason of his or her employment may be charged to tax on the cash equivalent of the benefit for the year (TA 1988 s 160, Sch 7).

From 6 April 1994, there is no charge to tax if either:
(a) all the beneficial loans provided by reason of the employment; or
(b) all the beneficial loans, excluding loans qualifying for tax relief, do not exceed £5,000.

The cash equivalent is calculated using the difference between the interest paid (if any) and the official rate of interest.

In January 2000 it was announced that the official rate of interest will be set, in advance, for the whole of the following tax year (although this policy may be changed if typical mortgage rates fall sharply during the year). Under this policy, the official rate of interest is set to remain at 6.25% for 1999-00 and 2000-01: (2000) SWTI 95.

The official rate of interest is set out below.

Date	Rate
From 6 March 1999	6.25%
6 August 1997–5 March 1999	7.25%
6 November 1996–5 August 1997	6.75%
6 June 1996–5 November 1996	7%
6 February 1996–5 June 1996	7.25%
6 October 1995–5 February 1996	7.75%
6 November 1994–5 October 1995	8%
6 January 1994–5 November 1994	7·5%
6 March 1993–5 January 1994	7·75%
6 January 1993–5 March 1993	8·25%
6 December 1992–5 January 1993	9%
6 November 1992–5 December 1992	9·75%
6 June 1992–5 November 1992	10·5%
6 March 1992–5 June 1992	10·75%
6 October 1991–5 March 1992	11·25%
6 August 1991–5 October 1991	11·75%
6 July 1991–5 August 1991	12·25%
6 May 1991–5 July 1991	12·75%
6 April 1991–5 May 1991	13·5%
6 March 1991–5 April 1991	14·5%
6 November 1990–5 March 1991	15·5%
6 November 1989–5 November 1990	16·5%
6 July 1989–5 November 1989	15·5%
6 January 1989–5 July 1989	14·5%
6 October 1988–5 January 1989	13·5%
6 August 1988–5 October 1988	12%
6 May 1988–5 August 1988	9·5%
6 December 1987–5 May 1988	10·5%
6 September 1987–5 December 1987	11·5%
6 June 1987–5 September 1987	10·5%
6 April 1987–5 June 1987	11·5%
6 October 1982–5 April 1987	12%

	1993–94	1994–95	1995–96	1996–97	1997–98	1998–99
Average official rate of interest	7·688%	7·7%	7·79%	6·93%	7·08%	7·16%

Note
From 6 April 1994, loans made on commercial terms by employers who lend predominantly to the general public are generally exempt.

Foreign currency loans

Currency	Date	Rate
Swiss franc	From 6 July 1994	5·5%
	6 June 1994 – 5 July 1994	5·7%
Japanese yen	From 6 June 1994	3·9%

Loans of computer equipment

From 6 April 1999 onwards: No taxable benefit in respect of loan to employees (provided loans are not restricted to directors or senior staff) of computer equipment for private home use, the value of the equipment and related expenses not to exceed £2,500 (TA 1988; s 156A; FA 1999, s 45).

Relocation expenses and benefits

Qualifying removal benefits and expenses[1]

Date of move	Limit
After 5 April 1993	£8,000

[1] The statutory relief covers the following expenses and benefits (TA 1988 Sch 11A) —

  (a) *disposal expenses and benefits* (legal and advertising expenses in connection with the disposal of accommodation, penalty for redeeming a mortgage, auctioneers' and estate agents' fees, disconnection of public utilities, rent, maintenance and insurance costs while the property is unoccupied);

  (b) *acquisition expenses and benefits* (legal expenses in connection with the acquisition of an interest in a new main residence, loan fees, mortgage indemnity insurance costs, survey and land registry fees, stamp duty, connection of public utilities). (NB: similar expenses and benefits are covered in respect of abortive acquisitions, if the property would have been the employee's new residence but the acquisition does not proceed either for reasons outside the employee's control or because he or she reasonably declines to proceed);

  (c) *transportation of domestic belongings* (including insurance costs);

  (d) *travelling and subsistence expenses and benefits* (for temporary visits to new residence before relocation; travel from old residence to new place of work or from new residence to old place of work where date of move and relocation of work do not coincide; subsistence and travel costs of child under 19 relocating before or after parents for educational reasons; benefit of a car or van for use in connection with the relocation where it is not otherwise available for private use);

  (e) *bridging loan expenses and beneficial bridging loans* (relief is given on any charge to interest at the official rate on a beneficial loan to the extent that the aggregate value of other qualifying benefits and expenses falls short of the maximum exempt amount);

  (f) *duplicate expenses and benefits in respect of new residence* (replacement domestic items).

Employers' contributions for moves to higher cost housing areas (before 6 April 1993)[1]

Date of move	Maximum contribution £
2 February 1993–5 April 1993	13,440
1 November 1991–1 February 1993	18,060
1 June 1991–31 October 1991	20,370
1 December 1990–31 May 1991	22,680
6 April 1990–30 November 1990	24,150
1 December 1989–5 April 1990	22,890
1 February 1989–30 November 1989	21,210

[1] Exempt amounts under Concession A67. Under transitional provisions, the concessionary relief continued to be available, as an alternative to the statutory relief (see above), where the employee was committed to relocate before 6 April 1993 and actually started work at the new location before 1 August 1993.

Disturbance allowances (before 6 April 1993)[1]

Category	Maximum amount	
	1.4.91–31.3.92 £	1.4.92–5.4.93 £
Married householder	2,550	2,655
Single householder	1,550	1,615
Single non-householder	600	625

[1] Exempt amounts under Concession A5. Under transitional provisions, the concessionary relief continued to be available, as an alternative to the statutory relief (see above), where the employee was committed to relocate before 6 April 1993 and actually started work at the new location before 1 August 1993.

Approved employee share schemes

Inland Revenue share schemes web page: www.inlandrevenue.gov.uk/shareschemes

All-employee share scheme

(It is proposed that the scheme will be introduced in the 2000 Finance Bill: (1999) SWTI 447, 1803, Budget Resolution 29)

Free share plan

	Annual maximum
From 2000-01	£3,000

Partnership share plan

	Annual maximum
From 2000-01	£1,500

Matching shares

From 2000-01	Maximum number of shares given by employer to employee for each partnership share bought	2

Reliefs

Where the conditions of the scheme are complied with–
(a) Free share plans: employers can give shares to employees free of income tax and national insurance contributions. (Some or all of these shares may be awarded for reaching performance targets.)
(b) Partnership share plans: employees may allocate part of their pre-tax salary to buy shares in their employing company without income tax or national insurance contributions being payable.
(c) Generally, all shares held in a plan for five years, will be free of income tax and national insurance contributions.
(d) No capital gains tax is payable on the withdrawal of shares from the plan and they are deemed to be acquired at their market value at that time.
(e) If shares are taken out of a plan within between three and five years, income tax and national insurance contributions will be payable on the lower of their initial value and their value on leaving the plan.
(f) Dividends paid on the shares are tax free (up to a £1,500 annual limit) provided they are used to acquire additional shares in the company.
(g) The costs of the plan will be deductible from profits for tax purposes.

Main conditions for relief

1 There is a limit on the value of the shares that can be purchased or allocated under the scheme.
2 Free and matching shares must normally be kept in the plan for at least three years. (Employees can take partnership shares out of the plan at any time.)
3 Shares must be taken out of the plan when the employee ceases to be employed by the company. (Some employees may lose their free and matching shares if they leave within thee years of getting the shares.)

Approved profit sharing schemes

(TA 1988 ss 186, 187, Sch 9, 10)

Profit sharing schemes will continue to be approved where applications for approval are received by the Revenue before 6 April 2001. Tax free awards of shares under approved schemes will continue to be allowed up to 5 April 2002 (2000) SWTI 387.)

Annual limit on shares appropriated

From 1991–92:	Greater of £3,000 or 10% of salary, up to £8,000
1989–90 and 1990–91:	Greater of £2,000 or 10% of salary, up to £6,000
1988–89:	Greater of £1,250 or 10% of salary, up to £5,000

Schedule E charge on early disposal or receipt of capital from shares

Time of disposal or capital receipt	Percentage charge[1]
Before 3rd anniversary of appropriation[2]	100%[3]

[1] Calculated on the appropriate percentage of the initial market value of the shares when appropriated (or the sales proceeds if less).

[2] If that anniversary falls on or after 29 April 1996. If the 3rd anniversary of the appropriation falls before that date but the 5th anniversary falls after it, the 100% charge arises if the disposal or capital receipt takes place before 29 April 1996. Where the 5th anniversary fell before 29 April 1996, the following charges applied:

Time of disposal or capital receipt	Percentage charge
Before 4th anniversary of appropriation	100%[4]
Between 4th and 5th anniversary of appropriation	75%[4]
After 5th anniversary of appropriation	nil

[3] The charge is reduced to 50% where the employee reaches the retirement age specified in the scheme rules or leaves the employment due to injury, disability or redundancy before the shares are sold or capital is received.

[4] The charge was reduced to 50% where the employee reached the retirement age specified in the scheme rules or left the employment due to injury, disability or redundancy within 5 years of the appropriation.

Approved employee share schemes — continued

Reliefs

Where the conditions of the scheme are satisfied, no Schedule E charge arises on the employee in respect of –

    (a) the value of the shares at the time of appropriation;

    (b) any increase in the value of the shares; or

    (c) any gain on the disposal of the shares (although capital gains tax is chargeable on any gain over the market value on appropriation).

Main conditions for relief

1   Shares in a company (or its parent company) must be acquired by trustees of the scheme and allocated to employee participants.

2   All employees must be eligible to participate on similar terms (subject to a minimum service requirement of up to 5 years and material interest exclusions).

3   The annual value of shares appropriated must not exceed the statutory maximum (see above).

4   The shares used in the scheme must be fully paid up, not redeemable and not subject to special restrictions.

5   Participants must permit the scheme trustees to hold the shares for the retention period (two years from the date of appropriation, unless the participant ceases to be employed before that date by reason of injury, disability, redundancy, retirement or death).

6   Shares disposed of within a specified period are subject to a Schedule E charge (see above).

Approved savings related share option schemes

(TA 1988 ss 185, 187, Sch 9)

Monthly contributions to SAYE scheme

	Maximum £	Minimum £
1 October 1998[3]	250	5–10[2]
1 April 1996–30 September 1998[1]	250	5–10[2]
1 September 1991–31 March 1996[1]	250	10 or under
1 September 1989–31 August 1991	150	10 or under

[1] The Treasury issued a new prospectus in April 1996: Booklet IR98 para 5.4.
[2] The company may choose a minimum savings contribution between £5 and £10.
[3] The Treasury issued a new prospectus applying from 1 October 1998 (see (1998) SWTI 1118)

Approved SAYE contracts: bonus and interest payments on termination

Date of termination	Amount payable – contracts to 30 September 1998	Amount payable – contracts from 1 October
3-year contract		
After at least 1 but less than 3 years	Refund of contributions plus simple interest at 3% p.a.	Refund of contributions plus simple interest at 3% p.a.
After 3 years	Refund of contributions plus bonus of 3 months' contributions	Refund of contribuitions plus bonus of 2·75 times the monthly contributions
5-year contract		
After at least 1 but less than 5 years	Refund of contributions plus simple interest at 3% p.a.	Refund of contributions plus simple interest at 3% p.a.
After 5 years	Refund of contributions plus bonus of 9 months' contributions	Refund of contributions plus bonus of 7·5 times the monthly contributions
After at least 5 but less than 7 years	Refund of contributions plus bonus of 9 months' contributions and compound interest at 3% p.a. for period after first 5 years	Refund of contributions plus bonus of 7·5 times the monthly contributions and compound interest at 3% p.a. for period after first 5 years
After 7 years	Refund of contributions plus bonus of 18 months' contributions	Refund of contributions plus bonus of 13·5 times the monthly contributions

Reliefs

Where the conditions of the scheme are complied with, no Schedule E charge arises on the employee in respect of –

    (a) the grant of an option to acquire shares;

    (b) the exercise of the option; or

    (c) any increase in the value of the shares.

Capital gains tax is chargeable on disposal of the shares: the CGT base cost is the consideration given by the employee for both the shares and the option.

Approved employee share schemes — continued

Main conditions for relief

1 All full time employees must be eligible to participate on similar terms (subject to a minimum service requirement of up to 5 years and material interest exclusions).
2 The scheme must provide for shares to be paid for with an amount of money not exceeding the repayments, bonuses and interest payments made under a linked SAYE scheme.
3 The scheme shares must be fully paid up, not redeemable and not subject to special restrictions.
4 Subject to cessation of employment due to injury, disability, redundancy, retirement or death, share options must not be exercised before the bonus date under the SAYE scheme (3, 5 or 7 years after its commencement, see above).
5 The purchase price of the shares must be stated at the time the option is granted and must not be manifestly less than 80% of their market value.

Company share option plans

(TA 1988 ss 185, 187 and Sch 9; FA 1996 s 114 and Sch 16)

Limit on value of shares under option held by employee at any one time

From 29 April 1996	£30,000

Reliefs

Where the conditions of the scheme are complied with, no Schedule E charge arises on the employee in respect of –
   (a) the grant of an option to acquire shares;
   (b) the exercise of the option; or
   (c) any increase in the value of the shares.
Capital gains tax is chargeable on disposal of the shares: the CGT base cost is the consideration given by the employee for both the shares and the option.

Main conditions for relief

1 There is a limit (see above) on the value of shares under option held by an employee at any one time (the value being that of the shares at the time the options are granted).
2 Options must be granted at a share price not manifestly less than the market value at the date of the grant.
3 The scheme shares must be fully paid up, not redeemable and not subject to special restrictions.
4 Only full time directors or qualifying employees may participate in the scheme.
5 Options must be exercised between 3 and 10 years after the grant, and not less than 3 years after the last exercise by the participator of an option (under the same or another approved company share option plan).

Enterprise management incentives

(It proposed that the scheme will be introduced in the 2000 Finance Bill: see (1999) SWTI 1804)

To take effect from the date of Royal Assent to FA 2000.
It is proposed that independent trading companies with gross assets not exceeding £15 million will be able to grant share options to up to 15 key employees, each receiving options over shares worth up to £100,000 at the time of the grant. The share options will normally be free of income tax for the employee and there will normally be no national insurance charges for employer or employee. Capital gains tax will be payable when the shares are sold, but business assets tapering relief (see p 37) will be available and will begin to run from the date on which the options are granted.

Executive share option schemes

(TA 1988 ss 185, 187, Sch 9)

NOTE: The income tax relief in respect of the grant and exercise of options under executive schemes was withdrawn with effect for options granted after 17 July 1995, subject to transitional provisions (see Revenue Press Release dated 28 November 1995). In general, options granted under an approved scheme after 16 July 1995 qualify for tax relief only if they meet the conditions for approved company share option plans (see above).

Limit on market value of unexercised options

Greater of £100,000 or 4 times emoluments subject to PAYE (excluding benefits).

Reliefs

Where the conditions of the scheme are satisfied, no Schedule E charge arises on the employee in respect of –
   (a) the grant or exercise of the option; or
   (b) any increase in value of the shares.
Capital gains tax is chargeable on disposal of the shares: the CGT base cost is the consideration given by the employee for both the shares and the option.

Main conditions for relief

1 The market value of shares over which a participant holds unexercised options must not exceed the statutory limit (see above).
2 The purchase price of the shares must be stated at the time the option is granted and must not be manifestly less than 85% of their market value.
3 The scheme shares must be fully paid up, not redeemable and not subject to special restrictions.
4 Only full time directors or qualifying employees may participate in the scheme.
5 Options must be exercised between 3 and 10 years after the grant, and not less than 3 years after the last exercise by the participator of an option (under the same or another approved executive scheme).

Profit-related pay schemes

(TA 1988 ss 169–184, Sch 8; FA 1997, s 61; FA 1998 s 62)

Limit on tax-free pay

Profit period beginning	Exempt amount
After 31 December 1999	no relief
1 January 1999–31 December 1999	lowest of: profit-related pay, 20% of earnings[1] and £1,000
1 January 1998–31 December 1998	lowest of: profit-related pay, 20% of earnings[1] and £2,000
31 March 1991–31 December 1997	lowest of: profit-related pay, 20% of earnings[1] and £4,000
1 April 1989–31 March 1991	lowest of: half profit-related pay, 10% of earnings[1] and £2,000
Before 1 April 1989	lowest of: half profit-related pay, 10% of earnings[1] and £1,500

[1] Emoluments within PAYE (excluding benefits) plus profit-related pay.

Main conditions for relief

1 The scheme must be registered. Schemes can only be established for private sector employments.
2 A scheme must relate to an employment unit (all or part of a business).
3 A scheme must define eligible employees and include at least 80% of the employees in the employment unit.
4 The scheme must operate by reference to defined profit periods and must define the method of calculation of the distributable pool of profit-related pay.

Payments on termination or variation of employment

Exempt lump sum payments

(a) Payments in connection with the cessation of employment on the death, injury or disability of the employee.
(b) Payments under unapproved retirement benefits schemes where the employee has been taxed on the actual or notional contributions to provide the benefit.
(c) Payments under approved retirement benefits schemes which can properly be regarded as a benefit earned by past service.
(d) Certain payments of terminal grants to members of the armed forces.
(e) Certain benefits under superannuation schemes for civil servants in Commonwealth overseas territories.
(f) Payments in respect of foreign service where the period of foreign service comprises –
   (i) 75% of the whole period of service; or
  (ii) the whole of the last 10 years of service; or
 (iii) where the period of service exceeded 20 years, one-half of that period, including any 10 of the last 20 years.
Otherwise, a proportion of the payment is exempt, as follows –

$$\frac{\text{length of foreign service}}{\text{length of total service}} \times \text{amount otherwise chargeable}$$

(g) The first £30,000 of genuine ex gratia payments (where there is no "arrangement" by the employer to make the payment).
(h) Statutory redundancy payments (included in computing £30,000 limit in (f) above).

Personal pension schemes and retirement annuities

Approval of contracts

Trades and professions for which an early retirement age has been agreed by the Revenue under TA 1988 s 620(4)(c) for the purpose of the approval of retirement annuity contracts are set out below. Under the personal pension schemes legislation, individuals may not take benefits from their pension arrangements before the age of 50. The trades and professions listed below for which the Revenue has approved an earlier retirement age of 30, 35, 40 or 45 have been approved under TA 1988 s 634(3)(b) for the purposes of personal pension schemes.

Retirement age	Profession or occupation		
30	skiers (downhill) *(personal pension schemes only)*		
35	athletes badminton players boxers cyclists dancers	footballers ice hockey players models national hunt jockeys Rugby League players Rugby Union players squash players	table tennis players tennis players (including real tennis) wrestlers
40	cricketers divers (saturation, deep sea and free swimming)	golfers motocross motorcycle riders motorcycle road racing riders	motor racing drivers speedway riders trapeze artists WPBSA snooker players
45	jockeys (flat racing)	Members of the reserve forces	

50	circus animal trainers
	croupiers
	interdealer brokers
	martial arts instructors
	moneybroker dealers
		newscasters (ITV)
		off-shore riggers (mechanical
		  fitters, pipe fitters, riggers,
		  platers, welders and
		  roustabouts)
			Royal Navy reservists
			Rugby League referees
			territorial army members

55	air pilots
	brass instrumentalists
	distant water
	  trawlermen
	firemen (part-time)
	health visitors (female)
		inshore fishermen
		midwives (female)
		moneybroker dealer
		  managers and directors
		nurses (female)
		physiotherapists (female)
			psychiatrists (who are also
			  maximum part time
			  specialists employed
			  within the NHS solely
			  in the treatment of the
			  mentally disordered)
			singers

Maximum limits for qualifying premiums

Personal pension schemes	
1989–90 to 2000–01	
Age in years at beginning of year of assessment	*Maximum percentage*
35 and below	17½
36 to 45	20
46 to 50	25
51 to 55	30
56 to 60	35
61 or more	40

1994–95 earnings cap £76,800
1995–96 earnings cap £78,600
1996–97 earnings cap £82,200
1997–98 earnings cap £84,000
1998–99 earnings cap £87,600
1999–00 earnings cap £90,600
2000–01 earnings cap £91,800

Retirement annuities	
1987–88 to 2000–01	
Age in years at beginning of year of assessment	*Maximum percentage*
50 and below	17½
51 to 55	20
56 to 60	22½
61 or more	27½

Note *retirement annuities:* contracts for dependants or life insurance—maximum percentage 5%; *personal pension schemes:* life insurance—maximum percentage 5%.

Partnership retirement annuities

The earned income limit for a retirement annuity paid to a former partner is 50% of the average of his or her share of the partnership profits in the best 3 of the last 7 years in which he or she was a partner (TA 1988 s 628).

From 1980–81 the limit is increased by the percentage increase in the RPI from the December in the year of retirement to the December preceding the year of assessment.

From 1982–83 the former partner's share of the profits in the first 6 of the last 7 years in which he or she was a partner is increased by the percentage increase in the RPI from the December in the relevant year to the December in the seventh year.

The retail prices index is printed on p 50.

Maintenance payments

From 6 April 2000: The transitional relief for payments under pre 15 March 1988 arrangements is ended. Payments are treated in the same way as payments under maintenance arrangements set up on or after 15 March 1988. Tax relief will only be given after 5 April 2000 if one or both parties to the marriage is aged 65 or over at 5 April 2000 (the test that applies for the receipt of a married person's allowance after that date, see p 54).

For court orders or agreements made on or after 15 March 1988, or applied for before 15 March but made after 30 June 1988, relief is given to the payer only up to an amount equal to the minimum annual married couple's allowance (£2,000 for 2000-01) and provided that the payment is to *the divorced or separated spouse*. The payments are made gross and the recipient is exempt from tax in respect of them.

Before 1994–95 the relief was given as a deduction from total income. From 1994–95 onwards it is given as a reduction in tax liability calculated as the appropriate percentage of the amount of the relief.

For 1994–95, the tax relief given to the payer was limited to the 20% lower rate. From 1995–96 the tax relief was limited to 15% and for 1999-2000 it was limited to 10%.

Medical insurance premiums

From 6 April 1990 to 1 July 1997, individuals were entitled to tax relief on premiums paid under an eligible contract for private medical insurance for UK resident individuals aged 60 or over (FA 1989 s 54). For premiums paid after 5 April 1994 relief was restricted to the basic rate, given by deduction from the premium; there was no higher rate relief. Until that date basic rate relief was given by deduction at source and higher rate relief had to be claimed.

Tax relief on such premiums is abolished for policies taken out, or renewed, after **1 July 1997** (except where arrangements were made before 2 July 1997 and the relevant contract was made, with the premium being at least partly paid, before 1 August 1997 or where a contract that had come to an end before 2 July 1997 is renewed before 1 August 1997 and the premium is at least partly paid by that date). See F(No2)A 1997 s 17.

National Savings Bank interest

First £70 of interest on deposits (other than investment deposits) is exempt (TA 1988 s 325).

Rent-a-room scheme

Subject to a maximum, gross annual receipts from letting furnished accommodation in the only or main home are exempt from tax. If the receipts exceed the maximum, the taxpayer can pay tax on the gross receipts after deduction of expenses or on the amount by which the receipts exceed the maximum, without relief for the actual expenses. An individual's maximum is halved if during the basis period for the year some other person received income from letting accommodation in that property. (F(No 2) A 1992 Sch 10.)

	Maximum amount
6 April 1997 onwards	£4,250
6 April 1992–5 April 1997	£3,250

Schedule E assessments

Persons domiciled in UK	Services performed			
	Wholly in UK	Partly in UK	Partly abroad	Wholly abroad
Non-resident	All	That part	None	None
Resident but not ordinarily resident	All	That part	Remittances	Remittances
Resident and ordinarily resident	All	All[1]	All[1]	All[1]
Persons domiciled outside UK	UK employer	As for person domiciled in UK.		
	Foreign employer	*Non-resident* All UK earnings. *Resident (not ordinarily resident)*—All UK earnings. (Remittances for duties performed outside UK.) *Resident (and ordinarily resident)* All earnings. (Remittances if all duties performed outside UK.)		

[1] Before 17 March 1998, exempt if qualifying period of over 364 days mostly abroad. The relief for seafarers continues after that date (FA 1998 s 63). Special relief for employees forced to return early from Kuwait or Iraq who had intended to work abroad for over 364 days.

Thresholds: PAYE and national insurance

	1993–94	1994–95	1995–96	1996–97	1997–98	1998-99	1999-2000	2000-01
PAYE[1]: Weekly	£66·50	£66·50	£68·00	£72·50	£78·00	£80·50	£83·00	£84·00
Monthly	£287·00	£287·00	£294·00	£314·00	£337·00	£350·00	£361·00	£365·00
National Insurance[2]: Weekly	£56·00	£57·00	£58·00	£61·00	£62·00	£64·00	£66·00	£76·00
Monthly	£243·00	£247·00	£252·00	£265·00	£269·00	£278·00	£286·00	£329.00

[1] From 1999-2000 these are also the earnings thresholds for employers for national insurance contributions.
[2] For employees only from 1999-2000.

Uniform allowances[1]

	1992–93 £	1993–94 £	1994–95 £	From 1995–96 £
Royal Navy and Royal Marines				
RN officers of flag rank and equivalent RM officers..	1,026·72	1,043·52	1,068·94	1,071·00
RN and RM below flag rank	790·68	802·08	798·84	792·12
WRNS officers (non-seagoing)	540·12	583·56	514·20	680·52
WRNS officers (seagoing)	609·12	661·56	646·56	853·80
Women medical and dental officers RN	455·76	516·36	452·16	567·48
QARNNS officers: female officers: matron and above..	588·00	731·88	572·88	544·68
below matron	875·64	963·48	821·28	828·00
male officers:				
chief nursing officer and above	475·08	488·40	527·28	489·36
below chief nursing officer	444·00	454·92	493·56	456·48
Army				
Officers serving at mounted duty with Household Cavalry and King's Troop RHA	909·92	973·93	1,012·88	1,012·88
Male dismounted officers: colonel and above	665·75	720·95	749·78	749·78
below colonel	623·22	566·63	673·19	673·19
Household Division	—	647·30	—	—
except Household Division.	—	566·63	589·29	589·29
Female QARANC: nursing officers colonels and above	623·24	627·76	671·48	671·48
non-nursing officers colonels and above	—	—	—	—
nursing officers below colonel	606·18	645·66	652·87	652·87
non-nursing officers below colonel	—	—	—	—
Female officers: colonels and above (except QARANC above)	—	480·62	499·84	499·84
below colonel (except QARANC above)	—	469·52	488·30	488·30
WRAC women officers: colonel and above	466·35	—	—	—
below colonel	438·03	—	—	—
RAMC and RADC women officers: colonel and above	—	—	—	—
below colonel	—	—	—	—
Male officers SSVC, SSLC	167·44	179·38	186·55	186·55
Women officers SSVC, SSLC	186·54	193·47	201·20	201·20
RAF				
RAF and PMRAFNS (male):				
air officers	375·48	375·48	445·68	422·76
group captains	363·60	363·60	427·56	402·72
wing commanders and below	336·36	336·36	392·52	361·10
PMRAFNS (female): air officers	461·16	461·16	624·00	589·16
group captains	445·20	445·20	621·00	586·00
wing commanders and below	439·68	439·68	615·24	579·70
WRAF and RAF (female):				
air officers	406·56	406·56	500·16	477·98
group captains	392·64	392·64	452·40	460·74
wing commanders and below	347·52	347·52	443·40	421·69

[1] Allowances have not changed from 1995-96 pending a review of the system for the provision of allowances.

Charities

Gift aid
(FA 1990 s 25)
The gift aid scheme was introduced with effect from 1 October 1990. It gives higher rate relief for an individual donor and corporation tax relief for a corporate donor. The charity claims repayment of basic rate income tax on the grossed up amount of the donation.

Extension of gift aid from 6 April 2000
(2000 Budget Resolutions 25, 26; (2000) SWTI 467)
From 6 April 2000, gift aid is extended to all donations to charity, including one-off gifts, made by UK-taxpayers (individuals or companies). There is no minimum limit for donations. Donors (who may be resident or non-resident) will have to make a declaration that they are UK taxpayers if the charity is to claim the repayment of basic rate income tax on the gift. One declaration can cover a series of donations to the same charity. Donors will be able to join the scheme by phone or the internet. It is no longer necessary for companies to deduct income tax from their donations and for the recipient charity to claim back the tax.

Limits on relief

Individuals and close companies	Minimum	Maximum
From 6 April 2000	—	—
16 March 1993–5 April 2000	£250	—
7 May 1992–15 March 1993	£400	—

Millennium gift aid
Introduced by FA 1998 s 48 and extended by FA 1999 s 56. Tax relief is given on donations by individuals to charities undertaking education and anti-poverty projects in 80 'low income countries'. The charities must be registered with the Revenue. The scheme was set up to run from 31 July 1998 to 31 December 2000 (SI 1998 No 1868). FA 1999 extended Millennium gift aid to gifts of money to relieve refugee poverty. Gifts made by instalment are aggregated and treated as a single payment made in the tax year in which the first instalment was made (FA 1999 s 57).

Limits on relief

	Minimum
Single gift or aggregate of smaller gifts made by individual in one tax year	£100

See now 'Extention of gift aid from 6 April 2000' above.

Covenants
(2000 Budget Resolution 27)
Because of the extension of the gift aid scheme from 6 April 2000, charitable covenants are in effect treated as regular donations by gift aid. For payments under a charitable covenant falling due before 6 April 2000 to be tax-effective, the covenant had to be for a period capable of exceeding three years (there are no monetary limits). With the introduction of the extended gift aid provisions, however, the separate tax relief for payments under covenants is withdrawn and all relief for such payments falling due on or after 6 April 2000 is given under the gift aid scheme.

Payroll giving
(TA 1988 s 202; SI 1986 No 2211; (2000) SWTI 337, 467)
Under the payroll giving scheme, employees authorise their employer to deduct charitable donations from their pay and receive tax relief on their donation at their top rate of tax. The government will add a supplement to donations for three years from April 2000.

Limits on relief

	Maximum
From 6 April 2000	—
6 April 1996–5 April 2000	£1,200
6 April 1993–5 April 1996	£900
6 April 1990–5 April 1993	£600

Government supplement

6 April 2000–5 April 2003	10%

Gifts in kind
Relief introduced by FA 1991 (TA 1988, s 84) for gifts by traders to educational establishments of plant or machinery either manufactured and sold or used for the purposes of the trade.
Millennium Gift Aid Scheme, tax relief introduced by FA 1998 s 47 for businesses to donate goods to help education projects and projects undertaken for medical purposes in eighty "low income countries" from 31 July 1998. From 27 July 1999, this relief is extended by FA 1999 s 55 (TA 1988, s 83A) to donations of goods or plant and machinery to any type of charity.

Gifts of shares and securities
From 6 April 2000, relief is available where a person disposes of listed shares and securities, unit trust units, AIM shares, etc. to a charity by way of a gift or sale at an undervalue. The amount deductible from total income is the market value of the shares etc. on the date of disposal plus incidental disposal costs less any consideration or vlaue of benefits received by the donor or a connected person. This is in addition to any capital gains tax relief. ((1999) SWTI 1819; (2000) SWTI 337, 467).

Inheritance tax relief see p 81.
Capital gains tax see p 36.

Reliefs for investments

Enterprise investment scheme

(Shares issued after 31 December 1993: TA 1988 ss 289–312; FA 1997 Sch 8 as revised from 1998–99 by FA 1998 ss 70, 71, 74, Sch 13 and as amended from 1999–2000 by FA 1999, ss 71–73, Schs 7, 8; 2000 Budget Resolution 36.)

Relief on investment

Maximum investment:	From 1998–99	£150,000
	1994–95	£100,000
	1993–94	£40,000[1]
Minimum investment:	From 1993–94	£500
Maximum carryback to preceding year	From 1998–99	½ amount invested between 6 April and 5 October (maximum £25,000)
	1994–95	½ amount invested between 6 April and 5 October (maximum £15,000)
Rate of relief	From 1993–94	20%[2]

[1] Applied to total enterprise investment and business expansion scheme investments for 1993–94.
[2] Given as a reduction in income tax liability.

Other reliefs

(a) Gains on the first disposal of shares on which EIS relief has not been withdrawn are exempt from capital gains tax.

(b) Reinvestment relief (ie deferral relief under TCGA 1992 Sch 5B) is available for gains on assets where the disposal proceeds are reinvested in eligible shares in a qualifying company. (It was announced in the 1999 Budget that CGT tapering relief will be calculated in accordance with the combined periods of ownership of the first and second investments (and any subsequent qualifying periods of reinvestment) where the shares in the first EIS company were issued after 5 April 1998 and disposed of after 5 April 1999: see (1999) SWTI 450.)

(c) A loss on the first disposal of shares from which EIS relief has not been withdrawn may be relieved against income tax or capital gains tax.

Main conditions for relief

1 The relief is available for subscriptions in cash to new ordinary fully paid-up shares in a qualifying company with no present or future right of redemption and no present or future preferential right to dividends or to the company's assets on a winding-up, throughout a five-year period from the date of issue.

2 The investor must hold the shares for three years from the date of issue where shares are issued after 5 April 2000. (The previous limit was five years.) He or she must not be connected with the issuing company, or receive value from it, at any time during the period beginning two years before the date of the share issue and ending five years after the share issue date.

3 The money subscribed must be used wholly for the purpose of a qualifying business activity within 12 months of the share issue date (or, where the company commences a qualifying trade within 12 months of the share issue date, within 12 months of the commencement).

4 The business activity must be carried on wholly or mainly in the UK for three years after the share issue date (or after the commencement of the trade, if later), unless there is a bona fide liquidation or receivership.

5 Throughout the period beginning with the share issue date and ending three years after that date (or, if later, three years after the date on which its qualifying business activity commences), the company must

(a) be unquoted;

(b) exist for a qualifying purpose;

(c) have fully paid up capital; and

(d) not be controlled by another company, or control another company (apart from a qualifying subsidiary). Under the provisions of FA 1997 Sch 8, a parent company may qualify if non-qualifying activities do not form a substantial part of the group's activities *as a whole.*

6 For shares issued after 1 July 1997, no arrangement must exist before or at the time of issue for the disposal of shares in the company, the disposal of the company's assets, the ending of the company's trade or a guarantee of the shareholders' investment.

Business expansion scheme

(Shares issued before 1 January 1994: TA 1988 ss 289–312 as originally enacted)

Relief on investment

Maximum investment:	£40,000[1]
Minimum investment:	£500
Maximum carryback to preceding year	½ amount invested between 6 April and 5 October (maximum £5,000)
Rate of relief	Up to 40%[2]

[1] Applied to total enterprise investment and business expansion scheme investments for 1993–94.
[2] Given as a deduction from total income.

Reliefs for investments — continued

Other reliefs

Capital gains relief: gains on the first disposal of shares on which BES relief has not been withdrawn are exempt from capital gains tax.
Loss relief (shares issued after 18 March 1986): none.

Main conditions for relief

As for the enterprise investment scheme (see above), except that the investor had to be UK resident and ordinarily resident in the year in which the shares were issued and the company had to be UK resident throughout the three-year period from the share issue date. There was no time limit for using the funds raised.

Venture capital trusts

(TA 1988 ss 332A, 842AA, Sch 15B, Sch 28B; TCGA 1992 ss 151A, 151B, Sch 5C; FA 1997 Sch 9; FA 1998 ss 70, 72, 73, Sch 12; FA 1999 ss 69, 70; 2000 Budget Resolution 37.)

Relief on investment

Maximum annual investment:	From 1995–96	£100,000
Rate of relief:	From 1995–96	20%[1]

[1] Given as a reduction in income tax liability. The rate of relief is an amount equal to the 'lower rate' of income tax for the year of assessment in respect of which the claim is made (TA 1988 Sch 15B para 1). The lower rate of income tax for 1999-2000 is 20% as defined by TA 1988 ss 1A, 832(1); FA 1999 s 22.

Other reliefs

(a) Dividends on shares within investment limit exempt from income tax (unless the investor's main purpose is tax avoidance – from 9 March 1999).
(b) Gains on share disposals exempt from capital gains tax (subject to investment limit).
(c) Reinvestment relief is available for gains on assets where the disposal proceeds are reinvested in a venture capital trust.

Main conditions for relief

1   The investment must be in new eligible shares: that is, ordinary shares which, in the five-year period from the issue date, carry no present or future preferential right to dividends or to a return of assets on the winding-up of the trust and no present or future right to redemption.
2   The investor must be an individual, aged 18 or over. He or she must hold the shares for three years from the date of issue where the shares are issued after 5 April 2000. (The previous minimum holding period was five years.)
3   The trust must satisfy the following conditions for approval by the Revenue –
  (a)   it must not be a close company;
  (b)   its income must be derived wholly or mainly (at least 70%) from investments in shares or securities;
  (c)   at least 70% by value of its investments must comprise "qualifying holdings" (newly issued shares in unquoted companies carrying on qualifying trades – the provisions relating to parent companies are relaxed by FA 1997). Special provisions apply where a company in which the VCT has invested goes into bona fide liquidation or receivership, or where the company is sold, merges or undergoes a capital reconstruction;
  (d)   at least 30% by value of its qualifying holdings must comprise "eligible shares" (see above);
  (e)   it may not hold more than 15% by value of its total investment portfolio in any one company;
  (f)   each class of its shares must be quoted on the Stock Exchange;
  (g)   it must distribute at least 85% of the income derived from shares and securities and 100% of income derived from other sources in each accounting period;
  (h)   at least 10% of the total investment in any one company must be held in ordinary, non-preferential shares (accounting periods ending after 1 July 1997);
  (i)   no part of a qualifying holding may consist of securities relating to a guaranteed loan (accounting periods ending after 1 July 1997).

Corporate venturing scheme see p 51.

Personal equity plans

(Subscriptions made **before 6 April 1999**: TA 1988 s 333; FA 1998 s 76; SI 1989/469; SI 1998/1869)

Subscription limit

	General plan £	Single company plan £
From 1991–92	6,000	3,000[1]
1990–91	6,000	—
1989–90	4,800	—

[1] Available from 1 January 1992.

Limit on investments in unit and investment trusts

	Qualifying investments £	Permitted non-qualifying investments £
From 1993–94	6,000	1,500
1992–93	6,000[1]	1,500[1]
1991–92	3,000[1]	1,500[1]
1990–91	3,000[1]	900[1]
1989–90	2,400	—

[1] For the years 1990–91 to 1992–93, the limit on investments in permitted non-qualifying holdings operated as an alternative to the limit on investments in qualifying unit and investment trusts. For 1993–94 and subsequent years, investment in one category does not preclude investment in the other category up to the respective limits.

Individuals aged 18 or over who are UK resident and ordinarily resident may subscribe to one general plan and (from January 1992) one single company plan in any tax year.

Reliefs

(a) Dividends on shares held in a plan are exempt from income tax.

(b) Interest on plan investments is exempt from income tax if reinvested; interest on cash deposits is paid gross.

(c) Gains on the disposal of assets held in a plan are exempt from capital gains tax.

(d) PEPs held at 5 April 1999 can be held outside the new ISA, but with the same tax advantages as the ISA (1998) SWTI 388; FA 1998 ss 75, 76.

(e) 10% tax credits paid until 5 April 2004 on dividends from UK equities.

Eligible investments (general plans)

(a) Ordinary shares in a UK incorporated company listed on a recognised stock exchange in an EU member state or dealt in on the USM.

(b) Units in an authorised unit trust or shares in an investment trust.

(c) Qualifying EC shares.

(d) Cash held on deposit for investment.

(e) (From 6 July 1995) UK quoted preference and convertible preference shares and EU equivalent shares.

(f) (From 6 July 1995) certain corporate bonds and convertible bonds of UK quoted companies (other than authorised credit institutions).

Eligible investments (single company plans)

(a) Ordinary shares in a UK incorporated company (or, following a reorganisation, shares representing those shares).

(b) Qualifying EC shares (or, following a reorganisation, shares representing those shares).

(c) Paired shares, one of which was issued by the designated company.

(d) Shares acquired by the investor under an approved profit sharing or savings-related share option scheme.

(e) Cash held on deposit for investment.

Tax exempt special savings accounts

(Accounts opened **before 6 April 1999**: TA 1988 ss 326A–326C; FA 1998 s 78)

Maximum deposit (from 1 January 1991)

First 12 months	£3,000[1]
Subsequent 12 month periods	£1,800
Overall limit	£9,000

[1] But the full amount of capital invested in a mature TESSA can be immediately reinvested in a new TESSA.

Reliefs

Interest and bonuses payable on the account over a five-year period from the date on which it was opened are exempt from income tax.

Main conditions for relief

1   An individual aged 18 or over may hold one TESSA.
2   The TESSA must be a bank or building society deposit account or a building society share account. From 2 January 1996 European authorised institutions may operate TESSAs (SI 1995/3239 and concession A92).
3   No capital may be withdrawn from the account during the initial five-year period.
4   After five years the account ceases to be tax exempt, but the capital (ie a maximum of £9,000) may be reinvested in full within six months in another TESSA.
5   TESSAs may be opened until 5 April 1999. Payments into them may be made under the above rules for the full five-year period. The capital in a TESSA that matures between 6 January 1999 and 5 April 1999 may be transferred into an ISA after 5 April 1999 rather than invested into another TESSA before that date. (See below.)

Individual savings accounts

(TA 1988 s 333; FA 1998 s 75; SI 1998 No 1870; SI 1998 No 1871; SI 1998 No 1869; SI 1998 No 1872; SI 2000 No 809)

In the 2000 Budget it was announced that the overall annual subscription limit will remain at £7,000 and the cash limit will remain at £3,000 for 2000-01: (2000) SWTI 406.

(From 6 April 1999)

Overall annual subscription limit	1999–2000 and 2000-01 6 April 2001 onwards	£7,000 £5,000
Cash limit	1999-2000 and 2000-01 6 April 2001 onwards	£3,000 £1,000
Life insurance limit	6 April 1999 onwards	£1,000

Reliefs

(a) Investments under the scheme will be free from income tax and capital gains tax.
(b) 10% tax credit paid until 5 April 2004 on dividends from UK equities.
(c) Withdrawals may be made without loss of tax relief.

Main conditions for relief

1   The account can include three components:
    (a)   cash (including National Savings),
    (b)   life insurance,
    (c)   stocks and shares.
2   Savers are subject to the subscription limits set out above. If the subscription limit is reached in a year, no further subscriptions can be made in that year, irrespective of any amounts withdrawn.
3   Accounts must be administered by a single manager or by separate managers for each component.

Inheritance tax

Delivery of accounts: due dates

Type of transfer	Due date
Chargeable lifetime transfers	Later of – (a) 12 months after the end of the month in which the transfer took place; and (b) 3 months after the date on which the person delivering the account became liable
PETs which become chargeable	12 months after the end of the month in which the transferor died
Gifts with reservation chargeable on death	12 months after the end of the month in which the death occurred
Transfers on death	Later of – (a) 12 months after the end of the month in which the death occurred; and (b) 3 months after the date on which the personal representatives first act or the person liable first has reason to believe that he is liable to deliver an account
National heritage property	6 months after the end of the month in which the chargeable event occurred

Delivery of accounts: excepted estates

Date of transfer or death	1 April 1991–5 April 1995	6 April 1995–5 April 1996	6 April 1996–5 April 1998	After 5 April 1998
Excepted transfers:	*Value below:*	*Value below:*	*Value below:*	*Value below:*
Total chargeable transfers since 6 April	£10,000	£10,000	£10,000	£10,000
Total chargeable transfers during last 10 years[2]	£40,000	£40,000	£40,000	£40,000
Excepted estates:				
Total gross value	£125,000	£145,000	£180,000[1]	£200,000[1]
Total gross value of property outside UK	£15,000	£15,000	£30,000	£50,000
Total gross value of chargeable transfers of cash, quoted shares or quoted securities within 7 years before death	nil	nil	£50,000	£75,000

[1] This limit applies to the aggregate gross value of the estate and of chargeable transfers of cash, quoted shares and quoted securities within 7 years before death.

[2] This limit remains the same for applicable periods prior to 1 April 1991.

Rates of tax

From 6 April 2000: Death rates

Cumulative chargeable transfers (gross)	Rate on gross	Tax on band	Cumulative tax	Cumulative chargeable transfers (net)	Rate on net fraction
£	%	£	£	£	
0 – 234,000	0	0	0	0 – 234,000	nil
234,000 +	40	—	—	234,000 +	$\frac{2}{3}$

Lower rates

Cumulative chargeable transfers (gross)	Rate on gross	Tax on band	Cumulative tax	Cumulative chargeable transfers (net)	Rate on net fraction
£	%	£	£	£	
0 – 234,000	0	0	0	0 – 234,000	nil
234,000 +	20	—	—	234,000 +	$\frac{1}{4}$

6 April 1999-5 April 2000: Death rates

Cumulative chargeable transfers (gross)	Rate on gross	Tax on band	Cumulative tax	Cumulative chargeable transfers (net)	Rate on net fraction
£	%	£	£	£	
0 – 231,000	0	0	0	0 – 231,000	nil
231,000 +	40	—	—	231,000 +	$\frac{2}{3}$

Lower rates

Cumulative chargeable transfers (gross)	Rate on gross	Tax on band	Cumulative tax	Cumulative chargeable transfers (net)	Rate on net fraction
£	%	£	£	£	
0 – 231,000	0	0	0	0 – 231,000	nil
231,000 +	20	—	—	231,000 +	$\frac{1}{4}$

6 April 1998-5 April 1999: Death rates

Cumulative chargeable transfers (gross)	Rate on gross	Tax on band	Cumulative tax	Cumulative chargeable transfers (net)	Rate on net fraction
£	%	£	£	£	
0 – 223,000	0	0	0	0 – 223,000	nil
223,000 +	40	—	—	223,000 +	$\frac{2}{3}$

Lower rates

Cumulative chargeable transfers (gross)	Rate on gross	Tax on band	Cumulative tax	Cumulative chargeable transfers (net)	Rate on net fraction
£	%	£	£	£	
0 – 223,000	0	0	0	0 – 223,000	nil
223,000 +	20	—	—	223,000 +	$\frac{1}{4}$

6 April 1997–5 April 1998 : Death rates

Cumulative chargeable transfers (gross)	Rate on gross	Tax on band	Cumulative tax	Cumulative chargeable transfers (net)	Rate on net fraction
£	%	£	£	£	
0 – 215,000	0	0	0	0 – 215,000	nil
215,000 +	40	—	—	215,000 +	$\frac{2}{3}$

Lower rates

Cumulative chargeable transfers (gross)	Rate on gross	Tax on band	Cumulative tax	Cumulative chargeable transfers (net)	Rate on net fraction
£	%	£	£	£	
0 – 215,000	0	0	0	0 – 215,000	nil
215,000 +	20	—	—	215,000 +	$\frac{1}{4}$

6 April 1996–5 April 1997: Death rates

Cumulative chargeable transfers (gross)	Rate on gross	Tax on band	Cumulative tax	Cumulative chargeable transfers (net)	Rate on net fraction
£	%	£	£	£	
0 – 200,000	0	0	0	0 – 200,000	nil
200,000 +	40	—	—	200,000 +	$\frac{2}{3}$

Lower rates

Cumulative chargeable transfers (gross)	Rate on gross	Tax on band	Cumulative tax	Cumulative chargeable transfers (net)	Rate on net fraction
£	%	£	£	£	
0 – 200,000	0	0	0	0 – 200,000	nil
200,000 +	20	—	—	200,000 +	$\frac{1}{4}$

6 April 1995–5 April 1996: Death rates

Cumulative chargeable transfers (gross)	Rate on gross	Tax on band	Cumulative tax	Cumulative chargeable transfers (net)	Rate on net fraction
£	%	£	£	£	
0 – 154,000	0	0	0	0 – 154,000	nil
154,000 +	40	—	—	154,000 +	$\frac{2}{3}$

Lower rates

Cumulative chargeable transfers (gross)	Rate on gross	Tax on band	Cumulative tax	Cumulative chargeable transfers (net)	Rate on net fraction
£	%	£	£	£	
0 – 154,000	0	0	0	0 – 154,000	nil
154,000 +	20	—	—	154,000 +	$\frac{1}{4}$

10 March 1992–5 April 1995: Death rates

Cumulative chargeable transfers (gross)	Rate on gross	Tax on band	Cumulative tax	Cumulative chargeable transfers (net)	Rate on net fraction
£	%	£	£	£	
0 – 150,000	0	0	0	0 – 150,000	nil
150,000 +	40	—	—	150,000 +	$\frac{2}{3}$

Lower rates

Cumulative chargeable transfers (gross)	Rate on gross	Tax on band	Cumulative tax	Cumulative chargeable transfers (net)	Rate on net fraction
£	%	£	£	£	
0 – 150,000	0	0	0	0 – 150,000	nil
150,000 +	20	—	—	150,000 +	$\frac{1}{4}$

6 April 1991–9 March 1992: Death rates

Cumulative chargeable transfers (gross)	Rate on gross	Tax on band	Cumulative tax	Cumulative chargeable transfers (net)	Rate on net fraction
£	%	£	£	£	
0 – 140,000	0	0	0	0 – 140,000	nil
140,000 +	40	—	—	140,000 +	$\frac{2}{3}$

Lower rates

Cumulative chargeable transfers (gross)	Rate on gross	Tax on band	Cumulative tax	Cumulative chargeable transfers (net)	Rate on net fraction
£	%	£	£	£	
0 – 140,000	0	0	0	0 – 140,000	nil
140,000 +	20	—	—	140,000 +	$\frac{1}{4}$

6 April 1990–5 April 1991: Death rates

Cumulative chargeable transfers (gross)	Rate on gross	Tax on band	Cumulative tax	Cumulative chargeable transfers (net)	Rate on net fraction
£	%	£	£	£	
0 – 128,000	0	0	0	0 – 128,000	nil
128,000 +	40	—	—	128,000 +	$\frac{2}{3}$

Lower rates

Cumulative chargeable transfers (gross)	Rate on gross	Tax on band	Cumulative tax	Cumulative chargeable transfers (net)	Rate on net fraction
£	%	£	£	£	
0 – 128,000	0	0	0	0 – 128,000	nil
128,000 +	20	—	—	128,000 +	$\frac{1}{4}$

Reliefs

The following is a summary of the main reliefs and exemptions for 2000–01 under the Inheritance Tax Act 1984. The legislation should be referred to for conditions and exceptions.

Agricultural property
Transfer with vacant possession (or right to obtain it within 12 months); transfer on or after 1 September 1995, of land let (or treated as let) on or after that date. 100% of agricultural value
Any other case 50% of agricultural value
(Under IHTA 1984 s 124C, as inserted by FA 1997 s 94, land managed according to terms of certain Habitat Schemes is treated as farm land, and qualifies for relief after 26 Nov. 1996.)

Charges arising and transfers occurring after 9 March 1992 and before 1 September 1995:
Transfer with vacant possession (or right to obtain within 12 months) 100% of agricultural value
Most other cases 50% of agricultural value

Note: The 100% relief is extended in limited circumstances by Concession F17.

Annual exemption
From 6 April 1981 £3,000

Business property
Unincorporated business
Unquoted shares (including shares in AIM or USM companies) (held for 2 years or more)[1]
Unquoted securities which alone, or together with other such securities and unquoted shares, give the transferor control of the company (held for 2 years or more)[1] — 100%
Settled property used in life tenant's business

Controlling holding in fully quoted companies
Land, buildings, machinery or plant used in business of company or partnership — 50%

[1] Tax charges arising and transfers occurring after 5 April 1996. 10 March 1992–5 April 1996 minority holding of shares or securities of up to 25% in unquoted or USM company qualified for 50% relief; larger holdings qualified for 100% relief.

Charities, gifts to
From 15 March 1983 Exempt

Marriage gifts
Made by: parent £5,000
remoter ancestor £2,500
party to marriage £2,500
other person £1,000

Political parties, gifts to
From 15 March 1988 Exempt

Quick succession relief
Estate increased by chargeable transfer followed by death within 5 years
Death within first year 100%
Each additional year: decreased by 20%

Small gifts to same person
From 6 April 1981 £250

Spouses with separate domicile (one not being in the UK)
Total exemption £55,000

Tapering relief
The value of the estate on death is taxed as the top slice of cumulative transfers in the 7 years before death. Transfers on or within 7 years of death are taxed on their value at the date of the gift on the death rate scale, but using the scale in force at the date of death, subject to the following taper—

Years between gift and death	Percentage of full charge at death rates
0–3	100
3–4	80
4–5	60
5–6	40
6–7	20

National insurance: State benefits

Taxable and non-taxable state benefits

State benefits of an income nature are in principle taxable in the same way as other sources of income, but the majority of such benefits are not in fact taxed.

Benefits taxed under Schedule E as earned income

(Income support[1] payments made to people who had to sign on,[2] or to certain claimants[3] involved in a trade dispute)
Incapacity benefit[4]
Industrial death benefit pensions
Invalid care allowance[5]
Jobseeker's allowance

Retirement pension[5]
Statutory maternity pay
Statutory sick pay
(Unemployment benefit[1 and 6])
Widowed mothers' allowance[5]
Widows' pension

Notes:
[1] Income support paid to unemployed people and unemployment benefit were replaced by the jobseeker's allowance in October 1996.
[2] Although taxable, income support paid to an unemployed person who is aged 60 or over, or is a lone parent with a child under 16 or is someone who has to stay at home to look after a severely disabled person, is not in fact taxed (see leaflet IR41: Income tax and the unemployed).
[3] Where the claimant is one of a married or unmarried couple and he (though not his partner) is involved in a trade dispute.
[4] Payments made during the initial 28-week period, and that part of the benefit which represents a child addition, are exempt (see below).
[5] Child dependency additions are not taxable (see (2) below).
[6] Additions for children, housing and exceptional circumstances are excluded.

Benefits which are not taxed

(1) *Short-term benefits*
   Maternity allowance

(2) *Benefits in respect of children*
   Child benefit
   Child dependency additions paid with retirement pension, widows' benefit, incapacity benefit, invalidity benefit, invalid care allowance, severe disablement allowance, higher-rate industrial death benefit, unemployability supplement and sickness (or, formerly, unemployment benefit) if beneficiary over pension age
   Child's special allowance
   Guardian's allowance
   One-parent benefit

(3) *Industrial injury benefits*
   Constant attendance allowance
   Industrial disablement benefit
   Pneumoconiosis, byssinosis and miscellaneous disease benefits
   Workmen's compensation supplement

(4) *War disablement benefits*
   Constant attendance allowance
   Disablement pension
   Severe disablement allowance

(5) *Other benefits*
   Attendance allowance

Christmas bonus
Council tax benefit
Disability living allowance
Disability working allowance (replaced by disabled person's tax credit from 5 October 1999)
Earnings top-up
Family credit (replaced by working families tax credit from 5 October 1999)
Housing benefit
Incapacity benefit (initial 28-week period *only*)
Income support (other than payments made to people who had to sign on or strikers before 7 October 1996: introduction of jobseeker's allowance. In practice, payments to an unemployed person who was (a) aged 60 or over, (b) a lone parent with a child under 16, or (c) someone staying at home to look after a severely disabled person, were not taxed: IR41.)
Invalidity benefit (replaced by incapacity benefit in April 1995)
Jobfinder's grant
Redundancy payment
Social fund payments
Vaccine damage (lump sum)
War widow's or dependant's pension
Widow's payment

Statutory maternity pay
Rates: from 10 April 2000

Higher weekly rate of statutory maternity pay	Lower weekly rate of statutory maternity pay	Daily rate of statutory maternity pay
9/10ths of employee's average weekly earnings	£60·20	—
Paid for a maximum of 18 weeks.	Earnings threshold: £67	

Statutory sick pay
Rates: from 10 April 2000

Average weekly earnings	Weekly rate of statutory sick pay	Daily rate of statutory sick pay
Under £67·00	nil	Weekly rate divided by number of qualifying days in week[1] in which day to be paid occurs
£67·00 or more	£60·20 (standard)	
[1] Commencing on the Sunday		

Benefits taxed under Schedule E

	Weekly 12.4.99 onwards £	Total 1999-2000 (52 weeks) £	Weekly 10.4.00 onwards £	Total 2000-01 (52 weeks) £
Retirement pensions				
Single person	66·75	3,471·00	67.50	3,510.00
Married couple:				
both contributors—each	66·75	3,471·00	67.50	3,510.00
wife not contributor—addition	39·95	2,077·40	40.40	2,100.80
wife not contributor—joint	106·70	5,548·40	107.90	5,610.80
Age addition (over 80)—each	0·25	13·00	0.25	13.00
Hospital downrating				
20% rate (persons with dependants)	13·35	varies	13.50	varies
40% rate (no dependants)	26·70	varies	27.00	varies
Widow's benefits				
Widows' pension—standard	66·75	3,471·00	67.50	3,510.00
Widowed mothers' allowance	66·75	3,471·00	67.50	3,510.00
Non-contributory retirement pension				
Single person (category C or D)	39·95	2,077·40	40.40	2,100.80
Married couple (category C)	63·85	3,320·20	64.55	3,356.60
Married couple (category D—over 80)	79·90	4,154·80	80.80	4,201.60
Age addition	0·25	13·00	0.25	13.00
Incapacity benefit				
Long-term	66·75	3,471·00	67.50	3,510.00
Increased for age: Higher rate	14·05	730·60	14.20	738.40
Lower rate	7·05	366·60	7.10	369.20
Short-term[1] (under pension age) higher rate	59·55	—	60.20	—
(over pension age) higher rate	66·75	—	67.50	—
Invalidity allowance when paid with retirement pension (transitional)				
Higher rate	14·05	730·60	14.20	738.40
Middle rate	8·90	462·80	9.00	468.00
Lower rate	4·45	231·40	4.50	234.00
Industrial death benefit				
Widow's pension:				
Higher permanent rate	66·75	3,471·00	67.50	3,510.00
Lower permanent rate	20·03	1,041·56	20.25	1,053.00
Invalid care allowance				
Each qualifying individual	39·95	2,077·40	40.40	2,100.80
Earnings limit	50·00	—	50.00	—
Adult dependency increase	23·90	1,242·80	24.15	1,255.80
Jobseeker's allowance				
Single: under 18	30·95	—	31.45	—
18 to 24	40·70	—	41.35	—
25 or over	51·40	—	52.20	—

[1] Lower rate (tax-free) paid up to week 28 (see below). Higher rate (taxable) paid weeks 29 to 52. New claims cannot be made by persons over pensionable age.

Child dependency additions (from 10.4.00): £9·85 a week for child for whom higher rate child benefit payable
£11·35 a week for each other child (tax free).

The Revenue generally apply the basis of 52 weeks at the new rate. In certain cases, however, it may be to the advantage of the recipient to calculate the amount actually received within the year of assessment where this includes one week at the old rate.

Tax-free rates (from 10.4.00):

Attendance allowance:	Higher rate	£53·55 a week
	Lower rate	£35·80 a week
Child benefit:	£15 for eldest eligible child (couple) (£15.50 from April 2001)	
	£17·55 for eldest eligible child (lone parent)	
	£10 (each) for other eligible children	
Disability living allowance:		
Care component:	Higher rate	£53·55 a week
	Middle rate	£35·80 a week
	Lower rate	£14·20 a week
Mobility component:	Higher rate	£37·40 a week
	Lower rate	£14·20 a week
Incapacity benefit:		
Short term (under pension age)	Lower rate	£50·90 a week
Maternity allowance:	Higher rate	£60·20 a week
	Lower rate	£52·25 a week
Widow's payment:	£1,000 lump sum	

Contributions

From 6 April 2000

Lower earnings limit: £67 a week £291 a month £3,484 a year		Upper earnings limit: £535 a week £2,319 a month £27,820 a year	
	Employees from 6.4.00	**Employers from 6.4.00**	
Class 1 Contributions **standard rate**		*(Earnings above £84 a week)*	
Earnings: £76–£535	10%	12·2%	
Over £535	no additional liability	12·2%	
Contracted out*		SR[1,3]	MP[2,3]
Earnings: £76–£535	8·4%[4]	9·2%	11·6%
Over £535	no additional liability	12·2%	12·2%
Reduced rate for married women and widows with valid certificate of election	3·85% (earnings £76 to £535)	(As above)	
Men over 65 and women over 60	Nil	(As above)	
Children under 16	Nil	Nil	

Class 2 Contributions: Self employed
Flat rate: £2 a week.
Share fishermen's special rate: £2.65 a week.
Small earnings exception: earnings under £3,825 a year.

Class 3 Voluntary Contributions: £6·55 a week.

Class 4 Contributions: 7% of profits or gains between £4,385 and £27,820 a year.
Exempt if pensionable age reached by beginning of year of assessment.

[1]Rates apply to salary-related schemes.
[2]Rates apply to money-purchase schemes.
[3]The lower rates apply to earnings between the earnings threshold of £84 and the upper earnings limit of £535. A deduction is made for the rebate that would have applied to NICs on earnings between the lower earnings limit £67 and the earnings threshold of £84. The rebate is 3% for salary-related schemes and 0.6% for money purchase schemes.
[4]A deduction is made from employee contributions for the rebate of 1.6% that would have applied to NICs on earnings between the lower earnings limit £67 and the primary earnings threshold of £76. Where the rebate reduces the employee's contributions to nil, the balance is offset against the employer's contributions.

From April 2001 (announced in 1999 Budget):
Full alignment of employees' NIC threshold with personal tax allowance.

6 April 1999-5 April 2000

Lower earnings limit: £66 a week £286 a month £3,432 a year		Upper earnings limit: (employees only)	£500 a week £2,167 a month £26,000 a year
	Employees from 6.4.99	**Employers from 6.4.99**	
Class 1 Contributions **standard rate**		*(Earnings above £83 a week)*	
Earnings: £66–£500	10%	12·2%	
Over £500	no additional liability	12·2%	
Contracted out*		SR[1,3]	MP[2,3]
Earnings: £66–£500	8·4%	9·2%	11·6%
Over £500	no additional liability	12·2%	12·2%
Reduced rate for married women and widows with valid certificate of election	3·85% (earnings £66 to £500)	(As above)	
Men over 65 and women over 60	Nil	(As above)	
Children under 16	Nil	Nil	

Class 2 Contributions: Self employed
Flat rate: £6·55 a week.
Share fishermen's special rate: £7·20 a week.
Small earnings exception: earnings under £3,770 a year.

Class 3 Voluntary Contributions: £6·45 a week.

Class 4 Contributions: 6% of profits or gains between £7,530 and £26,000 a year.
Exempt if pensionable age reached by beginning of year of assessment.

Notes: The employer NI contribution holiday of up to a year, which applied from 6 April 1996 (see p 86), is restricted to employments which began before 1 April 1999: (1998) SWTI 1705.
[1] Rates apply to salary-related schemes.
[2] Rates apply to money-purchase schemes.
[3] The lower rates apply to earnings between the earnings threshold of £83 and the upper earnings limit of £500. A deduction is made for the rebate that would have applied to NICs on earnings between the lower earnings limit of £66 and the earnings threshold £83. The rebate is 3% for salary-related schemes and 0.6% for money-purchase schemes.

6 April 1998-5 April 1999

Lower earnings limit: £64 a week			Upper earnings limit: £485 a week		
	£278 a month		**(employees only)**	£2,102 a month	
	£3,328 a year			£25,220 a year	

	Employees from 6.4.98		Employers from 6.4.98		
Class 1 Contributions					
standard rate	*On first £64*	*Remainder*	*(Rate applying to all earnings)*		
Earnings: £ 64·00–£109·99	2%	10%	3%		
£110·00–£154·99	2%	10%	5%		
£155·00–£209·99	2%	10%	7%		
£210·00–£485·00	2%	10%	10%		
Over £485	no additional liability		10%		
Contracted out*	*On first £64*	*Remainder*	*On first £64*	*Remainder*	
				SR[1]	MP[2]
Earnings: £ 64·00–£109·99	2%	8·4%	3%	Nil	1·5%
£110·00–£154·99	2%	8·4%	5%	2	3·5%
£155·00–£209·99	2%	8·4%	7%	4	5·5%
£210·00–£485·00	2%	8·4%	10%	7	8·5%
Over £485	no additional liability		10%	7% (to £485)	8·5% (to £485)
			10%	10% (over £485)	10% (over £485)
Reduced rate for married women and widows with valid certificate of election	3·85% (earnings to £485)		(As above)		
Men over 65 and women over 60	Nil		(As above)		
Children under 16	Nil		Nil		

Class 2 Contributions: Self employed
Flat rate: £6·35 a week.   Share fishermen's special rate: £7 a week.
Small earnings exception: earnings under £3,590 a year.

Class 3 Voluntary Contributions: £6·25 a week.

Class 4 Contributions: 6% of profits or gains between £7,310 and £25,220 a year.
Exempt if pensionable age reached by beginning of year of assessment.

[1] Rates apply to salary-related schemes. [2] Rates apply to money-purchase schemes.

6 April 1997–5 April 1998

Lower earnings limit: £62 a week			Upper earnings limit: £465 a week		
	£269 a month		**(employees only)**	£2,015 a month	
	£3,224 a year			£24,180 a year	

	Employees from 6.4.97		Employers from 6.4.97		
Class 1 Contributions					
standard rate	*On first £62*	*Remainder*	*(Rate applying to all earnings)*		
Earnings: £ 62·00–£109·99	2%	10%	3%		
£110·00–£154·99	2%	10%	5%		
£155·00–£209·99	2%	10%	7%		
£210·00–£465·00	2%	10%	10%		
Over £465	no additional liability		10%		
Contracted out*	*On first £62*	*Remainder*	*On first £62*	*Remainder*	
				SR[1]	MP[2]
Earnings: £ 62·00–£109·99	2%	8·4%	3%	Nil	1·5%
£110·00–£154·99	2%	8·4%	5%	2	3·5%
£155·00–£209·99	2%	8·4%	7%	4	5·5%
£210·00–£465·00	2%	8·4%	10%	7	8·5%
Over £465	no additional liability		10%	7% (to £465)	8·5% (to £465)
			10%	10% (over £465)	10% (over £465)
Reduced rate for married women and widows with valid certificate of election	3·85% (earnings to £465)		(As above)		
Men over 65 and women over 60	Nil		(As above)		
Children under 16	Nil		Nil		

Class 2 Contributions: Self employed
Flat rate: £6·15 a week.
Share fishermen's special rate: £6·80 a week.
Small earnings exception: earnings under £3,480 a year.

Class 3 Voluntary Contributions: £6·05 a week.

Class 4 Contributions: 6% of profits or gains between £7,010 and £24,180 a year.
Exempt if pensionable age reached by beginning of year of assessment.

[1] Rates apply to salary-related schemes. [2] Rates apply to money-purchase schemes.

6 April 1996–5 April 1997

Lower earnings limit: £61 a week £265 a month £3,172 a year		**Upper earnings limit:** **(employees only)**	£455 a week £1,972 a month £23,660 a year	

Class 1 Contributions	**Employees from 6.4.96**		**Employers from 6.4.96**	
standard rate	*On first £61*	*Remainder*	*(Rate applying to all earnings)*	
Earnings: £ 61·00–£109·99	2%	10%	3%	
£110·00–£154·99	2%	10%	5%	
£155·00–£209·99	2%	10%	7%	
£210·00–£455·00	2%	10%	10·2%	
Over £455	no additional liability		10·2%	
Contracted out*	*On first £61*	*Remainder*	*On first £61*	*Remainder*
Earnings: £ 61·00–£109·99	2%	8·2%	3%	Nil
£110·00–£154·99	2%	8·2%	5%	2%
£155·00–£209·99	2%	8·2%	7%	4%
£210·00–£455·00	2%	8·2%	10·2%	7·2%
Over £455	no additional liability		⎰10·2% 7·2% (to £455) ⎱ 10·2% (earnings over £455)	
Reduced rate for married women and widows with valid certificate of election	3·85% (earnings to £455)		(As above)	
Men over 65 and women over 60	Nil		(As above)	
Children under 16	Nil		Nil	

Class 2 Contributions: Self employed
Flat rate: £6·05 a week.
Share fishermen's special rate: £7.20 a week.
Small earnings exception: earnings under £3,430 a year.

Class 3 Voluntary Contributions: £5·95 a week.

Class 4 Contributions: 6% of profits or gains between £6,860 and £23,660 a year.
Exempt if pensionable age reached by beginning of year of assessment.

* Contracted out rates apply to members of contracted out occupational schemes only.
Note: From 6 April 1996 there is an employer NI contribution holiday of up to a year for individuals taken on who have been out of work for two years or more, trainees, and certain people who work intermittently during the qualifying period, who satisfy the conditions.

6 April 1995–5 April 1996

Lower earnings limit: £58 a week £252 a month £3,016 a year		**Upper earnings limit:** **(employees only)**	£440 a week £1,907 a month £22,880 a year	

Class 1 Contributions	**Employees from 6.4.95**		**Employers from 6.4.95**	
standard rate	*On first £58*	*Remainder*	*(Rate applying to all earnings)*	
Earnings: £ 58·00–£104·99	2%	10%	3%	
£105·00–£149·99	2%	10%	5%	
£150·00–£204·99	2%	10%	7%	
£205·00–£440·00	2%	10%	10·2%	
Over £440	no additional liability		10·2%	
Contracted out*	*On first £58*	*Remainder*	*On first £58*	*Remainder*
Earnings: £ 58·00–£104·99	2%	8·2%	3%	Nil
£105·00–£149·99	2%	8·2%	5%	2%
£150·00–£204·99	2%	8·2%	7%	4%
£205·00–£440·00	2%	8·2%	10·2%	7·2%
Over £440	no additional liability		⎰10·2% 7·2% (to £440) ⎱ 10·2% (earnings over £440)	
Reduced rate for married women and widows with valid certificate of election	3·85% (earnings to £440)		(As above)	
Men over 65 and women over 60	Nil		(As above)	
Children under 16	Nil		Nil	

Class 2 Contributions: Self employed
Flat rate: £5·75 a week.
Share fishermen's special rate: £7·30 a week.
Small earnings exception: earnings under £3,260 a year.

Class 3 Voluntary Contributions: £5·65 a week.

Class 4 Contributions: 7·3% of profits or gains between £6,640 and £22,880 a year.
Exempt if pensionable age reached by beginning of year of assessment.

Employers' contributions: benefits in kind

From *6 April 2000,* Class 1A national insurance contributions are payable by employers (at 12·2% for 2000-01) on all taxable benefits in kind, excluding benefits:

(1) which are covered by a dispensation; or
(2) included in a PAYE settlement agreement; or
(3) provided for employees earning less than £8,500 pa; or
(4) otherwise not required to be included on a PIID; or
(5) on which Class 1 national insurance contributions were due.

Expenses payments and the provision of childcare as a benefit in kind are not liable to Class 1A national insurance contributions. The first returns and payments are due under the new arrangements in July 2001 (see (1999) SWTI pp 400, 409, 1844).

Before 6 April 2000, national insurance contributions were payable by employers only where the benefits in kind were of cars and free fuel provided for the private use of employees (where the latter were liable to the income tax charge on cars). The benefit of cars and free fuel continues to be chargeable (see above). From 6 April 1994 the car benefit figure is calculated by reference to the list price of the car rather than by use of a table (see p 56), although a car fuel benefit table continues to be used.

Car benefits: private use
1994–95 onwards
Calculated by reference to the list price of the car, see p 58.

Car benefits: free fuel	
2000–01	
Cylinder capacity: 1,400cc or less	£207·40
(non-diesel cars) Over 1,400cc up to 2,000cc	£264·74
Over 2,000cc	£390·40
Cylinder capacity: 2,000cc or less	£264·74
(diesel cars) Over 2,000cc	£390·40
No internal combustion engine —	£390·40
1999–2000	
Cylinder capacity: 1,400cc or less	£147·62
(non-diesel cars) Over 1,400cc up to 2,000cc	£187·88
Over 2,000cc	£276·94
Cylinder capacity: 2,000cc or less	£187·88
(diesel cars) Over 2,000cc	£276·94
No internal combustion engine —	£276·94
1998–99	
Cylinder capacity: 1,400cc or less	£101·00
(non-diesel cars) Over 1,400cc up to 2,000cc	£128·00
Over 2,000cc	£189·00
Cylinder capacity: 2,000cc or less	£128·00
(diesel cars) Over 2,000cc	£189·00
No internal combustion engine —	£189·00
1997–98	
Cylinder capacity: 1,400cc or less	£80·00
(non-diesel cars) Over 1,400cc up to 2,000cc	£101·00
Over 2,000cc	£149·00
Cylinder capacity: 2,000cc or less	£74·00
(diesel cars) Over 2,000cc	£94·00
No internal combustion engine —	£149·00
1996–97	
Cylinder capacity: 1,400cc or less	£72·42
(non-diesel cars) Over 1,400cc up to 2,000cc	£90·78
Over 2,000cc	£134·64
Cylinder capacity: 2,000cc or less	£65·28
(diesel cars) Over 2,000cc	£83·64
No internal combustion engine —	£134·64

National insurance contributions leaflets

Leaflets regarding National Insurance contributions are issued by the Inland Revenue. They are available from the Inland Revenue website: http://www.inlandrevenue.co.uk and can be obtained from local Inland Revenue offices (including those which were Contributions Agency offices before 1 April 1999) except where indicated:

*Coastal Inland Revenue offices

**End of Year Section, HM Inspector of Taxes Cardiff 2, 15 North, Government Buildings, Ty LGlas Road, Llanishen, Cardiff CF4 5FN

†International Services, NICO, Longbenton, Newcastle-Upon-Tyne NE98 1ZZ

‡Contracted-out Employment Group, Inland Revenue National Insurance Contributions Office, Business Support, Room K2104, Newcastle-Upon-Tyne NE98 1ZZ

National Insurance

Leaflet	Date	Title
CA01	1999	National insurance contributions for employees
CA02	1999	National insurance contributions for self-employed people with small earnings
CA04	1999	National insurance contributions, Class 2 and Class 3: direct debit – the easier way to pay
CA07	1999	National insurance: unpaid and late-paid contributions
CA08	1999	NIC voluntary contributions
CA09	1999	NIC for widows
CA10	1999	NIC for divorced women
CA11*	1999	National insurance contributions for share fishermen
CA12	1999	NIC Training for further employment and your National Insurance record
CA13	1999	NIC for married women
CA14‡	1999	Termination of contracted-out employment: manual for salary related pension schemes and salary related parts of mixed benefits schemes
CA14A‡	1999	Termination of contracted-out employment: manual for money purchase pension schemes and money purchase parts of mixed benefits schemes
CA14B‡	1997	Contracted-out guidance for re-elections for salary related pension schemes and salary related overseas schemes
CA14C‡	1999	Contracted-out guidance for salary related pension schemes and salary related overseas schemes
CA14D‡	1999	Contracted-out guidance for money purchase pension schemes and money purchase overseas schemes
CA14E‡	1999	Contracted-out guidance for mixed benefit pension schemes and mixed benefit overseas schemes
CA14F‡	1999	Technical guidance on contracted-out decision making and appeals
CA15‡	1999	Cessation of contracted-out pension schemes manual
CA16‡	1999	Appropriate personal pension scheme manual – procedural guidance
CA16A‡	1999	Appropriate personal pension scheme manual – guidance for scheme managers
CA17‡	2000	Employees' guide to minimum contributions
CA19‡	1999	Using the accrued GMP liability service
CA20‡	1999	Using the contracted-out contributions/earnings information service
CA21‡	1999	Using the National Insurance number/date of birth checking service
CA22‡	1999	Contracted-out data transactions using magnetic media
CA23*	2000	NIC for mariners
CA24*	2000	NIC for masters and employers of mariners
CA25	1999	NIC for agencies and people finding work through agencies
CA26	1999	NIC for examiners and part-time lecturers, teachers and instructors
CA29	1999	Statutory Maternity Pay manual for employers
CA30	1999	Statutory Sick Pay manual for employers
CA33	1999	Cars and fuel – A manual for employers
CA34	1999	Application form to pay Class 1A NICs by alternative payment method
CA35/36	2000	Statutory sick pay tables and Statutory maternity pay tables
CA37	1999	Simplified deduction scheme for employers
CA38	2000	Not contracted out contributions for employers
CA39‡	2000	Contracted out contributions (for employers with contracted-out salary related schemes)
CA40	1999	Employee-only contributions for employers
CA42**	1999	National insurance tables: foreign going mariners and deep-sea fishermen
CA43‡	2000	Contracted-out contributions and minimum payments for employers with contracted out money purchase schemes
CA44	1999	Company directors – Manual for employers
CA47	1999	Charter for national insurance contributors
CA49	1999	Make your end of year easier – end of year returns by magnetic media
CA50	1999	Making year end returns on tape or disk. General guide
CA51/52	2000	Making year end returns on tape or disk. Technical guide
CA65†	1999	NIC for people working for embassies, consulates and overseas employers
CA66	1997	Surveys of NI records – a code of practice
CA69/IR 148	1999	Are your workers employed or self-employed? – construction workers
CA72	1999	National insurance contributions – deferring payments
CA76	1999	National insurance abroad – a guide for employers of employees from abroad
CA79	1999	Customer account service – helping employers to get end of year returns right first time
CA80	1997	Workers in building and construction. Help with NI for employees and self-employed, including agency workers
CA83	2000	NIC office – quality service through people
CWG1	1999	Employer's quick guide to PAYE and NICs
CWG2	1999	Employer's further guide to PAYE and NICs
CWG3	1999	The employer's annual pack
CWL1	1999	Starting your own business?
CWL2	1999	NI contributions for self-employed people, Class 2 and Class 4
CWL3	1997	Thinking of taking someone on?
CAT1		A catalogue of information, leaflets and posters
IR37	1999	Appeals against tax NI contributions, SSP and SMP
NE1	1999	First steps as a new employer
NI38	1999	Social security abroad
NI132	1999	National insurance for employers of people working abroad
NIC2	1999	NIC holiday scheme

Stamp duties

Ad valorem duty

Rounding. With effect from 1 October 1999, the charging provisions will be standardised to provide for the rounding up to the nearest £5 in all cases (where duty is currently rounded up to multiples of between 50p and £12) other than for SDRT. FA 1999 s 112, Sch 14.

Rates of duty (FA 1963 s 55; FA 1998 s 149; FA 1999 s 111, Sch 13; 2000 Budget Resolution 51; (2000) SWTI 393)

Consideration certified as:	Conveyance or transfer on sale with certificate of value	Lease premium where rent exceeds £600 p.a.	Conveyance etc without certificate of value	Stock transfers
28 March 2000[1]				
Not exceeding £60,000	Nil	1%		
£60,001–£250,000	1%	1%		
£250,001–£500,000	3%	3%	}4%	}0·5%
£500,001 or more	4%	4%		
16 March 1999[2] to 27 March 2000				
Not exceeding £60,000	Nil	1%		
£60,001–£250,000	1%	1%		
£250,001–£500,000	2·5%	2·5%	}3·5%	}0·5%
£500,001 or more	3·5%	3·5%		
17 March 1998[3] to 15 March 1999				
Not exceeding £60,000	Nil	1%		
£60,001–£250,000	1%	1%		
£250,001–£500,000	2%	2%	}3%	}0·5%
£500,001 or more	3%	3%		

[1] Unless transfer is pursuant to a contract made before 22 March 2000.
[2] Unless transfer is pursuant to a contract made before 10 March 1999.
[3] Unless transfer is pursuant to a contract made before 18 March 1998.

Leases

Any agreement for a lease entered into after 19 March 1984 is chargeable to duty as if it were the actual lease irrespective of the length of the term.

Premiums. If the consideration for the lease includes a premium, this is charged to ad valorem duty in accordance with the Table above. The nil rate of duty does not apply if the average rent reserved by the lease exceeds £600 p.a.

Rent. From 28 March 2000: *Leases not exceeding 7 years*, or for an indefinite term, are not chargeable to duty on the rent where this does not exceed £5,000[4] p.a. If the rent exceeds £5,000[4] p.a., the duty is—

For a lease of furnished residential
accommodation for a definite term of
less than 1 year...£5 from 1 October 1999 (previously £1)[5]
Other cases .... 1% from 1 October 1999 (previously 50p per £50 or part)

[4] 2000 Budget Resolution 52. the previous limit was £500.

Leases exceeding 7 years—

Rent	Over 7 yrs up to 35 yrs	Over 35 yrs up to 100 yrs	Over 100 yrs
From 1 October 1999	2%	12%	24%
Previously	£	£	£
£5 or less	0·10	0·60	1·20
Over £5 up to £10	0·20	1·20	2·40
Over £10 up to £15	0·30	1·80	3·60
Over £15 up to £20	0·40	2·40	4·80
Over £20 up to £25	0·50	3·00	6·00
Over £25 up to £50	1·00	6·00	12·00
Over £50 up to £75	1·50	9·00	18·00
Over £75 up to £100	2·00	12·00	24·00
Over £100 up to £150	3·00	18·00	36·00
Over £150 up to £200	4·00	24·00	48·00
Over £200 up to £250	5·00	30·00	60·00
Over £250 up to £300	6·00	36·00	72·00
Over £300 up to £350	7·00	42·00	84·00
Over £350 up to £400	8·00	48·00	96·00
Over £400 up to £450	9·00	54·00	108·00
Over £450 up to £500	10·00	60·00	120·00
Over £500; for every £50 or fraction of £50	1·00	6·00	12·00

Fixed duties

Stamp Act 1891 Sch 1	From 1 October 1999[5]	Previously
Leases (other than as described above)	£5	£2
Declaration of trust; duplicate or counterpart exchange or partition; release or renunciation; surrender	£5	50p

CREST: For instruments executed after 30 June 1996 there is no fixed stamp duty charge on deposits of shares into CREST, although there may be a liability to SDRT: see FA 1996 s 186.

[5] The minimum fixed stamp duty is £5 with effect from 1 October 1999 (previously 50p) (FA 1999, s 112, Sch 14).

Interest and Penalties

For instruments executed from 1 October 1999, interest will be payable on the amount of unpaid duty where the instrument is not stamped within 30 days of execution. A penalty will apply where the instrument is not presented for stamping within 30 days after execution (or if executed outside the UK, the day on which it is first received in the UK). If presented within one year after the end of the 30 day period, the penalty will be the lower of £300 or the amount of the unpaid duty, and if presented more than one year after the end of the 30 day period, it will be the greater of £300 or the amount of the unpaid duty (Stamp Act 1891 ss 15-15B). The Stamp Duty (Collection and Recovery of Penalties) Regulations SI 1999/2537 came into effect on 1 October 1999.

Value added tax

Annual accounting scheme

The taxable person must have been registered for at least one year at the date of application for authorisation (SI 1995/2518 Pt VII as amended). The taxable person must have reasonable grounds for believing that the value of taxable supplies in the year beginning at the date of application will not exceed a prescribed figure.

	Taxable turnover
From 9.4.91	£300,000

Registration limits
UK taxable supplies

	Past turnover[1]		Future turnover[1]
	1 year	*Unless turnover for next year will not exceed:*	*30 days*[2]
30.11.94–28.11.95	£46,000	£44,000	£46,000
29.11.95–26.11.96	£47,000	£45,000	£47,000
27.11.96–29.11.97	£48,000	£46,000	£48,000
30.11.97–31.3.98	£49,000	£47,000	£49,000
1.4.98–31.3.99	£50,000	£48,000	£50,000
1.4.99–31.3.2000	£51,000	£49,000	£51,000
1.4.2000 onwards	£52,000	£50,000	£52,000

[1] Value of taxable supplies (at zero and positive rates).
[2] Where there are reasonable grounds for believing that limit will be exceeded in this period.

Supplies from other EC countries

	Cumulative total[1] from beginning of calendar year
1.1.93 onwards	£70,000

[1] Value of supplies made by persons in other EU member states to non-taxable persons in the UK.

Acquisitions from other EC countries
VATA 1994 Sch 3

	Past acquisitions[1]	Future acquisitions[1]
	Cumulative total from 1 January	*30 days*[2]
1.1.95–31.12.95	£46,000	£46,000
1.1.96–31.12.96	£47,000	£47,000
1.1.97–31.12.97	£48,000	£48,000
1.1.98–31.3.98	£49,000	£49,000
1.4.98–31.3.99	£50,000	£50,000
1.4.99–31.3.2000	£51,000	£51,000
1.4.2000 onwards	£52,000	£52,000

[1] Value of acquisitions of taxable goods from suppliers in other EU member states.
[2] Where there are reasonable grounds for believing that limit will be exceeded in this period.

Deregistration limits

UK taxable supplies

Future turnover	Annual limit
30.11.94–28.11.95	£44,000
29.11.95–26.11.96	£45,000
27.11.96–29.11.97	£46,000
30.11.97–31.3.98	£47,000
1.4.98–31.3.99	£48,000
1.4.99-31.3.2000	£49,000
1.4.2000 onwards	£50,000

Unless during the year, the person will cease making taxable supplies (or suspend making taxable supplies for 30 days or more).

Supplies from other EC countries

	Past supplies[1]	Future supplies[1]
	Supplies in preceding calendar year	*Supplies in following calendar year*[2]
1.1.93 onwards	£70,000	£70,000

[1] Value of supplies made by persons in other EU member states to non-taxable persons in the UK.
[2] Where C & E are satisfied that limit will not be exceeded in this period.

Acquisitions from other EC countries
VATA 1994 Sch 3

	Past acquisitions[1]	Future acquisitions[1]
	Acquisitions in preceding calendar year	*Acquisitions in following calendar year*[2]
1.1.95–31.12.95	£46,000	£46,000
1.1.96–31.12.96	£47,000	£47,000
1.1.97–31.12.97	£48,000	£48,000
1.1.98–31.3.98	£49,000	£49,000
1.4.98–31.3.99	£50,000	£50,000
1.4.99-31.3.2000	£51,000	£51,000
1.4.2000 onwards	£52,000	£52,000

[1] Value of acquisitions of taxable goods from suppliers in other EU member states.
[2] Where C & E are satisfied that limit will not be exceeded in this period.

Rate of tax

	Standard rate	VAT fraction	Reduced rate[1]	VAT fraction
1.9.97 onwards	17.5%	7/47	5%	1/21
1.4.94–31.8.97	17.5%	7/47	8%	2/27
1.4.91–31.3.94	17.5%	7/47	n/a	n/a
18.6.79–31.3.91	15%	3/23	n/a	n/a

[1] Applies to supplies of fuel and power for domestic, residential or non-business charity use. Extended to the installation of energy-saving materials under certain grant schemes from 1 July 1998: SI 1998/1375 and to the installation of energy saving materials (including solar panels) in all homes from 1 April 2000 (see (2000) SWTI 470, 478, Budget Resolution 18).
The 5% reduced rate will be extended to women's sanitary products from January 2001 (see (2000) SWTI 471).

Flat rate scheme for farmers: 4% flat rate addition to sale price.

Penalties and surcharges

Offence	Penalty
Failure to pay tax due under the payment on account scheme on time (VATA 1994 s 59A)	(From 1.6.96) Default surcharge
Failure to submit return or pay tax due within time limit. (After 30.9.93, where a return is late but the tax is paid on time or no tax is due, a default is recorded but no surcharge arises) (VATA 1994 s 59)	Default surcharge: (defaults after 30.9.93) the greater of £30 and a specified percentage of outstanding VAT for period, depending on number of defaults in surcharge period– 1st default in period: 2% 2nd default: 5% 3rd default: 10% 4th default: 15% Further defaults: 15%
Evasion of VAT: conduct involving dishonesty (VATA 1994 s 60)	Amount of tax evaded or sought to be evaded (subject to mitigation)
Issuing incorrect certificate as to zero-rating (or, from 27 July 1999 as to eligibility to receive reduced-rate fuel and power) (VATA 1994 s 62; FA 1999 s 17)	Difference between tax actually charged and tax which should have been charged NB: Surcharge assessments are not issued for sums of less than £200 unless the rate of the surcharge is 10% or more
Misdeclaration or neglect (VATA 1994 s 63)	(After 9.3.92) 15% of VAT which would have been lost if inaccuracy had not been discovered
Repeated misdeclarations (VATA 1994 s 64)	(After 30.11.93) 15% of VAT which would have been lost if second and subsequent inaccuracies within penalty period had not been discovered
Material inaccuracy in EC sales statement (VATA 1994 s 65)	£100 for each material inaccuracy in 2 year penalty period (which commences following notice of second material inaccuracy)
Failure to submit an EC sales statement (VATA 1994 s 66)	Greater of £50 and a daily penalty (for no more than 100 days) depending on number of failures in default period– 1st failure: £5 2nd failure: £10 3rd and further failures: £15
Failure to notify liability for registration or change in nature of supplies by person exempted from registration (VATA 1994 s 67) (From 1.1.96 reintroduced for failure to notify liability for registration when business transferred as going concern)	(From 1.1.95) Greater of £50 and a specified percentage of the tax for which the person would have been liable, depending on the period of failure– 9 months or less: 5% Over 9, up to 18 months: 10% Over 18 months: 15% Where a liability to surcharge is established, Customs & Excise will not issue a surcharge assessment at the 2% or 5% rates for amounts of less than £200.
Unauthorised issue of invoices (VATA 1994 s 67)	(From 1.1.95) Greater of £50 and 15% of amount shown as or representing VAT
Breach of walking possession agreement (VATA 1994 s 68)	50% of VAT due and amount recoverable
Failure to preserve records for prescribed period (VATA 1994 s 69)	£500
Breaches of regulatory provisions, including failure to notify cessation of liability or entitlement to be registered, failure to keep records and non-compliance with any regulations made under VATA 1994 (VATA 1994 s 69)	Greater of £50 and a daily penalty (for no more than 100 days) of a specified amount depending on number of failures in preceding two years– No previous failures: £5 per day 1 previous failure: £10 per day 2 or more: £15 per day
Breaches of regulatory provisions involving failure to pay VAT or submit return by due date (VATA 1994 s 69)	Greater of £50 and a daily penalty (for no more than 100 days) of a specified amount depending on number of failures in preceding two years– No previous failures: greater of £5 and $\frac{1}{6}$% of VAT due 1 previous failure: greater of £10 and $\frac{1}{3}$% of VAT due 2 or more: greater of £15 and $\frac{1}{2}$% of VAT due
Failure to comply with statutory responsibility to pay correct amount of tax on time (FA 1997 ss 51,52)	(From 1 July 1997) Distress and attachment (poinding and sale and arrestment in Scotland)
Failure to comply with VAT tribunal directions or summons (VATA 1994 Sch 12 para 10)	Up to £1,000
Failure by person to whom an attachment notice has been given and who is or becomes indebted to the defaulter to pay the required amount (FA 1997)	£250 plus £20 for each day failure continues after payment has become due
Failure to comply with the accounting, invoicing, record-keeping and notification requirements for supplies involving investment gold ((2000) SWTI 472).	From date of Royal Assent to FA 2000 17.5% of the value of transactions concerned.

Default interest

The prescribed rate of interest for the purposes of VATA 1994 s 74 (the provisions of which were operative from 1 April 1990) has varied as follows:

	Rate
From 6 February 2000	8.5%
6 March 1999–5 February 2000	7.5%
6 January 1999–5 March 1999	8.5%
6 July 1998–5 January 1999	9.5%
6 February 1996–5 July 1998	6.25%
6 March 1995–5 February 1996	7%
6 October 1994–5 March 1995	6·25%
6 January 1994–5 October 1994	5.5%
6 March 1993–5 January 1994	6.25%
6 December 1992–5 March 1993	7%
6 November 1992–5 December 1992	7.75%
6 October 1991–5 November 1992	9.25%
6 July 1991–5 October 1991	10.00%
6 May 1991–5 July 1991	10.75%
6 March 1991–5 May 1991	11.5%
6 November 1990–5 March 1991	12.25%
1 April 1990–5 November 1990	13%

Interest on VAT overpaid in cases of official error

(VATA 1994 s 78)

	Rate		Rate
From 6 February 2000	5%	1 May 1988–31 July 1988	9.5%
6 March 1999–5 February 2000	4%	1 December 1987–30 April 1988	11%
6 January 1999–5 March 1999	5%	1 November 1987–30 November 1987	11.25%
1 April 1997–5 January 1999	6%	1 April 1987–31 October 1987	11.75%
6 February–31 March 1997	8%	1 January 1987–31 March 1987	12.25%
16 October 1991–5 February 1993	10.25%	1 August 1986–31 December 1986	11.5%
1 April 1991–15 October 1991	12%	1 April 1984–31 July 1986	12%
1 November 1989–31 March 1991	14.25%	1 April 1983–31 March 1984	12.5%
1 January 1989–31 October 1989	13%	1 July 1982–31 March 1983	13%
1 November 1988–31 December 1988	12.25%	1 March 1982–30 June 1982	14%
1 August 1988–31 October 1988	11%		

Zero rating

A zero-rated supply is a taxable supply, but the rate of tax is nil.
(References are to VATA 1994 Sch 8)

Group 1—Food.
Group 2—Sewerage services and water.
Group 3—Books etc.
Group 4—Talking books for the blind and handicapped and wireless sets for the blind.
Group 5—Construction of buildings etc.
Group 6—Protected buildings.
Group 7—International services.
Group 8—Transport.
Group 9—Caravans and houseboats.
Group 10—Gold.
Group 11—Bank notes.
Group 12—Drugs, medicines, aids for the handicapped etc.
Group 13—Imports, exports etc.
Group 15—Charities etc.
Group 16—Clothing and footwear.

Exempt supplies

No tax is chargeable on an exempt supply, and input tax cannot be recovered except as allowed under the partial exemption provisions (SI 1995/2518 Pt XIV; VAT Notice 706).
(References are to VATA 1994 Sch 9)

Group 1—Land.
Group 2—Insurance.
Group 3—Postal services.
Group 4—Betting, gaming and lotteries.
Group 5—Finance.
Group 6—Education.
Group 7—Health and welfare.
Group 8—Burial and cremation.
Group 9—Subscriptions to trade unions, professional and other public interest bodies.
Group 10—Sport, sports competitions and physical education.
Group 11—Works of art etc.
Group 12—Fund-raising events by charities and other qualifying bodies.
Group 13—Cultural services etc.
Group 14—Supplies of goods where input tax cannot be recovered.
Group 15—Investment gold

Partial exemption

De minimis limit for application of partial exemption rules
SI 1995/2518 reg 106

	Exempt input tax not exceeding
Tax years beginning after 30.11.94	(a) £625 per month on average; and (b) 50% of total input tax for prescribed accounting period
Periods beginning between 1.4.92 and 30.11.94	£600 per month on average

Capital goods scheme

Input tax adjustment following change in taxable use of capital goods
VATA 1994 s 34, SI 1995/2518 regs 112-116 (77/388/EEC art 20), SI 1999/599 reg 6.
From 1 April 1990

Item	Value	Adjustment period
Computer equipment	£50,000 or more	5 years
Land and buildings	£250,000 or more	10 years (5 years where interest had less than 10 years to run on acquisition)

Adjustment formula

$$\frac{\text{Total input tax on item}}{\text{Length of adjustment period}} \times \text{adjustment percentage}$$

The adjustment percentage is the percentage change in the extent to which the item is used (or treated as used) in making taxable supplies between the first interval in the adjustment period and a subsequent interval. (The first interval generally ends on the last day of the tax year in which the input tax was incurred.)

Car fuel

From 6 April 1987, VAT-inclusive scale figures are used to assess VAT due on petrol provided at below cost price for private journeys by registered traders or their employees, where the petrol has been provided from business resources. The high business-mileage discount was abolished from 1993-94.

	12 months	VAT due per car	3 months	VAT due per car	1 month	VAT due per car
2000–01						
Diesel engine						
Cylinder capacity: 2,000cc or less	£930	£138·51	£232	£34·55	£77	£11·46
more than 2,000cc	£1,180	£175·74	£295	£43·93	£98	£14·59
Any other type of engine						
Cylinder capacity: 1,400cc or less	£1,025	£152·65	£256	£38·12	£85	£12·65
Over 1,400cc up to 2,000cc	£1,300	£193·61	£325	£48·40	£108	£16·08
Over 2,000cc	£1,915	£285·21	£478	£71·19	£159	£23·68
1999–2000						
Diesel engine						
Cylinder capacity: 2,000cc or less	£785	£116·91	£196	£29·19	£65	£9·68
more than 2,000cc	£995	£148·19	£248	£36·93	£82	£12·21
Any other type of engine						
Cylinder capacity: 1,400cc or less	£850	£126·59	£212	£31·57	£70	£10·42
Over 1,400cc up to 2,000cc	£1,075	£160·10	£268	£39·91	£89	£13·25
Over 2,000cc	£1,585	£236·06	£396	£58·97	£132	£19·65
1998–99						
Diesel engine						
Cylinder capacity: 2,000cc or less	£785	£116·91	£196	£29·19	£65	£9·68
more than 2,000cc	£995	£148·19	£248	£36·93	£82	£12·21
Any other type of engine						
Cylinder capacity: 1,400cc or less	£850	£126·59	£212	£31·57	£70	£10·42
Over 1,400cc up to 2,000cc	£1,075	£160·10	£268	£39·91	£89	£13·25
Over 2,000cc	£1,585	£236·06	£396	£58·97	£132	£19·65
1997–98						
Diesel engine						
Cylinder capacity: 2,000cc or less	£740	£110·21	£185	£27·55	61	9·08
more than 2,000cc	£940	£140·00	£235	£35·00	78	11·61
Any other type of engine						
Cylinder capacity: 1,400cc or less	£800	£119·14	£200	£29·78	66	9·82
Over 1,400cc up to 2,000cc	£1,010	£150·42	£252	£37·53	84	12·51
Over 2,000cc	£1,490	£221·91	£372	£55·40	124	18·46

HM Customs and Excise: VAT notices

New notices no longer carry a designation of the year of issue or revision, but this is retained here as a guide to the year of publication of the latest version. Several leaflets and notices contain Update inserts, published from time to time.

(Cancelled leaflets have been deleted from the list.)

Notice		Date	Title
48		1999	Extra-statutory concessions
400		1999	**HM Customs and Excise Charter Standards**
431		1999	**Visiting forces**
700		1996	**The VAT guide**
	700/1	1997‡	Should I be registered for VAT?
	700/1W	1997	Ddylwnifod wedi fy nghofrestru am TAW?
	700/1A	1997	Should I be registered for VAT? Distance selling
	700/1AW	1997	Ddylwnifod wedify nghofrestru am TAW? – Gweythmo bell
	700/1B	1997	Should I be registered for VAT? Acquisitions
	700/1BW	1997	Ddylwnifod wedify nghofrestru am TAW? – Caffaeliadau
	700/2	1999	Group treatment
	700/3	1998	Registration for VAT: Corporate bodies organised in divisions
	700/4	1997	Registration for VAT: non-established taxable persons
	700/5	1985	Hire-purchase and conditional sale: repossessions and transfers of agreements
	700/7	1994	Business promotion schemes
	700/9	1996	Transfer of a business as a going concern
	700/9W	1996	Trosglwyddo busnes fel busnes byw
	700/11	1998	Cancelling your registration
	700/12	1995	Filling in your VAT return
	700/12W	1995	Llanwi'ch ffurflen TAW
	700/14	1999	Video cassette films: rental and part-exchange
	700/15	1995	The Ins and Outs of VAT
	700/15W	1995	Manylion TAW
	700/17	1996	Funded pension schemes
	700/18	1997	Relief from VAT on bad debts
	700/21	1995	Keeping records and accounts
	700/21W	1995	Cadw cofnodion a chyfrifon
	700/22	1989	Admissions
	700/24	1994	Postage and delivery charges
	700/25	1984	Taxis and hire cars
	700/28	1994	Estate agents
	700/31	1999	Pawnbrokers: disposals of pledged goods
	700/33	1995	Government funded training programmes and schemes to help the unemployed
	700/34	1994	Staff
	700/35	1997	Business gifts and samples
	700/41	1995	Late registration penalty
	700/41W	1995	Dirwy am gofrestru yn hwyr
	700/42	1993	Serious misdeclaration penalty
	700/43	1996	Default interest
	700/44	1993	Barristers and advocates: tax point on ceasing to practise
	700/45	2000	How to correct VAT errors and make adjustments or claims
	700/45W	1999	Sut i gywiro gwallau y dewch o hyd iddynt ar eich ffurflenni TAW
	700/46	1993	Agricultural flat rate scheme
	700/47	1993	Confidentiality in VAT matters (Tax advisers) – Statement of practice
	700/50	1997	Default surcharge
	700/50W	1997	Gordal diffyg talu
	700/51	1995	VAT enquiries guide
	700/51W	1995	Arweiniad ar ymholiadau TAW
	700/52	1996	Notice of requirement to give security to Customs and Excise
	700/52W	1996	Hysbysiad o'r angen i roi gwarant i'r Tollau Tramor o Chartref
	700/55	1993	VAT input tax appeals: luxuries, amusements and entertainment
	700/56	1999	Insolvency
	700/57	1999	VAT – administrative agreements entered into with trade bodies
	700/58	1998	Treatment of VAT repayment returns and VAT repayment supplements
	700/59	1994	VAT refunds on surrendered road licences
	700/60	1996	Payments on account
	700/61	1997	Artificial separation of business activities: statement of practice
	700/64	1996	Motoring expenses
	700/65	1996	Business entertainment
	700/66	1999	List of VAT business advice centres
	700/67	1997	The VAT registration scheme for racehorse owners
701			
	701/1	1995‡	Charities
	701/5	1990	Clubs and associations
	701/6	1997	Charity-funded equipment for medical, veterinary etc. uses
	701/7	1994‡	VAT reliefs for people with disabilities
	701/8	1997	Postage stamps and philatelic supplies
	701/9	1985	Terminal markets: dealings with commodities
	701/10	1999	Liability of printed and similar matter
	701/12	1996†	Sales of antiques, works of art etc from stately homes
	701/13	1995	Gaming and amusement machines
	701/14	1997	Food
	701/15	1995	Food for animals

Notice		Date	Title
	701/16	1999	Water and sewage services
	701/19	1995	Fuel and power
	701/20	1996†	Caravans and houseboats
	701/21	2000	Gold
	701/21A	2000	Investment gold coins
	701/22	1995	Tools for the manufacture of goods for export
	701/23	1995	Protective boots and helmets
	701/24	1992	Parking facilities
	701/26	1995	Betting and gaming
	701/27	1997	Bingo
	701/28	1997	Lotteries
	701/29	1992	Finance
	701/30	1997	Education and vocational training
	701/31	1992	Health
	701/32	1997	Burial, cremation and the commemoration of the dead
	701/33	1997	Trade unions, professional bodies and learned societies
	701/34	1989	Competitions in sport and physical recreation
	701/35	1995	Youth clubs
	701/36	1997	Insurance
	701/37	1994	Live animals
	701/38	1999	Seeds and plants
	701/39	1999	VAT liability law
	701/40	1999	Abattoirs
	701/41	1995	Sponsorship
	701/43	1993	Financial futures and options
	701/44	1998	Securities
	701/45	1994	Sport and physical education
	701/46	1996	Schools and school photographs
	701/47	1996	Culture
	701/48	1997	Corporate purchasing cards
702		1998	**Imports**
			(Single Market supplement)
	702/4	1994	Importing computer software
	702/6	1991	Import VAT certificates
	702/7	1993	Import VAT relief for goods supplied onward to another country in the European Community
	702/9	1998	Warehousing and free zones
703		1996	**Exports**
	703/1	1995	Supply of freight containers for export or removal from the UK
	703/2	1999	Sailaway boats supplied for export outside the European Community
	703/3	1999	Sailaway boat scheme
704		1999	**Retail exports**
	704/1	1999	VAT refunds for travellers departing from the European Community
	704/2	1999	Traveller's guide to the retail export scheme
705		1995	**Personal exports of new motor vehicles to destinations outside the European Community from 1 January 1993**
705A		1995	**VAT: Supplies of vehicles under the personal export scheme for removal from the EC**
706		1999	**Partial exemption**
	706/1	1992	Self-supply of stationery
	706/2	1990	Capital goods scheme – input tax on computers, land and buildings acquired for use in your business
708		1997	**Buildings and construction**
	708/5	1997	Registered social landlords (Housing Associations, etc)
709	709/1	1987	Industrial, staff and public sector catering
	709/2	1991	Catering and take-away food
	709/3	1993	Hotels and holiday accommodation
	709/4	1988	Package holidays and other holiday services
	709/5	1998	Tour operators' margin scheme
	709/6	1997	Travel agents
710	710/1	1991	Theatrical agents and Nett Acts
	710/2	1983	Agencies providing nurses and nursing auxiliaries
714		1995	**Young children's clothing and footwear**
714A		1995	**Young children's clothing and footwear: schedule of maximum sizes for zero-rating**
718		1999	**Margin schemes for secondhand goods, works of art, antiques and collectors' items**
719		1996	**VAT refunds for DIY builders and converters**
723		1996	**Refunds of VAT in the European Community for EC and non-EC traders**
725		1998	**VAT: the Single Market**
727		1997	**Retail schemes†**
	727/2	1997	Bespoke retail schemes
	727/3	1997	How to work the point of sale scheme
	727/4	1997	How to work the apportionment schemes

Notice		Date	Title
	727/5	1997	How to work the direct calculation schemes
	727/6	1997	Choosing your retail scheme
728		2000	**Motor vehicles, boats, aircraft: intra-EC movements by private persons**
730		1994	**Civil evasion penalty investigations: Statement of practice**
731		1999	**Cash accounting†**
732		1996	**Annual accounting**
741		1998	**Place of supply of services**
742		1995	**Land and property†**
	742/1	1990	Letting of facilities for sport and physical recreation
	742/2	1992	Sporting rights
	742/3	1995	Scottish land law terms
742C		1995	**Land and property: law**
744A		1996	**Passenger transport**
744B		1997	**Freight transport and associated services**
744C		1997	**Ships, aircraft and associated services**
744D		1996	**International services – zero rating**
747		1998	**VAT notices having the force of law**
749		1997	**Local authorities and similar bodies**
750		1998	**Community/Common transit**
759		1998	**An introduction to Customs Freight Simplified Procedures**
760		1998	**Customs freight simplified procedures (CFSP)**
761		1998	**Visits by Customs and Excise Officers to traders using Customs Freight Simplified Procedures**
770		1998	**Imported goods: End-use relief**
920		1999	**The single currency**
930		1999	What if I don't pay?
989		1997	**Visits by Customs and Excise officers**
999		2000	**Catalogue of publications**
1000		1999	**Complaints and putting things right**
CWLI		1999	Starting your own business?
–		1995	Welcome to VAT
Explanatory leaflet:		1999	Appeals and applications to the tribunals

Information sheets: available also at http://www.hmce.gov.uk.

4/93	Intra-EC processing of goods: simplification
1/94	Vendor control: special VAT retail scheme for tax free shops/airlines/ferry operators
2/94	VAT: recalculation of misdeclaration penalty
2/95	Trade with Austria, Finland and Sweden
5/95	VAT – changes to tour operators' margin scheme
6/95	VAT – NHS dispensing doctors
8/95	Late registration – incorrect assessment of penalty
9/95	VAT – valuation of imported works of art, antiques and collectors' pieces
10/95	Changes to liability of buildings
14/95	VAT registration in Austria, Finland and Sweden
1/96	VAT – filling in your EC sales list (Form VAT 101)
3/96	Tour operators' margin scheme – practical implementation of the airline charter option following the changes which came into effect on 1 January 1996
4/96	Tour operators' margin scheme – practical implementation of the agency option following the changes which came into effect on 1 January 1996
5/96	VAT – supplies by dentists
1/97	Tour operators' margin scheme – practical implementation of the 'trader to trader (wholesale) option'
6/97	Drugs, medicine and aids for the handicapped – liability with effect from 1 January 1998
2/98	Export house VAT provisions: withdrawal
3/98	Local authorities and NHS joint stores depots
5/98	Local authorities: supplies to new unitary authorities under local government reorganisation (transitional arrangements)
6/98	Local authority pension funds: VAT treatment and administrative concession
7/98	Local authorities: amendments to section 33 refund method
8/98	Charities – supply, repair and maintenance of relevant goods (including adapted motor vehicles)
9/98	VAT relief on the installation of energy saving materials
1/99	Local Authorities: community projects and VAT
2/99	Local Authorities: agreement of section 33 recovery methods
3/99	VAT: new deal programme
4/99	VAT: education action zones
5/99	VAT: School Standards and Framework Act 1998
6/99	Charities: liabilities of routine domestic tasks
7/99	Construction services: new rule for accounting for VAT
8/99	Opticians: Apportionment of charges for supplies of spectacles and dispensing
9/99	Imported works of art, antiques and collectors' pieces: changes to the reduced rate of VAT
10/99	Financial exemptions: changes brought about by the 1999 Finance Order
11/99	VAT - exemption of subscriptions to political, religious, patriotic, philosophical, philanthropic and civic bodies
12/99	VAT on business cars–charges to take effect on 1 December 1999
Video and booklet	1995 Welcome to VAT

† Publications having legal or quasi-legal force.   ‡ Now available in large print.

22% grossing-up table

Am't	Grossed at 22%	Am't	Grossed at 22%	Am't	Grossed at 22%	Am't	Grossed at 22%	Am't	Grossed at 22%	Am't	Grossed at 22%	Am't	Grossed at 22%	Am't	Grossed at 22%
£	£	£	£	£	£	£	£	£	£	£	£	£	£	£	£
1	1·28	71	91·03	141	180·77	211	270·51	281	360·26	351	450·00	421	539·74	491	629·49
2	2·56	72	92·31	142	182·05	212	271·79	282	361·54	352	451·28	422	541·03	492	630·77
3	3·85	73	93·59	143	183·33	213	273·08	283	362·82	353	452·56	423	542·31	493	632·05
4	5·13	74	94·87	144	184·62	214	274·36	284	364·10	354	453·85	424	543·59	494	633·33
5	6·41	75	96·15	145	185·90	215	275·64	285	365·38	355	455·13	425	544·87	495	634·62
6	7·69	76	97·44	146	187·18	216	276·92	286	366·67	356	456·41	426	546·15	496	635·90
7	8·97	77	98·72	147	188·46	217	278·21	287	367·95	357	457·69	427	547·44	497	637·18
8	10·26	78	100·00	148	189·74	218	279·49	288	369·23	358	458·97	428	548·72	498	638·46
9	11·54	79	101·28	149	191·03	219	280·77	289	370·51	359	460·26	429	550·00	499	639·74
10	12·82	80	102·56	150	192·31	220	282·05	290	371·79	360	461·54	430	551·28	500	641·03
11	14·10	81	103·85	151	193·59	221	283·33	291	373·08	361	462·82	431	552·56	510	653·85
12	15·38	82	105·13	152	194·87	222	284·62	292	374·36	362	464·10	432	553·85	520	666·67
13	16·67	83	106·41	153	196·15	223	285·90	293	375·64	363	465·38	433	555·13	530	679·49
14	17·95	84	107·69	154	197·44	224	287·18	294	376·92	364	466·67	434	556·41	540	692·31
15	19·23	85	108·97	155	198·72	225	288·46	295	378·21	365	467·95	435	557·69	550	705·13
16	20·51	86	110·26	156	200·00	226	289·74	296	379·49	366	469·23	436	558·97	560	717·95
17	21·79	87	111·54	157	201·28	227	291·03	297	380·77	367	470·51	437	560·26	570	730·77
18	23·08	88	112·82	158	202·56	228	292·31	298	382·05	368	471·79	438	561·54	580	743·59
19	24·36	89	114·10	159	203·85	229	293·59	299	383·33	369	473·08	439	562·82	590	756·41
20	25·64	90	115·38	160	205·13	230	294·87	300	384·62	370	474·36	440	564·10	600	769·23
21	26·92	91	116·67	161	206·41	231	296·15	301	385·90	371	475·64	441	565·38	610	782·05
22	28·21	92	117·95	162	207·69	232	297·44	302	387·18	372	476·92	442	566·67	620	794·87
23	29·49	93	119·23	163	208·97	233	298·72	303	388·46	373	478·21	443	567·95	630	807·69
24	30·77	94	120·51	164	210·26	234	300·00	304	389·74	374	479·49	444	569·23	640	820·51
25	32·05	95	121·79	165	211·54	235	301·28	305	391·03	375	480·77	445	570·51	650	833·33
26	33·33	96	123·08	166	212·82	236	302·56	306	392·31	376	482·05	446	571·79	660	846·15
27	34·62	97	124·36	167	214·10	237	303·85	307	393·59	377	483·33	447	573·08	670	858·97
28	35·90	98	125·64	168	215·38	238	305·13	308	394·87	378	484·62	448	574·36	680	871·79
29	37·18	99	126·92	169	216·67	239	306·41	309	396·15	379	485·90	449	575·64	690	884·62
30	38·46	100	128·21	170	217·95	240	307·69	310	397·44	380	487·18	450	576·92	700	897·44
31	39·74	101	129·49	171	219·23	241	308·97	311	398·72	381	488·46	451	578·21	710	910·26
32	41·03	102	130·77	172	220·51	242	310·26	312	400·00	382	489·74	452	579·49	720	923·08
33	42·31	103	132·05	173	221·79	243	311·54	313	401·28	383	491·03	453	580·77	730	935·90
34	43·59	104	133·33	174	223·08	244	312·82	314	402·56	384	492·31	454	582·05	740	948·72
35	44·87	105	134·62	175	224·36	245	314·10	315	403·85	385	493·59	455	583·33	750	961·54
36	46·15	106	135·90	176	225·64	246	315·38	316	405·13	386	494·87	456	584·62	760	974·36
37	47·44	107	137·18	177	226·92	247	316·67	317	406·41	387	496·15	457	585·90	770	987·18
38	48·72	108	138·46	178	228·21	248	317·95	318	407·69	388	497·44	458	587·18	780	1,000·00
39	50·00	109	139·74	179	229·49	249	319·23	319	408·97	389	498·72	459	588·46	790	1,012·82
40	51·28	110	141·03	180	230·77	250	320·51	320	410·26	390	500·00	460	589·74	800	1,025·64
41	52·56	111	142·31	181	232·05	251	321·79	321	411·54	391	501·28	461	591·03	810	1,038·46
42	53·85	112	143·59	182	233·33	252	323·08	322	412·82	392	502·56	462	592·31	820	1,051·28
43	55·13	113	144·87	183	234·62	253	324·36	323	414·10	393	503·85	463	593·59	830	1,064·10
44	56·41	114	146·15	184	235·90	254	325·64	324	415·38	394	505·13	464	594·87	840	1,076·92
45	57·69	115	147·44	185	237·18	255	326·92	325	416·67	395	506·41	465	596·15	850	1,089·74
46	58·97	116	148·72	186	238·46	256	328·21	326	417·95	396	507·69	466	597·44	860	1,102·56
47	60·26	117	150·00	187	239·74	257	329·49	327	419·23	397	508·97	467	598·72	870	1,115·38
48	61·54	118	151·28	188	241·03	258	330·77	328	420·51	398	510·26	468	600·00	880	1,128·21
49	62·82	119	152·56	189	242·31	259	332·05	329	421·79	399	511·54	469	601·28	890	1,141·03
50	64·10	120	153·85	190	243·59	260	333·33	330	423·08	400	512·82	470	602·56	900	1,153·85
51	65·38	121	155·13	191	244·87	261	334·62	331	424·36	401	514·10	471	603·85	910	1,166·67
52	66·67	122	156·41	192	246·15	262	335·90	332	425·64	402	515·38	472	605·13	920	1,179·49
53	67·95	123	157·69	193	247·44	263	337·18	333	426·92	403	516·67	473	606·41	930	1,192·31
54	69·23	124	158·97	194	248·72	264	338·46	334	428·21	404	517·95	474	607·69	940	1,205·13
55	70·51	125	160·26	195	250·00	265	339·74	335	429·49	405	519·23	475	608·97	950	1,217·95
56	71·79	126	161·54	196	251·28	266	341·03	336	430·77	406	520·51	476	610·26	960	1,230·77
57	73·08	127	162·82	197	252·56	267	342·31	337	432·05	407	521·79	477	611·54	970	1,243·59
58	74·36	128	164·10	198	253·85	268	343·59	338	433·33	408	523·08	478	612·82	980	1,256·41
59	75·64	129	165·38	199	255·13	269	344·87	339	434·62	409	524·36	479	614·10	990	1,269·23
60	76·92	130	166·67	200	256·41	270	346·15	340	435·90	410	525·64	480	615·38	1,000	1,282·05
61	78·21	131	167·95	201	257·69	271	347·44	341	437·18	411	526·92	481	616·67	2,000	2,564·10
62	79·49	132	169·23	202	258·97	272	348·72	342	438·46	412	528·21	482	617·95	3,000	3,846·15
63	80·77	133	170·51	203	260·26	273	350·00	343	439·74	413	529·49	483	619·23	4,000	5,128·20
64	82·05	134	171·79	204	261·54	274	351·28	344	441·03	414	530·77	484	620·51	5,000	6,410·26
65	83·33	135	173·08	205	262·82	275	352·56	345	442·31	415	532·05	485	621·79	6,000	7,692·31
66	84·62	136	174·36	206	264·10	276	353·85	346	443·59	416	533·33	486	623·08	7,000	8,974·36
67	85·90	137	175·64	207	265·38	277	355·13	347	444·87	417	534·62	487	624·35	8,000	10,256·41
68	87·18	138	176·92	208	266·67	278	356·41	348	446·15	418	535·90	488	625·64	9,000	11,538·46
69	88·46	139	178·21	209	267·95	279	357·69	349	447·44	419	537·18	489	626·92	10,000	12,820·51
70	89·74	140	179·49	210	269·23	280	358·97	350	448·72	420	538·46	490	688·21	11,000	14,102·56

34% grossing-up table

(*The rate applicable to trusts remains at 34% for 2000-01.*)

Am't	Grossed at 34%	Am't	Grossed at 34%	Am't	Grossed at 34%	Am't	Grossed at 34%	Am't	Grossed at 34%	Am't	Grossed at 34%	Am't	Grossed at 34%	Am't	Grossed at 34%
£	£	£	£	£	£	£	£	£	£	£	£	£	£	£	£
1	1·52	71	107·58	141	213·64	211	319·70	281	425·76	351	531·82	421	637·88	491	743·94
2	3·03	72	109·09	142	215·15	212	321·21	282	427·27	352	533·33	422	639·39	492	745·45
3	4·55	73	110·61	143	216·67	213	322·73	283	428·79	353	534·85	423	640·91	493	746·97
4	6·06	74	112·12	144	218·18	214	324·24	284	430·30	354	536·36	424	642·42	494	748·48
5	7·58	75	113·64	145	219·70	215	325·76	285	431·82	355	537·88	425	643·94	495	750·00
6	9·09	76	115·15	146	221·21	216	327·27	286	433·33	356	539·39	426	645·45	496	751·52
7	10·61	77	116·67	147	222·73	217	328·79	287	434·85	357	540·91	427	646·97	497	753·03
8	12·12	78	118·18	148	224·24	218	330·30	288	436·36	358	542·42	428	648·48	498	754·55
9	13·64	79	119·70	149	225·76	219	331·82	289	437·88	359	543·94	429	650·00	499	756·06
10	15·15	80	121·21	150	227·27	220	333·33	290	439·39	360	545·45	430	651·52	500	757·58
11	16·67	81	122·73	151	228·79	221	334·85	291	440·91	361	546·97	431	653·03	510	772·73
12	18·18	82	124·24	152	230·30	222	336·36	292	442·42	362	548·48	432	654·55	520	787·88
13	19·70	83	125·76	153	231·82	223	337·88	293	443·94	363	550·00	433	656·06	530	803·03
14	21·21	84	127·27	154	233·33	224	339·39	294	445·45	364	551·52	434	657·58	540	818·18
15	22·73	85	128·79	155	234·85	225	340·91	295	446·97	365	553·03	435	659·09	550	833·33
16	24·24	86	130·30	156	236·36	226	342·42	296	448·48	366	554·55	436	660·61	560	848·48
17	25·76	87	131·82	157	237·88	227	343·94	297	450·00	367	556·06	437	662·12	570	863·64
18	27·27	88	133·33	158	239·39	228	345·45	298	451·52	368	557·58	438	663·64	580	878·79
19	28·79	89	134·85	159	240·91	229	346·97	299	453·03	369	559·09	439	665·15	590	893·94
20	30·30	90	136·36	160	242·42	230	348·48	300	454·55	370	560·61	440	666·67	600	909·09
21	31·82	91	137·88	161	243·94	231	350·00	301	456·06	371	562·12	441	668·18	610	924·24
22	33·33	92	139·39	162	245·45	232	351·52	302	457·58	372	563·64	442	669·70	620	939·39
23	34·85	93	140·91	163	246·97	233	353·03	303	459·09	373	565·15	443	671·21	630	954·55
24	36·36	94	142·42	164	248·48	234	354·55	304	460·61	374	566·67	444	672·73	640	969·70
25	37·88	95	143·94	165	250·00	235	356·06	305	462·12	375	568·18	445	674·24	650	984·85
26	39·39	96	145·45	166	251·52	236	357·58	306	463·64	376	569·70	446	675·76	660	1,000·00
27	40·91	97	146·97	167	253·03	237	359·09	307	465·15	377	571·21	447	677·27	670	1,015·15
28	42·42	98	148·48	168	254·55	238	360·61	308	466·67	378	572·73	448	678·79	680	1,030·30
29	43·94	99	150·00	169	256·06	239	362·12	309	468·18	379	574·24	449	680·30	690	1,045·45
30	45·45	100	151·52	170	257·58	240	363·64	310	469·70	380	575·76	450	681·82	700	1,060·61
31	46·97	101	153·03	171	259·09	241	365·15	311	471·21	381	577·27	451	683·33	710	1,075·76
32	48·48	102	154·55	172	260·61	242	366·67	312	472·73	382	578·79	452	684·85	720	1,090·91
33	50·00	103	156·06	173	262·12	243	368·18	313	474·24	383	580·30	453	686·36	730	1,106·06
34	51·52	104	157·58	174	263·64	244	369·70	314	475·76	384	581·82	454	687·88	740	1,121·21
35	53·03	105	159·09	175	265·15	245	371·21	315	477·27	385	583·33	455	689·39	750	1,136·36
36	54·55	106	160·61	176	266·67	246	372·73	316	478·79	386	584·85	456	690·91	760	1,151·52
37	56·06	107	162·12	177	268·18	247	374·24	317	480·30	387	586·36	457	692·42	770	1,166·67
38	57·58	108	163·64	178	269·70	248	375·76	318	481·82	388	587·88	458	693·94	780	1,181·82
39	59·09	109	165·15	179	271·21	249	377·27	319	483·33	389	589·39	459	695·45	790	1,196·97
40	60·61	110	166·67	180	272·73	250	378·79	320	484·85	390	590·91	460	696·97	800	1,212·12
41	62·12	111	168·18	181	274·24	251	380·30	321	486·36	391	592·42	461	698·48	810	1,227·27
42	63·64	112	169·70	182	275·76	252	381·82	322	487·88	392	593·94	462	700·00	820	1,242·42
43	65·15	113	171·21	183	277·27	253	383·33	323	489·39	393	595·45	463	701·52	830	1,257·58
44	66·67	114	172·73	184	278·79	254	384·85	324	490·91	394	596·97	464	703·03	840	1,272·73
45	68·18	115	174·24	185	280·30	255	386·36	325	492·42	395	598·48	465	704·55	850	1,287·88
46	69·70	116	175·76	186	281·82	256	387·88	326	493·94	396	600·00	466	706·06	860	1,303·03
47	71·21	117	177·27	187	283·33	257	389·39	327	495·45	397	601·52	467	707·58	870	1,318·18
48	72·73	118	178·79	188	284·85	258	390·91	328	496·97	398	603·03	468	709·09	880	1,333·33
49	74·24	119	180·30	189	286·36	259	392·42	329	498·48	399	604·55	469	710·61	890	1,348·48
50	75·76	120	181·82	190	287·88	260	393·94	330	500·00	400	606·06	470	712·12	900	1,363·64
51	77·27	121	183·33	191	289·39	261	395·45	331	501·52	401	607·58	471	713·64	910	1,378·79
52	78·79	122	184·85	192	290·91	262	396·97	332	503·03	402	609·09	472	715·15	920	1,393·94
53	80·30	123	186·36	193	292·42	263	398·48	333	504·55	403	610·61	473	716·67	930	1,409·09
54	81·82	124	187·88	194	293·94	264	400·00	334	506·06	404	612·12	474	718·18	940	1,424·24
55	83·33	125	189·39	195	295·45	265	401·52	335	507·58	405	613·64	475	719·70	950	1,439·39
56	84·85	126	190·91	196	296·97	266	403·03	336	509·09	406	615·15	476	721·21	960	1,454·55
57	86·36	127	192·42	197	298·48	267	404·55	337	510·61	407	616·67	477	722·73	970	1,469·70
58	87·88	128	193·94	198	300·00	268	406·06	338	512·12	408	618·18	478	724·24	980	1,484·85
59	89·39	129	195·45	199	301·52	269	407·58	339	513·64	409	619·70	479	725·76	990	1,500·00
60	90·91	130	196·97	200	303·03	270	409·09	340	515·15	410	621·21	480	727·27	1,000	1,515·15
61	92·42	131	198·48	201	304·54	271	410·61	341	516·67	411	622·73	481	728·79	2,000	3,030·30
62	93·94	132	200·00	202	306·06	272	412·12	342	518·18	412	624·24	482	730·30	3,000	4,545·45
63	95·45	133	201·52	203	307·58	273	413·64	343	519·70	413	625·76	483	731·82	4,000	6,060·61
64	96·97	134	203·03	204	309·09	274	415·15	344	521·21	414	627·27	484	733·33	5,000	7,575·76
65	98·48	135	204·55	205	310·61	275	416·67	345	522·73	415	628·79	485	734·85	6,000	9,090·91
66	100·00	136	206·06	206	312·12	276	418·18	346	524·24	416	630·30	486	736·36	7,000	10,606·06
67	101·52	137	207·58	207	313·64	277	419·70	347	525·76	417	631·82	487	737·88	8,000	12,121·21
68	103·03	138	209·09	208	315·15	278	421·21	348	527·27	418	633·33	488	739·39	9,000	13,636·36
69	104·55	139	210·61	209	316·67	279	422·73	349	528·79	419	634·85	489	740·91	10,000	15,151·52
70	106·06	140	212·12	210	318·18	280	424·24	350	530·30	420	636·36	490	742·42	11,000	16,666·67

17.5% VAT (tax included in amount) – VAT fraction ⁷/₄₇

Am't	VAT incl. in Am't	Am't	VAT incl. in Am't	Am't	VAT incl. in Am't	Am't	VAT incl. in Am't	Am't	VAT incl. in Am't	Am't	VAT incl. in Am't
£ or p	£ or p	£ or p	£ or p	£ or p	£ or p	£ or p	£ or p	£ or p	£ or p	£ or p	£ or p
1	0·15	71	10·57	141	21·00	211	31·43	281	41·85	810	120·64
2	0·30	72	10·72	142	21·15	212	31·57	282	42·00	820	122·13
3	0·45	73	10·87	143	21·30	213	31·72	283	42·15	830	123·62
4	0·60	74	11·02	144	21·45	214	31·87	284	42·30	840	125·11
5	0·74	75	11·17	145	21·60	215	32·02	285	42·45	850	126·60
6	0·89	76	11·32	146	21·74	216	32·17	286	42·60	860	128·09
7	1·04	77	11·47	147	21·89	217	32·32	287	42·74	870	129·57
8	1·19	78	11·62	148	22·04	218	32·47	288	42·89	880	131·06
9	1·34	79	11·77	149	22·19	219	32·62	289	43·04	890	132·55
10	1·49	80	11·91	150	22·34	220	32·77	290	43·19	900	134·04
11	1·64	81	12·06	151	22·49	221	32·91	291	43·35	910	135·53
12	1·79	82	12·21	152	22·64	222	33·06	292	43·49	920	137·02
13	1·94	83	12·36	153	22·79	223	33·21	293	43·64	930	138·51
14	2·09	84	12·51	154	22·94	224	33·36	294	43·79	940	140·00
15	2·23	85	12·66	155	23·09	225	33·51	295	43·94	950	141·49
16	2·38	86	12·81	156	23·23	226	33·66	296	44·09	960	142·98
17	2·53	87	12·96	157	23·38	227	33·81	297	44·23	970	144·47
18	2·68	88	13·11	158	23·53	228	33·96	298	44·38	980	145·96
19	2·83	89	13·26	159	23·68	229	34·11	299	44·53	990	147·45
20	2·98	90	13·40	160	23·83	230	34·26	300	44·68	1,000	148·94
21	3·13	91	13·55	161	23·98	231	34·40	310	46·17	1,100	163·83
22	3·28	92	13·70	162	24·13	232	34·55	320	47·66	1,200	178·72
23	3·43	93	13·85	163	24·28	233	34·70	330	49·15	1,300	193·62
24	3·57	94	14·00	164	24·43	234	34·85	340	50·64	1,400	208·51
25	3·72	95	14·15	165	24·57	235	35·00	350	52·13	1,500	223·40
26	3·87	96	14·30	166	24·72	236	35·15	360	53·62	1,600	238·30
27	4·02	97	14·45	167	24·87	237	35·30	370	55·11	1,700	253·19
28	4·17	98	14·60	168	25·02	238	35·45	380	56·60	1,800	268·08
29	4·32	99	14·74	169	25·17	239	35·60	390	58·09	1,900	282·98
30	4·47	100	14·89	170	25·32	240	35·74	400	59·57	2,000	297·87
31	4·62	101	15·04	171	25·47	241	35·89	410	61·06	2,100	312·77
32	4·77	102	15·19	172	25·62	242	36·04	420	62·55	2,200	327·66
33	4·91	103	15·34	173	25·77	243	36·19	430	64·04	2,300	342·55
34	5·06	104	15·49	174	25·91	244	36·34	440	65·53	2,400	357·45
35	5·21	105	15·64	175	26·06	245	36·49	450	67·02	2,500	372·34
36	5·36	106	15·79	176	26·21	246	36·64	460	68·51	2,600	387·23
37	5·51	107	15·94	177	26·36	247	36·79	470	70·00	2,700	402·13
38	5·66	108	16·09	178	26·51	248	36·94	480	71·49	2,800	417·02
39	5·81	109	16·23	179	26·66	249	37·09	490	72·98	2,900	431·91
40	5·96	110	16·38	180	26·81	250	37·23	500	74·47	3,000	446·81
41	6·11	111	16·53	181	26·96	251	37·38	510	75·96	3,100	461·70
42	6·26	112	16·68	182	27·11	252	37·53	520	77·45	3,200	476·60
43	6·40	113	16·83	183	27·26	253	37·68	530	78·94	3,300	491·49
44	6·55	114	16·98	184	27·40	254	37·83	540	80·43	3,400	506·38
45	6·70	115	17·13	185	27·55	255	37·98	550	81·91	3,500	521·28
46	6·85	116	17·28	186	27·70	256	38·13	560	83·40	3,600	536·17
47	7·00	117	17·43	187	27·85	257	38·28	570	84·89	3,700	551·06
48	7·15	118	17·57	188	28·00	258	38·43	580	86·38	3,800	565·96
49	7·30	119	17·72	189	28·15	259	38·57	590	87·87	3,900	580·85
50	7·45	120	17·87	190	28·30	260	38·72	600	89·36	4,000	595·74
51	7·60	121	18·02	191	28·45	261	38·87	610	90·85	4,100	610·64
52	7·74	122	18·17	192	28·60	262	39·02	620	92·34	4,200	625·53
53	7·89	123	18·32	193	28·74	263	39·17	630	93·83	4,300	640·43
54	8·04	124	18·47	194	28·89	264	39·32	640	95·32	4,400	655·32
55	8·19	125	18·62	195	29·04	265	39·47	650	96·81	4,500	670·21
56	8·34	126	18·77	196	29·19	266	39·62	660	98·30	4,600	685·11
57	8·49	127	18·91	197	29·34	267	39·77	670	99·79	4,700	700·00
58	8·64	128	19·06	198	29·49	268	39·91	680	101·28	4,800	714·89
59	8·79	129	19·21	199	29·64	269	40·06	690	102·77	4,900	729·79
60	8·94	130	19·36	200	29·79	270	40·21	700	104·26	5,000	744·68
61	9·09	131	19·51	201	29·94	271	40·36	710	105·74	6,000	893·62
62	9·23	132	19·66	202	30·09	272	40·51	720	107·23	7,000	1,042·55
63	9·38	133	19·81	203	30·23	273	40·66	730	108·72	8,000	1,191·49
64	9·53	134	19·96	204	30·38	274	40·81	740	110·21	9,000	1,340·42
65	9·68	135	20·11	205	30·53	275	40·96	750	111·70	10,000	1,489·36
66	9·83	136	20·26	206	30·68	276	41·11	760	113·19	11,000	1,638·30
67	9·98	137	20·40	207	30·83	277	41·26	770	114·68	12,000	1,787·23
68	10·13	138	20·55	208	30·98	278	41·40	780	116·17	13,000	1,936·17
69	10·28	139	20·70	209	31·13	279	41·55	790	117·66	14,000	2,085·11
70	10·43	140	20·85	210	31·28	280	41·70	800	119·15	15,000	2,234·04

INDEX